A
WHOLE-SOULED
WOMAN

❖❖❖❖❖❖

Prudence Crandall and the
Education of Black Women

A
WHOLE-SOULED
WOMAN

❖❖❖❖❖❖

Prudence Crandall and the Education of Black Women

SUSAN STRANE

W·W·Norton & Company

NEW YORK   LONDON

Copyright © 1990 by Susan Strane

ALL RIGHTS RESERVED.

Printed in the United States of America.

The text of this book is composed in Monticello, with display type set in Caslon Openface. Composition by PennSet, Inc. Manufacturing by the Murray Printing Company.

Book design by Tere LoPrete.

FIRST EDITION

Library of Congress Cataloging-in-Publication Data

Strane, Susan. A whole-souled woman:
Prudence Crandall and the Education of Black Women / Susan Strane.—1st ed.
p. cm.
1. Crandall, Prudence, 1803–1890. 2. Afro-American teachers—Connecticut—Biography. I. Title.
LA2317.C73S77 1990
371.1′0092—dc20   89-36519

ISBN 0-393-02826-7

W. W. Norton & Company, Inc.
500 Fifth Avenue, New York, N. Y. 10110

W. W. Norton & Company Ltd.
37 Great Russell Street, London WC1B 3NU

1 2 3 4 5 6 7 8 9 0

To Elsa and Morgan

Acknowledgments

*R*esearching a minor historical figure like Prudence Crandall requires a lot of detective work. The following librarians and archivists have gone out of their way to be helpful: Mary Kent of the Shain Library, Connecticut College, New London; Anne Borg of the Kent Memorial Library, Suffield, Connecticut; Daniel Widawsky of the Bancroft Library at the University of California at Berkeley (Mark Twain Papers); Larry Jochims of the Kansas Historical Society, Topeka.

I would like to thank the following libraries for granting me access to their collections: the Boston Public Library; Houghton Library at Harvard University, Boston, Massachusetts; the Olin Library of Cornell University, Ithaca, New York; the History and Genealogy Library of the Connecticut State Library, Hartford; the Free Library, Kingston, Rhode Island; Special Collections, Columbia University, New York City. I am also indebted to the staffs of the following historical societies: the Connecticut Historical Society, Hartford; the Rhode Island Historical Society,

Providence; the Illinois Historical Society, Springfield; the New-York Historical Society, New York City.

Several local historians helped in the project, and I would like to thank them: Mrs. Phillip Benson of the Westerly, Rhode Island, Historical Society; Mr. J. P. Smith of the Canterbury Historical Society, Canterbury, Connecticut; Mrs. Hope Andrews of Hope Valley, Rhode Island; Mr. Eugene Newhouse of Rockwell City, Iowa.

Two women have been indispensable in completing this book. Kaz Koslowski, curator of the Prudence Crandall House and Museum in Canterbury, has patiently provided me with advice and guidance for several years. Marvis Olive Welch, a pioneer researcher of Prudence Crandall, has been a generous and encouraging mentor throughout the project.

I would also like to thank two descendants of Prudence Crandall: Mrs. Jessica Nashold of Mendota, Illinois, and Mrs. Lyle Black of Farnhamville, Iowa.

Special gratitude goes to Linda Strane Hutchinson and Howard Hutchinson for their outstanding generosity.

Last, I want to acknowledge the support of the following friends and relatives: my husband, William Starr; my editor, Susan Gaustad; Nellie Hester Bailey; Robin Corey; Anne Donaldson; Alice Hageman; Martha Vaughan; Nancy Trichter; Kathy Anderson.

Prologue:
Elk Falls, Kansas, 1886

"*I* searched for the truth my whole life," the eighty-four-year-old woman said as she sat before the fire with a wooden bowl in her lap, cutting wormholes out of apples. George Thayer, a young reporter, scribbled her words in his notebook with one hand and balanced a teacup in the other. He had slogged many miles across the rain-soaked prairie to meet her. He was writing a series for the Hartford *Evening Post* about his bicycle journey, "awheel and afoot," across the continent and back. Prudence Crandall was installment twenty-three.

The room in which they sat was sparsely furnished with several straight-backed chairs and an old pine desk piled with books. She was reading *Is Darwin Right?* by spiritualist William Denton, and she recommended that he read it too.

She was thin and bent and her face was very wrinkled. Her sandy gray hair was smoothed back with a common round comb and hung straight as if it had been cut all around with sheep shears. She wore what seemed to be a dress, George Thayer decided after he had stared at it a while, made of a single piece of black muslin with a hole cut out for her head. It was drawn in at the waist with some string. She wasn't particular for fashion, she said.

Prudence Crandall had been famous fifty years earlier, long before the Civil War, when she had conducted a school for black girls in Canterbury, Connecticut. By this act she had so enraged her neighbors that they had, among other things, set her house on fire while she was still inside, as though they were burning a witch on a very large pyre. Yet she was always glad to see someone from "good old Connecticut," she had said when the reporter showed up dripping wet at the door of her little frame house on Osage Avenue. She had settled him by the fire and stuffed him with ham and potatoes, bread and butter, apple pie and gingersnaps, and cup after cup of strong tea.

The Connecticut legislature in its recent session had formally apologized to her for that state's "cruel outrages," and George Thayer thought his readers would like to know what she thought of the news that had been sent to her on the new-fangled telegraph. "Tell them I am happy," she instructed him.

Her eyes sparkled intensely as she spoke. Old John Brown had glinty eyes like that, George Thayer recalled reading. He had heard that everyone in southeast Kansas was a little crazy, and he was ready to believe it. Prudence Crandall had already told him she regularly talked to spirits.

And now, she supposed, he wanted to hear all about Canterbury. She gazed at him with such concentration that she popped a wormhole into her mouth instead of a slice of apple and did not even notice. "My whole life has been one of opposition," she began.[1]

Canterbury

❖❖❖❖❖❖

Chapter One

*P*rudence Crandall was her father's daughter and Pardon Crandall was a difficult man. All the Crandalls were like that, proud, stubborn, "stiff-necked." They never seemed to be content; the taint of rebelliousness, passed down through the generations like original sin, defined them.

The first malcontented Crandall to arrive in the New World was John Crandall in 1635. An Anabaptist, he was soon banished from the Massachusetts colony along with Roger Williams and other Anabaptists to the wilderness that was to become Rhode Island. There, instead of withering away as his enemies had intended, he thrived among the Quakers and other outcasts. The Crandalls stayed in Rhode Island for a century and a half.

In 1799 John Crandall's descendant Pardon Crandall married Esther Carpenter from Hope Valley. Esther was the favorite and last child of her aged father Hezekiah. When he gave his fifteen-year-old daughter to Pardon, it was with the understanding that she would remain near her father. Hezekiah built the newlyweds a house next to his own, and from his iron mill he provided his daughter with all the boot scrapers, trivets, and cooking pots she could ever need, as if their weight would anchor her firmly next to him. In this house four children were born: Hezekiah in 1800, Prudence in 1803, Reuben in 1806, and Hannah Almira (called Almira) in 1813.

Pardon did not thrive in his father-in-law's shadow, where Esther was as much a daughter as a wife and where her friends and relatives had as many claims on her affection as he did. A story survives that illustrates his resentment. Esther wanted very much to attend a clambake on Long Island Sound. Pardon grudgingly consented, and they left the children with Esther's mother and set off at six in the morning. During the twelve-mile ride along the Pawcatuck River, Pardon maintained a sullen silence. As soon as they arrived at the beach, without allowing Esther to alight or even to greet her friends, he turned the wagon around and started back. His only words to her were "You wanted to go to the clam-bake. I took ye, didn't I?" When they reached home, he ate his dinner and went back off to the silence of his fields.[1]

Religious differences added to the strain between the Crandalls and the Carpenters. At her marriage, Esther had worn a black satin Empire-style frock finished with red and yellow satin at the hem. Over her shoulders she had draped a cape of scarlet. Sometime afterward, however, she and Pardon became Quakers and began addressing each other as "thee" and "thou." Esther packed away her worldly clothes, symbols of her pampered childhood, forever.

Finally, in 1813, within weeks of the birth of their fourth child, Pardon moved his family by oxcart thirty miles across the border into Windham County, Connecticut, to a red farmhouse near the prosperous village of Canterbury. Other Quakers had settled there already on Black Hill and in

Plainfield, the town across the turbulent Quinebaug River.[2]

Prudence and her siblings spent a happy childhood on this farm. Following the example of their mother, they found they could do almost anything if they were clever enough not to impose upon their father. For example, Pardon forbade spring housecleaning. It was part of his bias against "gathered-in" things, a Quaker term that referred to worldly possessions. He said it was totally unnecessary and disruptive of his peace of mind. Every year, however, he returned to Hopkinton, Rhode Island, on business. As soon as he had disappeared down the road, Prudence and Almira ran to fetch the neighbor women, who had been organized ahead of time by Esther. The women swooped into the house, flung open all the doors and windows, beat the rugs, aired the bedding, and did a hundred other forbidden things before Pardon returned. He never noticed.[3]

But in spite of his obstinacy in certain matters, Pardon was no tyrant. He was a responsible, hard-working man, anchored to his land, devoted to his family, and respected in the community. He prospered during these years, farming in the summer and taking his turn with other village fathers teaching in the district elementary school in the winter when there was no regular schoolmaster. But since he was a Quaker, he did not join the men of the place in their amusements. He did not march in the Masonic parades. He did not bet on horses at the Butts Bridge racecourse, frequent the taverns, or attend supper parties in the stately homes adjacent to the village green. Pardon was, however, the village overseer of the poor, and in a sense, he struggled upstream against the prevailing current.

He had moved westward, as John Crandall had done long before him, but had not found the physical and psychic space he craved. Several years later he would try another escape, but for the time being he invested in a brig called *The Hope*, whose voyages to Guadeloupe and Martinique he savored only in his imagination.

In time Hezekiah, his oldest son, married Clarissa Cornell, second cousin of the founder of Cornell University. This alliance linked the Crandalls with two of the oldest families in Canterbury, the Kinnes and the Coggswells.[4] Like the grandfather for whom he was named, Hezekiah was "brisk for business" and soon was running a small cotton mill on Mudhole Road. Reuben, six years younger than Hezekiah, chose to pursue the profession of medicine. Pardon sent him to Yale, and he later studied with Dr. Andrew Harris, one of Canterbury's leading physicians.

It was decided that Prudence, who was too inquisitive for her own good, should receive a "guarded" Quaker education. She was sent to Providence to the finest Quaker boarding school in existence, known as the New England Yearly Meeting School or more familiarly as the Brown Seminary. This imposing four-story school sat in the midst of forty-three donated acres of Moses Brown's homestead. Brown, then in his eighties, was one of Providence's most venerable citizens and a longtime abolitionist. There, unlike most finishing schools she might have been sent to, Prudence's curiosity was unleashed and she was allowed to pursue arithmetic, rhetoric, grammar, Latin, and the sciences all the way from the geological laboratory in the basement to the observatory on the roof.

The school was unique because its purpose was to produce not an intellectual elite, but broad-minded citizens who would make democracy work. To ensure this, girls as well as boys were admitted, poor children received scholarships, and students of other religious backgrounds were welcomed. Plain clothes, plain speech, and plain manners were the rule. The school's patron, ancient Moses Brown, sometimes toddled over from his Elmgrove mansion with vegetables from his garden for the school kitchen. Students were allowed to pick mulberries in his yard and on rare occasions were invited inside for refreshments.[5]

The school provided advanced opportunities for students of unusual qualifications, and when she was older Prudence may have been a "monitor" or apprentice teacher. When she left Providence around 1830, she returned to Connecticut and taught briefly in Lisbon before becoming a teacher at a boarding school in Plainfield, across the river from Canterbury.

Prosperous, bucolic Canterbury then appeared to be one of those quintessential New England villages described by Charles Dickens when he visited America: "Every little colony of houses had its church . . . peeping from among the white tops and shady trees; every house is the whitest of the white; every Venetian blind the greenest of the green; every fine day's sky the bluest of the blue."[6]

But Canterbury was in reality far more contentious. Important changes were taking place. For one thing, industrialization had disrupted the tranquil landscape with raucous little mill towns called Unionville, Packerville, and Centerville. In colonial days there had been laws against peddlers, itinerant preachers, and strangers in general who introduced disruptive diseases and infectious ideas. As late as 1829 a town committee urged Canterbury citizens to purchase "their domestic productions of the manufacturers and mechanics in our own town in preference to going abroad for the articles or encouraging foreigners to bring articles to us."[7] Now "foreigners and strangers" were coming in droves, while the lure of wild Ohio had taken many young men from established families away. Money, not land or one's longevity upon it, was the new measure of status.

It befuddled the older generation, who preferred to know without doubt who were the elite and who were the upstarts.

Once upon a time brandy and claret sat on the sideboards of every wealthy dining room in Canterbury. Hard cider was consumed by workers in the fields along with meat pies and custard. It was common to see "red-nosed idlers grouped about the door of the tavern, coughing and spitting after their morning drams."[8] But now a temperance society in Canterbury, the first in Windham County, preached that it was immoral and unhealthy to imbibe spirits. Prudence and Hezekiah's wife Clarissa joined the society, although they were not allowed to speak at meetings.

Traditionally, the most respected men of Canterbury attended Masonic meetings of the Moriah Lodge on the second floor of Johnson's Tavern and took part in Masonic parades and picnics. Now a faction in the village attacked the fraternal organization of freemasonry as secret and subversive, anti-American, antidemocratic, and even Papist. So strong were feelings on the issue, one chronicler wrote, that grave old men who had been neighbors all their lives quarreled and refused to speak to one another.[9]

Another big change was the advent of revival sects, which by 1830 had sprouted all over New England. The revivalists promised that all men and women, rich or poor, could obtain salvation by repenting their past sins and dedicating themselves, not to the accumulation of land and wealth, which had previously delineated the worthy, but to doing good works. In Hampden, just northwest of Canterbury, a group known as the Christ-ians were said to pray so loud they could be heard two miles away. These believers, in order to be humble, became literally like children and crawled on the floor. They spent so much time in meeting that they neglected to milk their cows.[10] Such behavior prompted

Alexis de Tocqueville, who toured America for ten months in 1831, to declare, "Religious insanity is very common in the United States."[11]

Itinerant preachers set up tents in groves outside the village, and drew flocks of people. Prudence more than once borrowed a chaise from storekeeper Stephen Coit and drove out to Lebanon or Voluntown to hear them.[12]

It was Prudence's enthusiasm for new ideas that prompted her brother Reuben, a doctor, to write to her in the summer of 1831 from Peekskill, New York, where he had established his medical practice. He had long ago despaired for the soul of his father after Pardon had slammed down the family Bible one night and roared, "It's a damn lie!"[13] Now Reuben feared his older sister, whom he considered a "very obstinate girl," was following a similar erratic course, having been baptized a Baptist not with a sprinkling of water but by full immersion in the Quinebaug River. "My mind has been very much exercised at times on your case and condition," he wrote, "and I sincerely hope that you use discretion in all your undertakings."[14]

What prompted Reuben to write was the fact that Prudence had recently been appointed director of the new Canterbury Female Seminary. Reuben did not want her to disgrace herself, and him in the process, with religious nonsense. If she, as principal, ran off to revival meetings every three or four days, he promised that he would have a "very poor opinion" of her.

Reuben was quite conventional in his manners and attitudes and sensed that his sister might not thrive, let alone survive, among the social elite of Canterbury. He therefore offered her copious advice on how to please the parents of the pampered girls she was soon to teach. He admonished her to stick to her task: "I wish you would endeavor to make your school your dependence for your living, and no man can make a living in any business without he attends strictly to it." He suggested she have Almira, who was to be her helper, gather the girls in a group "aside from regular school hours" and make them practice reading in turn. Reading well out loud, he wrote, was a requisite for a "finished and accomplished young lady." Her students should also write compositions every week because improvements in this area would be readily noticed by the parents and "be a source of greatest satisfaction to them."[15]

Although Reuben's anxiety about conflict between his sister and her clients eventually proved to be justified, it was premature. Everyone in Canterbury, from the humblest farmer to the richest squire, wanted the school because it would save them the expense of sending their daughters abroad after elementary school. The selectmen knew the school would elevate their village in the estimation of larger towns like Norwich, Litchfield, and Hartford, which had female academies of their own.[16] Prudence was no stranger in the village, and she traveled in and out of the mainstream of the elite provincial society of Canterbury with ease. Yet although she was among them, she was not really one of them.

The house she was about to buy was unlike any she had ever lived in before. The site of her new school was to be the stately Paine mansion, vacant since Luther Paine had fallen down dead while chopping wood in the backyard. It was situated on a corner of the village green at the intersection of two turnpikes, within a yard enclosed by a chaste white fence. This ample building, along with two others in the village, was acknowledged to be of such architectural distinction as to constitute a "Canterbury" style. The main part of the house, built by a gifted local architect by the name of Dyer, between 1801 and 1805, had four rooms on each floor and two interior chimneys. An archway beyond the center stairway led to additional small, low-ceilinged rooms in an ell extension that probably predated the rest of the house.

The white facade displayed graceful classical details that distinguished it from the more sober Georgian style to which it was related. Two-story pilasters stood at the corners of the building. Within the slightly projecting center gable, the six-paneled front door was dark green and framed with a fanlight and rectangle sidelights. On the second story, above the front door, was a tripartite Palladian window of great elegance. Each of the other symmetrical windows, of which there were eight in the front, had twenty-four panes of glass. Within the yard grew fruit trees, a kitchen garden, and in the spring, a profusion of day lilies.[17]

Opposite the Paine house on a slight hill was the home of Dr. Andrew Harris, Reuben's onetime teacher and patron, which boasted a conservatory that was "the wonder of the county."[18] Across the turnpike, flanking the side of the school like another paternal arm, was the new home of lawyer Andrew T. Judson, one of the most influential men in Canterbury. Judson anticipated that the new school would attract the daughters of some of the leading men of the state, a tantalizing situation considering the fact that he had ambitions to be governor. Therefore, he lost little time in implicating himself in the school's affairs. He composed a courtly letter to Prudence, which was signed by seventeen other gentlemen, assuring her of their "entire approbation" and offering their "efficient aid" and "cordial support."

These gentlemen, friends and colleagues all, decided among themselves who would serve on the Board of Visitors, the body designed to counsel and guide Prudence in decisions and policies. From the professional class the board included Dr. Harris and Canterbury's leading lawyers—Judson, Daniel Frost, Jr., and Rufus Adams, who was justice of the peace. Another member, axe manufacturer Samuel Hough, gave Prudence a $1,500 mortgage on the $2,000 purchase price of the house.[19] William Kinne, secretary of the Congregational Church on the green, represented an old landed family. The new Congregational minister of that church, the Reverend Dennis Platt, agreed to serve as chairman.

The Board of Visitors placed an advertisement in the *Brooklyn* (Connecticut) *Advertiser* stating that reading, writing, arithmetic, English grammar, geography, ancient and modern history "together with delineating maps," natural and moral philosophy, chemistry, and astronomy would be taught. There would be no vacation during the year. Therefore scholars could enter or leave at any time without interruption. Tuition was to be $3.00 per term plus $1.50 per week for board, which would include laundry done "in the family of the instructress." Every scholar was expected to attend public worship "somewhere" on the Sabbath. The ad ended with platitudes lauding Prudence's moral reputation and teaching ability.

Prudence moved into the house early in October 1831, and soon after that had about twenty students. Most of these, like Sarah Adams, Frances and Sarah Coit, Eliza and Phoebe Hough, Amy Baldwin, and Mary Clark of Canterbury, were day students.[20] Hannah Pearl, the daughter of state senator Phillip Pearl, came over from Hampton, Connecticut. Another student, H. B. Robbins, came from Lisbon, Connecticut.

At the end of January 1832, the Board of Visitors assessed the progress of the pupils and unanimously resolved that "the first quarterly examination of this school has given entire satisfaction." In an advertisement in the *Norwich*

Courier of March 21, Prudence expanded her list of subjects to include—for additional tuition—drawing, painting, piano, and French. The ad pronounced that "the location of the school possesses many natural advantages and is surrounded with good society."

Chapter Two

*O*n any day in the spring of 1832, the bonneted young ladies of the Canterbury Female Seminary could be seen taking a brisk stroll, two by two in an undeviating line, led by their admirable directess. But as Prudence's school flowered, another school, in New Haven, Connecticut, had withered in the bud. And though she didn't know it, the fate of this other school would have a direct bearing on the Canterbury Seminary.

On October 1, 1831, an editorial in the *New Haven Palladium* stated: "We will inform [our readers] that we mean, without any jesting, to say there has been an attempt, a serious attempt, to get up an institution in this place for the education of colored men." The notion of a school of higher education for black people was humorous at the time because they had not even been granted the right to an adequate elementary education. In 1827 *Freedom's Journal*, the first black newspaper in the United States, had noted that New Haven, with a black population of 800, had two black schools, which operated only three months of the year. Philadelphia, with a much larger black population of 20,000, had only three schools run by four overwhelmed teachers. New York had two schools for its black population of 15,000. Both Providence, with 1,500 blacks, and Hartford, with 500, had none. "Can the husbandman," asked the editors of *Freedom's Journal*, "if the fields be neglected during the time of ploughing and sowing, expect a harvest?"[1]

Higher education was not considered a "right" of black people, whose humanity, let alone citizenship, had not yet been conceded by the white majority. A surfeit of contemporary scriptural, scientific, and historical data could be conjured to "prove" black people were incapable of learning like white people. Furthermore, it was considered unwise to raise the hopes of black people unrealistically, for no matter how many degrees they might succeed in winning, the prejudice against them was so great they could never be accepted in society as equal with whites.

Many educated white people regretted the grievous, though profitable, historical "error" of bringing blacks to the country in the first place. Some of the most prominent of these men, including Andrew Jackson, Henry Clay, and Francis Scott Key, formed the American Colonization Society in 1816 to raise money to send the black people, starting with all those who were not docile and productive slaves, to a colony on the west coast of Africa called Liberia, where they might flourish among their own kind. To this superficially humane enterprise flocked many troubled liberals of the day as well as diehard racists. But the colonization scheme was never a resounding success in the South, and by 1830 the society was largely a Northern-based organization attempting to deal with a Northern "problem": the expanding communities of free black people living in urban areas who were, according to the *African Repository*, the official organ of the Colonization Society, "a greater nuisance than even slaves."[2]

Most free blacks, although they proposed their own schemes for repatriation from time to time, were strongly opposed to the Colonization Society. A meeting of "people of color" in Hartford on July 13, 1831, resolved: "The American Colonization Society is actuated by the same motivations which influenced the mind of Pharaoh when he ordered the male children of the Israelites to be destroyed." By and large, black Americans wanted to stay in their own country, and they wanted for their children the same things that white people wanted for theirs. One of these things was education.

The idea of a school for blacks in New Haven originated with the Reverend Simeon Jocelyn, the white minister of a black church. He planned to combine classical studies with a practical curriculum in the mechanical arts and agriculture. He convinced two vital but very different friends to join him in setting up the school—William Lloyd Garrison and Arthur Tappan, both of whom would play a large role in Prudence Crandall's life too.

Garrison was the young editor of a fiery abolitionist newspaper, *The Liberator*, which he had founded early in 1831 in Boston. Before coming to Boston, Garrison had lived in Baltimore, where he learned about slavery firsthand: while walking down the streets, he would hear cries and screams from behind closed shutters as slaves were beaten by their masters. He was originally sympathetic toward the Colonization Society, until black friends convinced him that the most rebellious slaves, therefore the potential leaders, would be the first ones taken to Africa. The purpose of the society in the South, they told him, was not to abolish the system but to make it run more efficiently.

Garrison was above all a man of action, and once he understood the problem, he longed to do something to end it. He seized an opportunity when he learned that a ship-owner originally from his native town of Newburyport, Massachusetts, was transporting slaves from Baltimore to New Orleans. He wrote an article in *The Genius of Universal Emancipation*, the paper he worked for in Baltimore, advertising the man as a robber and a murderer. The ship-owner, Francis Todd, immediately sued Garrison for libel and easily won the case in the sympathetic Southern court. Garrison, unable to pay the fine and court costs amounting to $100, went to jail. There he demonstrated the focused energy his enemies came to cite as evidence of his fanaticism. He wrote constantly—articles, sonnets (one entitled "The Guiltless Prisoner"), and an eight-page tract condemning his trial.

A copy of this tract landed among the invoices and orders on the desk of Simeon Jocelyn's other friend, Arthur Tappan. Tappan was a wealthy New York businessman whose family lived in New Haven. A staunch temperance man, he had also once belonged to the Colonization Society until he discovered that barrels of rum were accompanying the emigrants to Africa. Tappan was highly principled and religious, abstemious in his personal life—he habitually took a tumbler of water and a few dry biscuits for lunch—but generous with his time and money toward causes of moral uplift that ranged from distributing free Bibles to redeeming fallen women. Tappan was so moved by Garrison's plight that he immediately cabled money for his release. Garrison soon left Baltimore for Boston, where he founded *The Liberator*.

Jocelyn had convinced Tappan to be one of ten donors, the remaining nine as yet hypothetical, to contribute $1,000 each toward the school. He hoped to raise the same amount among blacks. He needed Garrison's journalistic talents as well. In May 1831 Jocelyn wrote to Garrison that a group of colored gentlemen meeting at the Reverend Peter Williams' St. Phillip's African Episcopal Church in New York City had voted to merge their own plans for a high school with his. Garrison agreed to accompany Jocelyn and Tappan to Philadelphia, where they could present the plan for their school to a convention of black people that was being held there.

At the convention Jocelyn asked the assembly to consider New Haven as the best site for the school. He told them Arthur Tappan had offered to buy a fine piece of land, and he fully expected to secure the support of the trustees and faculty of Yale. The enlightened citizens of New Haven would soon follow suit and approve the plan, he felt, because of their extensive trade ties with the West Indies, where emancipation was imminent. After a day of debate, the convention unanimously passed the proposal. Riding back from Philadelphia, the three men must have felt a sense of satisfaction, not knowing, as black leader Martin Delany would put it, they had just "promised a great deal more than they [would] ever [be] able half to fulfill in thrice the period in which they expected it."3

During the summer that followed, in 1831, while the Paine mansion was being readied for Prudence's arrival in Canterbury, Garrison lectured to black and white audiences in meeting halls and dim church basements across New England, asserting that the proposed college would prepare young black men to compete in society on an equal basis with whites. The school's unique combination of study and manual labor would produce literate laborers whose material success would destroy the prejudices against them. The logic of this argument was obvious to Garrison, who was optimistic by nature, but many Northerners believed the alternatives to slavery or colonization would be miscegenation or race war and not the fruitful coexistence Garrison envisioned.[4]

Garrison's ideas found a voice in Samuel Joseph May, the Unitarian minister (the first one in the state) in Brooklyn, Connecticut, the county seat six miles from Canterbury. May was an earnest young family man with an aristocratic Boston background. He was slight of build and gentle in manner, and there was little in his background and less in his appearance to indicate the passion of his broad-mindedness. May had met Garrison shortly after the journalist had escaped Baltimore for Boston. Garrison had resolved to educate Boston with his insight that slavery was a national and not a regional problem, but found to his astonishment that all the lecture halls and churches were shut against him. He was told by such noted liberal clergymen as Lyman Beecher that his zeal was "commendable" but his independent, "fanatical notions" were unacceptable.[5] Deeply frustrated, Garrison placed a want ad for a lecture hall in the newspapers, promising that if one did not become available, he would shout his message in the open air of the Boston Common, if only to an audience of squirrels. When a hall finally did materialize, May, who was visiting Boston at the time, attended the lecture. The impression made by Garrison's words that night, May wrote in his memoirs, "gave a new direction to my thoughts, a new purpose to my ministry."[6] May introduced himself to Garrison after the lecture, and the two men formed a friendship that lasted all their lives.

May's "new purpose" to his ministry became evident when, on the Fourth of July 1831, he startled his Brooklyn congregation with the text of Ezekiel 22, chapter 29: "The people of the land have used oppression, and exercised robbery, and have vexed the poor and needy." "It would become us," the articulate preacher began, "to lower our tone of rejoicing." Two million people were slaves in the land of the free, and all white people, North and South, who allowed their lawmakers to perpetuate the bondage were "partakers of the sin." One day, he warned, the slaves will rise and throw off their own shackles if white people do not unloose them first: "Some Moses, or at least a Petion, will be born among the children of Africa, who will teach them their rights, and lead them forth to their defence."[7]

On the same holiday in Washington, D.C., Francis Scott Key, a founder of the Colonization Society and the next District Attorney for the District of Columbia, evinced a quite different attitude as he congratulated an audience gathered in the rotunda of the Capitol: "Is not the face of our country right in the beauties of nature, the labors of industry, the profusion of plenty? . . . Are not the kingdoms of the earth looking at us with respect, as the nation 'that will neither do nor suffer wrong'? . . . And are not the oppressed of the world thronging to our shore? . . . What is there that is not improving?"[8]

But it was May's words that proved to be prophetic in the coming weeks. In the dark of the night of August 21, a slave preacher named Nat Turner climbed through a window of his master's house in Southampton, Virginia, and then unbarred the front door to his followers, who crept upstairs and murdered the entire Travis family as they slept. Then the band moved across the countryside, killing every white person in their path.

By August 23 the rebellion was crushed; about fifty-five white people had died. Turner eluded capture for nearly two months until he was discovered, half-starved, hiding in a woodpile. On November 11, 1831, calm and unrepentant, he was hung.

In the hysteria that followed the insurrection, innocent black people were tortured, maimed, and executed in reprisal. There was a deluge of punitive laws against efforts to "enlighten" or "improve" free blacks and slaves. Because Nat Turner read the Bible for inspiration, literacy was a sorcerous art. Garrison, Simeon Jocelyn, and Arthur Tappan found themselves advocating a black college at an unfortunate historical moment.

The mayor of New Haven called a city meeting for September 10 to deal with the school proposal, although some citizens' groups, while opposed to the school, called such an action "hasty." After impassioned speeches by leading citizens, the body voted 700 to 4 (one of these dissenters was Jocelyn) that the college was a dangerous interference in city life, was incompatible with the prosperity of Yale, and ought to be resisted by all lawful means. Their resolutions concluded, "that if the establishment of such a college in any part of the country were deemed expedient, it should never be imposed on any community without their consent." Prospects for the black school seemed dim.

Simeon Jocelyn responded with a bitter letter in *The Liberator* in which he accused "our high minded patriots, our law givers, our greedy politicians" of twisting and distorting the issue before the common people had had a chance to consider it.[9] But probably few of the voters at the New Haven town meeting read his words. *The Liberator* was not yet well known among Northern white people. It had, however, shocked the Southerners, and they blamed the paper in part for fomenting the Turner rebellion. (The editor of the Tarboro, North Carolina, *Free Press*, for example, declared that anyone associated with it ought to be "barbecued.") And *The Liberator* was quite well known to free black people, whose subscriptions and donations kept the paper afloat during its first precarious years. In addition, a host of black volunteers stepped forward to act as agents for the paper in their areas.

The agent for Canterbury was a black farmer named William Harris.[10] Harris had come to America as a youth from the West Indies, burning with the desire to acquire a formal education. This had never come to pass, but he nevertheless married, raised a large family, and prospered modestly. He passed his deferred dream on to his children.

The Harris family was one of about a dozen free black families in Canterbury in the early 1830s. Slavery had existed in the state until after the Revolutionary War, when laws were passed that called for its gradual demise. By 1830 there were still twenty slaves in the state of Connecticut, but there were none in Windham County. Slavery had never been as profitable and practical on small Connecticut farms as it had been in other New England states like Rhode Island, where there were large tobacco plantations.

Between the races in Canterbury there was superficial harmony if not equality. One chronicler wrote that racial feelings in the village were "dormant." Adults of different races did not mix socially, but their children sat side by side in the same dismal district schools and were permitted to play together "in those rare cases where the children of the Puritan community were allowed to play."[11] Also, during harvest time certain social taboos were set aside. Then temporary black farmhands sat alongside their employers and ate huge midday dinners.

Steady work for black men, however, was seasonal, and they could not be apprenticed in white men's trades, nor, of course, could they enter the professions. Day laborers, it was said, often had trouble collecting their wages. Virtually every black woman in the village worked as a domestic servant or a laundress. The mill owners, who sometimes sent wagons out into the countryside to recruit unmarried girls and children, would not hire black women.

Racist practices were common. When black people traveled to or from the village, they were obliged to ride on top of the stagecoach in all kinds of weather. It was said that when there was a real schoolmaster in the village for any length of time, he skipped the black families as he "boarded round."[12] There had once been an unpleasant incident across the Quinebaug River at the all-white Plainfield Academy. The prankish boys, bored at hoisting the headmaster's cow into the belfry, held a mock trial with a black boy as defendant and nearly hanged him.

There was also the ubiquitous tradition of segregating black families in the rear pews or second-story galleries of churches and meeting houses, while the white people sat up front. Over in Brooklyn, Samuel Joseph May, who did not respect hierarchies of any sort and would not even wear a ministerial black robe for fear it would separate him from his flock, had once challenged this Christian pecking order. A black family was overcrowded in their assigned pew, which was as far away from the rest of the congregation as it could be and still remain in the building. May invited them to use one of the large front pews in the side galleries that happened to be vacant. They were reluctant to accept this courtesy, but the minister insisted upon it. After the service an irate parishioner demanded to know what the "nigger" family was doing in the front of the church. May told the man the family was there at his invitation, and warned him that if he did or said anything to hurt the feelings of that worthy family, May would announce it to the congregation and shame him as much as he was able. The black family remained in their pew.

It was through William Harris, indirectly, that Prudence became acquainted with *The Liberator*. One of Harris' sons,

Charles, was engaged to Mariah Davis, who worked at the
new Canterbury Female Seminary as a servant, or rather,
in Prudence's words, as a "family assistant."[13] Mariah read
The Liberator, and one day Prudence saw a copy and asked
to borrow it. What she read there—that slavery was a sin
and must be immediately repudiated even if the process of
eradicating it turned out to be a gradual one—comple-
mented the revivalist preaching of people like Charles
Finney, who held that salvation demanded immediate re-
pentance from the sinner and a decision to turn from narrow
self-interest to wider benevolence toward one's fellow creatures. The articles in *The Liberator*, then, however blunt
and startling their language, were less a challenge to Prudence's sensibility than a confirmation.

Garrison's feminism was so unformed at the time that he
still thought women should not speak in public gatherings.
Nonetheless, he printed a speech made by a black woman,
Maria Stewart, before a mixed audience of men and women
in Boston in September 1832, which Prudence may have
read. It was racism, Stewart said, that kept black people
mired in menial work, and it was constant menial work that
deadened their minds and spirits. Black people had to push
themselves for betterment. They could not wait for whites
to confer it upon them. Black women, Stewart declared,
had an important role in the development of the race as
mothers and homemakers. Her statement was poignant because black women often lost their children in slavery and
even in freedom seldom had the chance to stay at home like
white women of the new middle class. Morality and worth
were not inherent to any particular race or class, Stewart
said. If black women had the same opportunities as genteel
white women, their intellects would be as bright, their manners as dignified, and consequently their children would be
qualified to assume any position in life. Stewart daringly

blamed black women's degradation not on their own un-
worthiness, not on the shiftlessness of black men, but on
the greed and rapacity of white men.

William Harris also had a seventeen-year-old daughter
named Sarah, who was very close to Mariah Davis, her
brother's fiancée. Like her other siblings, Sarah was part
white, part Indian, and part black. Her complexion was so
light that an English visitor who later met her remarked,
"She had, indeed, so small a portion of the prohibited fluid
in her veins that she might have escaped observation at a
soiree in London or Paris, except for her good looks and
graceful manner."[14] Sarah had noticed that when Mariah
had finished her chores, she was permitted by Prudence to
sit in on classes in the sunny classroom on the second floor.[15]
Sarah was very keen and had already been educated to the
limit of the district school. She was aware that without
further education she was destined to remain, as Alexis de
Tocqueville had expressed it, "a sojourner in the dwellings
of [her] master," in this case the dwelling of Mr. Jedidiah
Shepard.

Sometime in the second autumn of the school, 1832,
Sarah approached Prudence and told her she wanted to get
"a little more learning" so she could teach "colored children." She said she would not board at the school but would
walk several miles daily from her father's farm. If Prudence
admitted her, she would be forever obliged, but if such an
action might be a means of injury, she would not "insist
upon the favor."[16]

Prudence did not reply immediately, but said she would
like to think about it. It was harvest time, the time of plenty.
From her upstairs windows she could see the cows that had
been loosed in the stubby fields of timothy, oats, and barley
to glean what the reapers had left behind. Pumpkins yel-
lowed on the vine. In the orchards, apples reddened the

ground. From many porch posts hung "weighty strings of quartered apples, of sweet corn boiled on the cob for winter, and gaudy red peppers drying in the sun."[17] All day long could be heard the "muffled thump of flails" and the creaking cider presses. As Prudence moved through her mansion, she could hear laughter in the keeping room. Young girls carrying books or knitting ascended the staircase and curtsied to her as she passed. She need do nothing and all would continue in this peaceful, fulsome way.

But now she knew too much. Slavery was a sin. If she kept Sarah's mind in bondage when she had the chance to free it, then she was no better than the rankest slaveholder. She recalled a recent editorial in *The Liberator* in which William Lloyd Garrison had written that "two capital errors" deterred the advancement of black people: one was that men undervalued the power of women in the cause, and the second was that women undervalued themselves.[18]

She understood the Quaker way: do not fight with those who are wrong, but come to the aid of those who are oppressed. She summoned Sarah and told her that if she were injured on Sarah's account, she could bear it. Sarah might enter as one of her students.

Chapter Three

Sarah began to attend classes. At first it did not seem to matter to anyone. Then, indirectly, through her family, Prudence learned of the first stirrings of disapproval. Several families told Pardon they would withdraw their daughters if Prudence's bizarre whim continued much longer. Her practical older brother Hezekiah, whose wife Clarissa was expecting her fifth baby, worried that patronage at his cotton mill was falling off. Soon the first of many delegations arrived at the school's front door.

As Mariah served tea in the front parlor, Mrs. Peters, the wife of an Episcopal minister, summarily announced: "Miss Harris must be dismissed. We will not have our girls in a school with a 'nigger.' If you do not send her away, we will withdraw our daughters and your school will sink." Prudence had in some way expected this, but she presented to the assembly of well-dressed matrons a perfect poker face, despite any churning emotions she was experiencing. This ability was one of her gifts. "Then let it sink," she replied simply, "I will not dismiss her."[1] The ladies retreated in a huff, their bonnets bobbing indignantly as they hurried down the path and out the gate.

Abraham Payne, a young man in the village at the time and later a lawyer, maintained that initially few people cared much if Sarah attended classes or not. After all, Mariah had been doing it informally for some time. Payne supposed that if things had run their natural course, enough white families would have withdrawn their daughters one by one until the school died a natural pecuniary death. He blamed subsequent events on the intervention of abolitionists and on the machinations of Andrew T. Judson and the Board of Visitors. There was also the issue of Prudence's "stiff-necked" attitude, which grew even stronger in the months Sarah was attending classes. Not only did Prudence remain adamant about Sarah staying in school, she came up with a much more daring plan.

The only champion of black people that Prudence knew of at the time was William Lloyd Garrison. On January 13, 1833, she wrote to him in Boston. She apologized for her boldness in writing directly to him, unknown to him as she was, but "circumstances" dictated it. She described her situation and then told him the object of her inquiry: "I wish to know your opinion respecting changing white scholars for colored ones." Did he, she wondered, think she could obtain twenty to twenty-five "young ladies of color," if not from Boston alone, then from "all the large cities in several states"? She said she was coming to Boston in a few days to discuss the matter with him in person.[2]

No one, not even her family, had an inkling of her intentions to radically change the school and make it one exclusively for black students. She was off to Boston to visit "infant schools" and buy "infant school apparatus," she told shopkeeper Richard Fenner across his counter one day. Would he provide her with a letter of introduction, as she knew no one in that city? She asked the Reverend Dennis Platt, the new Congregational minister of the church on the green, and the Reverend Levi Kneeland, her own pastor at the Baptist Church in neighboring Packerville, for letters as well. Then she set off on her own for Massachusetts.

In 1833 Boston had a population of about 60,000. The city was on the brink of transformation. In a few years gas lighting would be installed, railroads would eclipse the maritime industry, and the trickle of Irish immigration would become a deluge. Everywhere new buildings were going up, and the main streets were newly paved with rocks from the beach, called cobblestones. Prudence checked into the Marlboro Hotel on Washington Street, a well-known "temperance house," and immediately sent off a message to Garrison: "The lady who wrote you a short time since would inform you she is now in town and should be very thankful if you would call this evening at 6 o'clock."[3]

Garrison and his partner Isaac Knapp were then living a spartan existence in their office, not far from the waterfront. They slept on pallets on the floor, ate day-old bread from a nearby bakery, and worked incessantly. The place was always dim because of the ink-spattered windows. The printing press stood in one corner, with the composing stand opposite. There were also a long cluttered mailing table, two or three straight-backed chairs, and a pine desk at which the editor sat late at night composing his vitriolic editorials.

The Liberator had been slowly gaining circulation in the two years of its existence, and the office had become a rendezvous for people of all walks of life sympathetic to the cause of abolition, from white intellectuals like David Lee Child and his wife Lydia Maria Child, a well-known author, to working black people who were barbers, stevedores, waiters, and shoemakers. In addition, an organization Garrison helped found, the New England Anti-Slavery Society, was having its first anniversary.

This bunch of "nobodies," as the Colonization Society referred to them, were busily researching the status of American slavery and exposing the wretched general condition of the Northern free black population. They were at war with the hypocritical American Colonization Society, whose members, Garrison wrote, could "love and benefit" black people "four thousand miles off, but not at home."[4] The New England Anti-Slavery Society's president, Arnold Buffum, a Quaker importer and manufacturer of hats, was busy as the organization's full-time lecturing agent. Garrison held the arduous position of corresponding secretary.

Garrison, Simeon Jocelyn, and others had not abandoned their hopes for a black manual labor college. On September 4, 1832, the New England Anti-Slavery Society had passed a resolution to send Garrison to England to solicit money for the project.[5] Small groups like the Colored Female Religious Moral Society of Salem and the Juvenile Garrison Independent Society of Boston had begun to collect money for his passage. "Garrison in England will do the cause more good in three months than twelve in America," declared Arnold Buffum. Prudence's letter proposing an advanced school for black girls fit well into the society's agenda.

In a quiet corner of the Marlboro Hotel lobby, or perhaps in a deserted side parlor, Prudence waited for Garrison to arrive, masking her trepidation with composure. There was the chance, after all, that he would be the totally unsavory character a contemporary had envisioned him to be, "a stout, rugged, dark-visaged desperado" somewhat like a pirate. What if he was a fast-talking snake oil vender? What if he was as deranged as many said he was, or the devil incarnate?

When Garrison arrived, Prudence saw in a moment that

he was none of these things but rather a somberly clothed young man, pale and handsome with features more patrician than piratical.[6] His manners were courteous and his words soft-spoken and deliberately chosen. As Harriet Martineau, the English radical who first met him in 1835, commented, his entire demeanor was very much like that of a Quaker.[7] His magnetism immediately engaged Prudence, as it had others. Samuel Joseph May's first words to him after hearing his lecture had been "Mr. Garrison, I am not sure that I can endorse all you have said this evening . . . but I am prepared to embrace *you*."[8] Lydia Maria Child remembered, "He got hold of the strings of my conscience and pulled me into reform work . . . I could not do otherwise so help me God."[9]

There was a risk to Garrison in supporting Prudence's proposition. A second failure to establish a school might prove insurmountable. Nevertheless, he agreed to run an advertisement for the school in *The Liberator* within a month. He promised to send Arnold Buffum to Canterbury to aid her, and he gave her the names of several black people whose daughters might become prospective students. One of these people was Elizabeth Hammond, a black woman living in Providence who had two daughters, and it was for this city that Prudence next set out.

Providence had a relatively small black community, and for this reason there were no black newspapers, no black professionals, and, unlike larger cities like Philadelphia, no affluent black families. Black men in Providence were cooks, waiters, gardeners, handymen, grooms, porters, and day laborers, and this last category was being usurped by Irish immigrants. As one black man said, "To drive a carriage, carry a market basket after the boss, and brush his boots or saw wood and run errands was as high as a colored man could rise."[10] Nevertheless, through the most stringent thrift and sacrifice, Providence blacks succeeded in many instances in acquiring small parcels of real estate.

The North End of Providence, where Elizabeth Hammond lived, was a rough and tumble area crowded with saloons, dance halls, and brothels frequented by sailors, white laborers, and other transients. It is doubtful that Prudence had ever been to the neighborhoods called Hardscrabble and Snowtown when she attended the Brown Seminary. The North End was also the home of most of the black population of the city. It was a high-crime area, and white violence against the black people was common. In September 1831 a brawl started by drunken sailors ignited five nights of white rioting in which five people died and much black property was destroyed.

Elizabeth Hammond was a widow whose husband Thomas had managed to acquire property valued at $2,000 at the time of his death in 1826. She owned a boarding house, which allowed her to make a living without journeying daily to distant white neighborhoods. It also allowed her to protect and supervise her daughters, Ann Eliza, age seventeen, and Sarah, age nine, in a decent home above the violent street below. During Prudence's visit, Mrs. Hammond introduced her to two white abolitionists, George Benson, a wool merchant, and his younger brother Henry, who was *The Liberator* agent for Providence.

The Benson boys were the sons of George Benson, Sr., a wealthy retired businessman formerly associated with the Moses Brown family in the lucrative firm of Brown, Benson, and Ives. The eight Benson children had grown up in a magnificent house on Angell Street in Providence, built on a lot originally owned by Moses Brown. The family had always been involved with progressive causes. The revolutionary hero the Marquis de Lafayette had once enjoyed the panorama of Providence from an upstairs window of this mansion. George Benson, Sr., decided in 1822 for principled reasons to withdraw from the combative arena of business and retire to a farm in Brooklyn, Connecticut, where he became close friends with Samuel Joseph May.

Young Henry Benson was impressed with Prudence's plan. He officially reported to Garrison that they had had a "pleasant interview" with her. "She is," he wrote, "I should [think] exactly the one for that purpose."[11]

Mrs. Hammond also took Prudence to visit three other black families with daughters. Prudence optimistically wrote to Garrison afterward, "They seem to feel much for the education of their daughters, and I think I shall be able to obtain six scholars from Providence."[12]

Prudence returned to Canterbury on a Saturday evening. The following Monday she confided in her friend Daniel Packer. Packer owned the mill in Packerville and had built the church Prudence attended so that his workers would have a religious center in their lives. He praised the school idea, but, practical Yankee that he was, he feared she would lack for students and be ruined as a result.[13] Taking this pessimistic view to heart, Prudence decided to start out on another recruiting mission immediately. She sent a note to Garrison asking him to inform his friends in New York that she would arrive on the next boat.

In New York she used Garrison's introduction to meet with the Reverend Peter Williams of St. Phillip's African Episcopal Church, and he agreed to be the New York liaison for the school. Then, fortuitously, on the returning packet boat she met Arthur Tappan, who was commuting to his home in New Haven. They talked about the ill-fated New Haven school and her own enterprise. Tappan pledged his support and gallantly added, "He did not know but he should come with the scholars when they entered school."[14]

She also stopped over in New Haven to meet Simeon Jocelyn, whose enthusiasm acted like a tonic on her.

When she arrived home she felt confident enough to satisfy the curiosity of her family and friends, which, after two mysterious trips, was considerable. To her "astonishment," and partly because the critical Reuben was far away in Peekskill, they received her news quietly and "exhibited but little opposition." Pardon, who valued his peace and privacy above all else, was cautious, but as he later remarked, "My family was the setters-up of that school and myself a supporter of my family."[15] Prudence casually dropped Arthur Tappan's name and found, as she had expected, that the weight of his reputation quashed many of their fears. She did not dwell upon the part William Lloyd Garrison was to play in the project. One of her friends, Dr. Roland Green from the Quaker community on Black Hill, had long agonized over the "culpable neglect" of the education of black children. Now he relayed the news of this exciting development to his good friend Samuel Joseph May in Brooklyn.

Soon afterward, probably on February 24, 1833, Prudence stood before her students and calmly announced that beginning with the next term their school would receive only young ladies of color. She had had a conversion of sorts, she explained, and intended to dedicate the rest of her life to the education of colored children, twenty of whom were already planning to attend the school.

That very night four of the most powerful men of the village, lawyer Daniel Frost, Jr., Dr. Andrew Harris, justice of the peace Rufus Adams, and merchant Richard Fenner decided to act without delay. By nine o'clock the next morning they were sitting in Prudence's parlor pressing her with inquiries. Had she considered the embarrassment she would cause at the Congregational Church if she arrived there with a score of black girls intending to worship? Her visitors knew that some of the local girls like Sarah Harris were members of the Congregational Church in the Westminster section of Canterbury, several miles away, and would probably want to attend the convenient church on the green. Prudence replied that she planned to invite "colored or white" preachers to hold services inside the school. The gentlemen were not satisfied with this solution and informed her they had resolved to do everything in their power to destroy her new venture and "that they could do it, and should do it."[16]

Prudence was considerably shaken by this call and hurriedly penned a letter to Simeon Jocelyn. If he could use his influence, she hinted, to persuade Arthur Tappan to come to Canterbury, it would mean a great deal, although she realized that would be "a favor too great to be expected." She told Jocelyn she was reminding Garrison to dispatch Arnold Buffum as he had promised. She closed her note with "Your opinion and advice will be thankfully received on this occasion and I hope you will by no means withhold it but write to me IMMEDIATELY." There was a postscript: "Please write to me IMMEDIATELY."[17]

Neither Tappan, Garrison, nor Jocelyn was able to come to her aid before the male delegation returned on March 1, this time officially representing the village. The group had regretted their hasty threats and this time had prepared a strategy of patient condescension. Their spokesman, Daniel Frost, Jr., the founder of the Canterbury Temperance Society, was accustomed to lecturing recalcitrant audiences. In a "kind and affecting manner," Frost explained to Prudence that they were perfectly willing that blacks be educated provided it was somewhere other than Canterbury. He urged her to consider the impropriety of going against "all their wishes" and predicted her "design" would bring disgrace upon them all. Then Dr. Harris declared that "if she received her expected scholars the blacks of the town . . . would begin to look up and claim an equality with the whites; and if they were all placed upon an equal footing *property and life* would no longer be safe."[18] It was then that Prudence, who had studied logic, uttered the didactic and politically ruinous retort "Moses had a black wife!"

Chapter Four

*T*he situation was more serious than the town committee had imagined. Prudence had not repented. Nor was she ashamed. They had scolded her and she had not even cried. It dawned on them that they had been fired as advisers, dismissed as summarily as the students.

This became perfectly clear when an advertisement appeared in the March 2, 1832, edition of *The Liberator*, not in the tiny-print classified section, but prominently displayed with a florid introduction by the editor. The ad thanked everyone who had previously patronized Prudence's school and informed them that on the first Monday of April, she would be receiving "young ladies and little misses of color." The shock of this information was compounded by the new list of sponsors: Arthur Tappan, Reverend Peter Williams, Reverend Theodore Wright, Reverend George Bourne, Reverend Heyborn, and Reverend Samuel Cornish from New York; James Forten and Joseph Cassey from Philadelphia; George Benson, Jr., from Providence; William Lloyd Garrison and Arnold Buffum from Boston; Reverend Samuel Joseph May from Brooklyn; and Daniel Packer from Canterbury. Most of these men were abolitionists who lived outside Connecticut. Many of them were black.

It was as if Prudence had dragged a delicate and private family squabble into the light of day like a berserk town crier. The *Brooklyn Advertiser Press* wanted to know how she could seek out William Lloyd Garrison, "who was an entire stranger to her," while at the same time she hid "the object of her visit" from the "kind and able advisors whom she had often eulogized for their warmth of friendship, and the interest they had manifested in her welfare."[1]

In Providence, George Benson's initial elation that the school was under way dissolved when he understood the severity of the criticisms against her. He left immediately for Canterbury, during a cold spell so severe that on the return trip he froze his fingers and couldn't write for a month. On his arrival in the village, he found that Prudence was "calm and undaunted."[2] Reassured, and rather impressed, Benson left for Brooklyn to visit his sisters and parents and to consult with Samuel Joseph May. As he was mounting his horse, he saw justice of the peace Rufus Adams tacking a notice onto the signpost in front of the Congregational Church: an emergency town meeting was called for Saturday night. It amazed Benson that the prevention of the school was considered an urgent enough matter to override Canterbury's traditional Blue Laws against work and business being conducted between sundown on Saturday and sunrise on Monday.

Benson knew Samuel Joseph May would find this meeting significant. May had already written to Prudence offering his support, and she had replied that she would welcome a visit, but as yet they had not met. May, whose unorthodox religious views had already generated a good deal of hostility in certain circles, worried that his presence might further alienate the Congregationalists in Canterbury. But he also knew Prudence could not stand alone against the whole village. May was a civil libertarian, and he believed in Prudence's right to open any kind of school she wished as much as he believed in abolitionism. "How can we stretch out our hands for the relief of the slave," he wondered, "if that hand is chained . . . it is then but a preliminary measure in the cause of the enslaved that we secure our own rights."[3]

May's views ran counter to the prevailing sentiments about women and politics, held by, among others, Catherine Beecher, an educator who would later denounce Prudence's school. Beecher, the articulate daughter of Boston's famed Reverend Lyman Beecher, wrote, "Whatever, in any measure, throws a woman into the attitude of a combatant, either for herself or others—whatever binds her in a party conflict—whatever obliges her in any way to exert coercive influences, throws her out of her appropriate sphere." When that happens, Beecher warned, "the sacred protection of religion" and "all the generous promptings of chivalry" no longer applied.[4]

After George Benson met with May in Brooklyn, the two men left for Canterbury. As they entered the village, several men confronted them and warned them they would be in personal danger if they meant to help the schoolteacher, but Benson and May continued on their mission anyway. Again, they found Prudence to be the very picture of tranquillity. "The effect of her Quaker discipline" seemed apparent "in every word she spoke and in every expression of her countenance."[5] The three of them agreed that Prudence could not go to the town meeting without offending everyone she hadn't offended already. Prudence therefore asked May if he would represent her at the meeting; he replied, "Certainly, come what will!"[6] This was an astute move on Prudence's part because everyone in the area knew May and respected him; even his enemies found him "a hard man to hate." Although he had gained but few converts to Unitarianism, May allowed every organization or group that needed a meeting place to use his church, the largest building in Brooklyn. May had founded the local chapter of the Colonization Society in 1829, and was active on the school committee, in the peace society, and in the temperance league. (He was, in fact, the person who saved lawyer Daniel Frost, Jr., from alcoholic ruin, and everyone in Canterbury knew it.)

First of all, it was decided, May would attempt to explain how Prudence had made her decision and how, having done so, she could not retract it without deeply wounding Sarah's feelings and "adding to the mountain load of injuries and insults already heaped upon the colored people of our country." In addition, May would offer to pay bonds for the students, as the clever triumvirate of Canterbury lawyers (Andrew T. Judson, Rufus Adams, and Daniel Frost, Jr.) had dug up an old pauper law made to "prevent any foreigners from being chargeable to the town." This 1650 law stated: "No master of a familye shall give interteinment or habietation to any younge man to sojourne in his familye, but by the allowance of the inhabitants of the towne where he dwells, under the penalty of twenty shillings per week."[7] In other words, no strangers could remain in the village for long unless the town authorities consented. May, the compromiser, also suggested delicately that Prudence consider moving her school to a "more retired situation" than on the village green at the junction of two turnpikes. Prudence concurred. She also decided that it would be best if Arnold Buffum, president of the New England Anti-Slavery Society, did not visit Canterbury for the time being.

George Benson conveyed all this information to Garrison and Buffum in Boston, and Garrison shot back a quick reply:

> Although distracted with cares, I must seize my pen to express my admiration of your generous and prompt defense of Miss Crandall from her pitiful assailants. . . . If possible, Miss C. must be sustained at all hazards. If we suffer the school to be put down in Canterbury, other places will partake of panic and also prevent its introduction in their vicinity. . . . The New Haven excitement has furnished a bad precedent, second must not be given.

Garrison was relieved to hear that May was going to the meeting. "If anyone can make them ashamed of their conduct he is the man, may the Lord give him courage, wisdom, and success."[8]

Shortly before the town meeting was to take place, Prudence learned that Arnold Buffum was lecturing in nearby Norwich, and on an impulse, she went there and begged him to come to Canterbury after all. Finally the fateful night of March 9 arrived. May was considerably nervous about his role and it was, therefore, with "surprize and joy" (and probably relief) that he found Arnold Buffum waiting for him in Prudence's front parlor. Prudence gave each of the gentlemen a letter of introduction to the chairman of the meeting requesting that they be heard as her attorneys. She promised to be bound by any agreement they saw fit to make on her behalf. Then the two men left, and Prudence watched them cross the road and merge into the throng of men making their way up the dark hill through the tangle of carts and carriages and into the church, which blazed with light in the wintry night.[9]

The Congregational Church could hold a thousand people if some of them stood, and that night many did. George and Henry Benson arrived from Providence just in time to secure two seats upstairs in the gallery near some black men. Henry wanted a good overview because he planned to take notes for an article for *The Liberator*. May and Buffum squeezed down a side aisle on the main floor and found space in a wall pew near the deacon's seat where the meeting's moderator, Ashael Bacon, was banging his gavel for order. Next to Bacon sat Andrew T. Judson. May looked about the room and recognized many men from neighboring villages; he also noted the "two or three decent looking colored men" sitting in the gallery near the Bensons.

Rufus Adams, justice of the peace, began the meeting by reading a "warning" in which he predicted that a flood of black people of "foreign jurisdiction" was about to break upon the village. Because the "characters and habits" of these people would be "various and unknown," they posed a threat to the "properties and reputations" of Canterbury citizens. Therefore the voices of the villagers must be raised in protest, Adams declared. A committee composed of the civil authority and selectmen should immediately point out to the "person" contemplating the establishment of the school the "incalculable evils" of the design and make her stop.

Then the venerable Andrew T. Judson rose. He was, in the current vernacular, "a gentleman of property and standing": the town clerk of Canterbury, the state attorney for Windham County, a former state senator, a director of the Windham County Bank, a director of the Windham County Mutual Fire Insurance Corporation, a pillar of the Congregational Church, and—not least—the former secretary of the Board of Visitors of the Canterbury Female Seminary.

Judson addressed his fellow citizens as if he were pros-

ecuting a crime and they were the jury. He drummed in
the notion of the indignity they had all suffered when Prudence advertised her new school in Garrison's outrageous
newspaper without consulting them. He alluded to Arthur
Tappan, one of the "powerful conspirators" directing her,
and asked the men of Canterbury if they were frightened
because Miss Crandall's friends had "a few thousand dollars." Judson bellowed that the idea of a school for "nigger
girls" across the street from his house was "insupportable."
In fact, he was not willing to give up "one corner" of the
village for such a purpose. He warned the fathers in the
audience that if the school went into operation as one had
in New Orleans—"where there is scarcely a *happy* person"—their sons and daughters would be ruined. He ex-
tolled the actions of the prudent men of New Haven in
thwarting a school for blacks there. After their example, he
challenged, "shall it be said *we* cannot, that we dare not
resist?" He triumphantly concluded that the old law relating
to the "introduction of foreigners" would make it so expensive for all concerned that the school would not be able to
function.

As Judson bowed to wild applause, May and Buffum
passed their letters to Rufus Adams, who handed them to
Judson. Judson glanced at them and then broke out into a
noisier tirade than before and accused the two of insulting
the town with their presence. Other men jumped to their
feet and began shouting. They waved their fists and warned
May and Buffum not to say a word or they would be arrested
or beaten. Pardon Crandall, who was also present, thought
the scene was like the Inquisition. May and Buffum sat
back down.

Henry Benson was so disgusted with the meeting he went
outside to cool down. Several men were standing about
stomping their feet to stay warm and earnestly discussing

Judson's remarks and how much it would cost to "[convey] the scholars out of town." Henry, who was only nineteen, blurted out that it would cost more than Mr. Judson imagined because he and others like him were prepared to take the case to the Supreme Court of America if they had to!

Inside, one lone man named George White, a tanner by trade, protested that everyone was so excited that they were not thinking straight. The old law, he argued, was never intended to shut down a school and never meant to be used against a good Christian woman like Prudence Crandall. White suggested they buy back the Paine house or otherwise help Prudence move to another part of the village. The whole time White was trying to be heard, the room was in the "utmost confusion." Solomon Paine, a prominent member of the church, kept jumping up from his seat and demanding the moderator declare White out of order. The black men in the gallery, it was noted, also made "a great disturbant" by boldly talking out loud.

Amid this tumult, Bacon, the moderator, called for a vote and then abruptly adjourned the meeting. At that, May jumped up on his pew and cried out, "Men of Canterbury, I have a word for you. Hear me!" He said that the school had no purpose other than education and that the prospective students came from fine and respectable families. He quickly introduced Arnold Buffum, but as Buffum began to speak, Judson yelled from the back of the church that everyone must leave. Many in the audience, however, decided to remain. Minutes later, the great church doors flew open and six men, headed by Dr. Andrew Harris, stomped down the aisle. "Out! Out!" they ordered as they herded the recalcitrants from the building. Then they slammed the doors and locked them.

May and Buffum lingered outside the church in the frosty night answering questions from a few men interested enough to listen to them. Finally they too went home. George and Henry Benson went to Bacon's tavern, where they had left their horses. Henry soon found himself baited by a half dozen men, several of them quite drunk. They taunted him about the law Judson had resurrected. For the second time that night, Henry said the law was unconstitutional and Miss Crandall's friends would spare no expense in proving it. The abolitionists, he promised, were willing to put up bonds for the scholars even if it took $10,000, $20,000 or—he got a little carried away—$100,000. One of the more intoxicated customers leered at Henry and said that if he was so sincere, he just ought to marry one of those black girls who were coming. All the men laughed and turned back to their drinks.

Chapter Five

*T*he matter could have been peacefully resolved. The village was far more embroiled in the anti-Mason issue than in antislavery. But, as Abraham Payne, a firsthand witness to the dispute, remembered, Andrew T. Judson "did not wish to have the case settled."[1]

Judson began to court, wheedle, and bully people to join his crusade against the school. The extent to which Judson was typical of his time and class can never be fully known, but he converted many willing followers. This son of a Congregational minister was in his late forties and had reached a crossroad in his life. He had not been born in Canterbury, but over the years he had become "the great man of the place."[2] Now he was ambitious for larger conquests. Abraham Payne described him as "a gentleman of pleasing manners and remarkable control of temper" who was "not easily defeated in any objective he set out."

Judson relished his position of authority in the village, and he also enjoyed being lord of his manor. His wife was very fastidious socially and gave lavish dinner parties for her friends. One day, according to a nineteenth-century Canterbury historian, Judson loudly ordered his wife, who was upstairs, to hurry down to meet a distinguished visitor. Mrs. Judson hastily preened herself and then sailed down her grand staircase only to "meet" a large bullfrog that had hopped in uninvited through the front hall. Judson's new home, which faced the broadside of Prudence's school, symbolized his position in the village. One of his worries was that his property value would plummet from exposure to the school, and not only his fortune but his status along with it.

Alexis de Tocqueville, after a year of observing American "men of property and standing," concluded that "the desire of acquiring the good things of this world" was "the prevailing passion with them." The fear of losing their identity, falling in status, and becoming anonymous was their nightmare.[3] Catherine Beecher articulated these mid-century anxieties when she wrote: "Everything is moving and changing. Persons in poverty are rising to opulence, and persons of wealth, are sinking to poverty . . . there is a mingling of all grades of wealth, intellect, and education. . . . All are thrown into promiscuous masses."[4] In his excited frame of mind, Judson imagined "promiscuous masses" living right across the street from his house.

Judson's justification for reviving the pauper law was his concern that, once educated, the black girls would not leave and Canterbury would become the "Liberia of America."[5] Their families would join them, but there would not be enough work to sustain them. The newcomers would quickly descend into poverty, the crime rate would soar, and the village would be ruined.

Ruination loomed also in the spector of amalgamation. Judson and his followers believed that when the differences between the black and white girls in the village became less obvious with acquired middle-class manners, fashion, and speech, the black girls would aspire to marry white men. "A Friend of the Colonization Society" wrote to a Norwich paper at the time, "They propose, by softening down the rough features of the African mind, in these wenches, to cook up a palatable morsel for our white bachelors." The Judsonites also thought the black men who would flock to Canterbury would seduce the white women. A spokesman warned Pardon shortly after the town meeting, "Mr. Crandall, in less than five years both your daughters will be married to negroes."[6]

Yet, as William Lloyd Garrison had pointed out again and again, amalgamation was already a reality. Amalgamation, or the more vulgar term "mongrelization," existed, primarily in the South, not because of intermarriage, but because white men owned and raped black women. This fantasy and possibility, no matter how repressed, existed in the minds of all men who upheld the institution of slavery. The threat to the purity of the white race, which was interpreted by men like Judson as a threat to the nation, came not from without but from within. Many white men supported the Colonization Society as the means to protect their better selves from their baser selves. They heartily approved of President Andrew Jackson's policy of pushing Native Americans westward to the wilderness as well as shipping blacks eastward to Africa.

It was not difficult to portray Prudence as an example of white womanhood gone astray, another threat to the purity of the nation. It had become apparent that, although she had initially agreed to move the school, she really did not want to. "Command of her premises" was her strength. The house had never been "bought and fitted up for her," May would remind the selectmen; she had been loaned money to buy it, and the lender had received "good security" for the repayment of the loan with interest. Therefore the village had no right to demand she return the building to its original use.[7] Pardon, who was being pressured by the authorities, tried to convince her to sell. "Not that I thought she had committed a crime or done anything which she had not a perfect right to do," he explained, "but I wanted peace and quietness." He threatened to sell the house out from under her, but she told him she would never turn over the title to him. The house, she said, was "commodious" and close to the market and the post office. Besides, she added, she had gone to "considerable expense" to furnish it.[8]

Prudence's unwillingness to cooperate with male authorities riled her opponents. She refused to accept her condition in life and seemed ready to impart the same defiance to the black girls. If she had planned to prepare her new students for their proper station as domestics with evening courses in cooking and sewing, it might have been tolerable. But she intended to teach the same curriculum offered at most of the elite private seminaries in the Northeast. There were to be recitals on the pianoforte, recitations of Shakespeare, and tea parties in the afternoon. Catherine Beecher, who had several years earlier directed her own seminary in Hartford, bristled when she read the advertisement for Prudence's school. Beecher thought it was outrageous that in a period when most white people did not receive a higher education, black girls should get it first: "There are not a dozen coloured families in New England, in such pecuniary circumstances, that if they were white it would not be thought ridiculous to attempt to give their daughters such a course of education, and Canterbury was a place where but few of the wealthiest families ever thought of furnishing such accomplishments for their children."[9]

Prudence's behavior was an inversion of the "natural order." The evolving notion of separate spheres for the sexes held that the stability and goodness of women in the home balanced, and thus legitimized, the aggression and selfishness of men abroad in the world. A woman like Prudence, who stepped out of her sphere, as does someone who insists on standing up in a crowded canoe, acted in a hostile or even antisocial way. When she engaged in "politics," Prudence was worse than a bluestocking, a maladjusted spinster, or a village idiot. She was aberrant and perverse. Her actions constituted a form of treason. Judson need no longer behave as a gentleman because Prudence was no longer a lady.

Judson's commitment to the battle against the school, however, was more than an emotional reaction to personal slights and threats. As Abraham Payne recalled, "Whatever he did or omitted to do, whatever he said or omitted to say, he was always grinding some axe of his own."[10] Judson did not view the affair merely as a local issue. The implications of the matter extended far beyond the boundaries of Canterbury, and so did Judson's ambitions. He wanted to be the Democratic governor of Connecticut at a time when his prospects for attaining such a goal were exceedingly remote.

In March 1830, Judson had complained to his friend Gideon Welles, editor of the Hartford *Times*, that opposition to their "Jackson party" was very strong in their part of the state. He blamed the Jackson administration itself: "Connecticut has been wholly overlooked by them. Every favor, and every consideration have passed by on the other side. No encouragements are given to the wavering, no hopes to the aspiring, no rewards to the faithful."[11]

On February 5, 1833, several weeks before Prudence made her radical announcement about admitting black students, Judson and other leading Democrats invited President Jackson to visit Connecticut's "revolutionary soil" on his upcoming tour and see firsthand their "virtuous population" and particularly their "seminaries of learning."[12] Jackson replied, however, that he and Vice-President Van Buren would be unable to visit the Hartford area.

Judson had noticed the publicity enjoyed by the coalition that successfully blocked the New Haven School.[13] Wishing to call attention to himself, Judson called his own "hasty" town meeting on March 9. His tirade during the meeting was deliberately theatrical. He whipped up the emotions of the audience so that the resolutions would pass without debate, and he manipulated their fears of amalgamation because he thought his stance would win him the alliance of Southern Democrats.[14]

There were, of course, ample reasons to think Prudence's school was linked to organized antislavery. For one thing, no one in Canterbury knew very much about antislavery, and this first manifestation in their midst caused far more panic than the subsequent formation of antislavery societies in Plainfield and Brooklyn.[15] Unable to identify or deal with the real tensions at work, men like Judson often blamed abolitionists, "foreigners," religious outcasts, and the like for the upheavals around them. In reality, the abolitionists of the early 1800s were not a cohesive, well-funded mass organization at all. Many of their greatest leaders were not yet upon the scene: Theodore Weld was a student out in "wild" Ohio, Wendell Phillips was on the debating team at Harvard, and Frederick Douglass was still a slave. Nevertheless, Judson had some evidence for his convictions. Prudence had advertised in William Lloyd Garrison's paper and had persuaded Arnold Buffum, president of the New England Anti-Slavery Society, to represent her. Most significantly, she had frequently dropped Arthur Tappan's name.

The villagers, led by Judson, envisioned a standoff against troops of big-city agitators primed by Tappan's legendary fortune. The emphasis on village prerogatives and state rights at the town meeting reflected this attitude of "us" against "them." Judson did not realize how much initiative actually came from local abolitionists—and amateurs at that—like Samuel Joseph May and the Bensons.[16]

When Judson claimed the school was an outpost of abolitionism, he implied it would participate in the abolitionists' war on the Colonization Society. The society, at the time, was the main object of Garrison's barbs. He regarded Liberia as little more than a refuse dump where "hundreds of worn-out slaves are annually turned out to die, like old horses."[17] Prudence had already denounced the society as "double-dealing" and "deceptive."[18] Until the school crisis, Judson had never joined the local society, which had been organized by Samuel Joseph May. Ironically, because of the crisis, May was seriously considering leaving it. Many important politicians belonged to the Colonization Society, and Judson had much to gain by appearing to fight a lonely battle in its name.

Through mutual civic activities, Judson and May had previously established a "pleasant acquaintance" which had almost become a "personal friendship."[19] Judson therefore decided to call upon the minister two days after the town meeting. May was, after all, a gentleman of influence from an old Boston family. Possibly because of May's ties with colonization, Judson thought he could still be swayed.

Judson apologized for using "certain epithets" at the public meeting but added that he thought May was "inconsiderately and unjustly" promoting the school. May replied that he wished the matter could be settled amicably. Given a little time, he was sure Prudence would remove herself from the green. Judson interrupted, saying that this was not the issue. He did not want the school anywhere in Canterbury, nor, for that matter, anywhere in the state. He was in favor of the colonization solution: "Let them be sent back there, or kept as they are here." May argued that considering the Colonization Society's limited resources and the unwillingness of most blacks to leave, there would never be fewer black people in the country than there were at the moment. The real question, as he saw it, was whether whites were going to give black people their rights or continue to hoard all the privileges of the society. The latter course would damn them before God in heaven and cause inevitable vindictive violence on earth. "I trust, sir," May said, "you will erelong come to see that we must accord to these men their rights, or incur justly the loss of our own."

Judson did not see. He threatened that he would block the school with his pauper law, but May countered that he would fight the law to the highest court. Judson laughed at this, but May assured him he would manage it somehow. "Mr. Judson left me in high displeasure," May remembered, "and I never met him afterwards but as an opponent."

Three days after this confrontation, a committee composed of selectmen and the civil authority visited Prudence and officially presented the resolutions passed at the town meeting to her. This time Pardon, Almira, and another woman were with her. Pardon noted the committee had a "furroner" of their own in tow, a lawyer from another town. Samuel Hough, the axe manufacturer who had given Prudence her mortgage, read the resolutions out loud. The strange lawyer, according to Pardon, insulted Prudence with various remarks, and then the officials turned on him. "Mr. Crandall," one of them said, "you are a man we have always esteemed. We feel sorry for you." Pardon received this condescension with "disdain" and put the insult, so to speak, "in his pocket."[20]

After the visitors left, Prudence composed a dignified response. She informed the committee that she would consider their resolutions, consult with her friends, and abide by their advice. (Part of the advice she would receive from George Benson was to deal with such men only in writing and never again let them through her front door.) Then she hurried over to Brooklyn where she stayed two or three days as a guest in the Bensons' large house near the center of town. There she deepened her friendship with the Benson girls, Anna, Charlotte, Mary, Frances, Sarah, and the youngest, Helen.

She also "consulted" with Samuel Joseph May, who was fast becoming "her sympathizer in all her sorrows."[21] May told her plainly that it was time to decide: if she was not afraid, she should proceed, but if she was, she should abandon the project. Prudence assured him she was not the least apprehensive either for herself or for her students. May likewise committed himself to continuing the struggle and promised to write a pamphlet refuting the town meeting resolutions. The decision was not altogether easy for him to make, for he already had many responsibilities, not the least of which was to his family.

Lucretia Coffin May, his wife, was overwhelmed with the burdens of motherhood and genteel poverty. She resented her husband's myriad projects, and she may well have resented Prudence. "I hope you will remember not to forget," she had written to him that very winter, "that you went to Boston *this time* to *see your father* and will not give all your time to emancipating slaves, settling all the quarrels in Christendom, and educating all the children."[22]

While the polarization of her friends and neighbors surprised Prudence, she was cheered that at least some of them had gravitated to her side. Her father was confused, but supportive. More firm in their commitments were Dr. Roland Green of Black Hill, William Kinne from Plainfield, and the Reverend Levi Kneeland, the minister from the Baptist church in Packerville.[23] George Benson was urging Simeon Jocelyn to engage counsel on behalf of any black parents who "might be molested." In Brooklyn, the entire Benson family was at her disposal. The stage was set.

Chapter Six

*T*he first salvo in the war of words came from the cannon of William Lloyd Garrison. *The Liberator* of March 16, 1833, carried an article about the Canterbury town meeting. The text was Henry Benson's, but the typesetting was pure Garrison. In huge black letters—"black as the infamy attached to them"—Garrison displayed the names of Andrew T. Judson, Rufus Adams, Solomon Paine, Captain Richard Fenner, and Dr. Andrew Harris beneath the heading "Heathenism Outdone." By way of introducing these men, who were mentioned prominently in Benson's article, the angry editor wrote, "To colonize these shameless enemies of their species in some desert country would be a relief and blessing to society."

Garrison's outrage on her behalf caught Prudence off balance. At the time, she was feeling that if it were not for her faith in God, she "should fall like the fading leaf before the northern blasts." Disconcerted that Garrison had chosen such an aggressive tack without consulting her, she entreated him "to handle the prejudices of the people of Canterbury with all the mildness possible as everything severe tends merely to heighten the flame of malignity amongst them."[1] Henry Benson also wrote to Garrison, although not necessarily with criticism: "Your remarks in the last *Liberator* were awfully cutting."[2]

Samuel Joseph May had often spoken to his good friend about his rhetoric, but to no avail; they were simply not of the same mind. Garrison's excesses on this occasion pained May so much that he disassociated himself from them. "I respect and love Mr. Garrison's fervent devotion to the cause of the oppressed," he wrote, but at the same time, "no one can disapprove, more than I do, the harshness of his epithets, and the bitterness of his invectives."[3] The disapproval of his friends did not persuade Garrison to retract his words, although he was moved to explain them. He defended *The Liberator*'s "hard language" and regretted the English tongue was so "lamentably weak and deficient." "I wish," he fervently stated, "its epithets were heavier—I wish it would not break so easily—I wish I could denounce slavery, and all its abettors, in terms equal to their infamy."[4]

Garrison was, much to his enemies' annoyance, an avowed pacifist or "non-resistant." Words were his bullets. He did not believe his paper was fomenting anarchy and violence, as his opponents maintained. For Garrison, the American system and all its institutions were already violent, and the symbol of that inherent violence was the Constitution of the United States, which had united the foundling nation by compromising on slavery.

But even at its most extreme, *The Liberator*'s language was not singular or even unusual for its day. Extravagant language prevailed in print and speech in the 1830s, especially in newspapers with a political slant. Soon after the *Liberator* article appeared, Almira Crandall gleefully quoted to Henry Benson from a letter her friend William Burleigh had submitted to the *Norwich Courier*. Young Burleigh, the current local district schoolteacher, came from an eccentric family in Plainfield, every one of whom was an abolitionist. Burleigh had consented to aid Prudence as a teacher in her school, and thus he rose to her defense. In his letter, which was not accepted for publication, Burleigh called Judson and his friends "the demons of Canterbury" and "devotees of the devil." He hoped "the cry of the oppressed" would "startle them from their sleep" and "haunt their dreams . . . depriving them of all rest, all peace—all comfort, until they shall cease to do evil and learn to do good."[5]

Abraham Payne observed that *The Liberator*'s "roll of infamy," contrary to Prudence's fears, did not produce any incendiary effect. "It was curious," he wrote, "to observe that the men whose names were on this roll were rather pleased with that distinction, and others were mortified because their names were left off."[6] Judson was one of the most delighted: it gave him the opportunity to sue Garrison for libel. (There was a local precedent for libel in the 1827 case of Fuller versus the Trustees of the Academic School in Plainfield. In that case a guest at a private party in the home of Levi Robinson, a member of the Board of Trustees at Plainfield, had pronounced the members of the board to be a set of rascals and scoundrels who were no more fit to act in that capacity than Port Hall, "an infamous black man well known to all then present.")[7]

But lawsuits "in bundles," as Pardon Crandall put it, were only part of Judson's plan of attack. In the March 27, 1833, *Norwich Courier* Judson publicly appealed to the Colonization Society for support, although he had never been active in the society. He deplored the opposition both he and the society had suffered from "certain individuals" who had formed an antislavery society. He identified Prudence as an enemy of colonization and a promoter of intermarriage. By this maneuver, he hoped to secure the sympathy of the many powerful men in Connecticut who were colonizationalists and also to motivate the moderate faction in Canterbury to tolerate the application of the pauper law.[8] Eleven selectmen and representatives of the civil authority signed Judson's Appeal to the Colonization Society along with him.

It fell to Samuel Joseph May to respond to Judson's charges. He wrote two long and vigorous letters that first appeared in the *Brooklyn Advertiser Press* and were subsequently reprinted as pamphlets, in which form they led a long and useful life as propaganda. In the first letter, May criticized Judson's behavior at the town meeting as ungentlemanly and unprofessional. As a lawyer, May wrote, accustomed to proceedings where no judgment is given until both sides are heard, Judson should have insisted someone speak in Prudence's behalf. May also defended his own presence at the meeting. "It is not true," he argued, "that *we* asked leave to address the meeting. Miss Crandall asked leave to be heard *by us*." Although he didn't live in the village, May said, he belonged to a larger community that was also affected. "I am, sir," he finished loftily, "not a stranger, but your fellow citizen."

The second letter resumed where the first one left off. May reminded Prudence's critics that the Canterbury folk had not conferred favors upon her, but merely encouraged her to open a school. The benefits, from the outset, had been mutual. He predicted that property values would not decline if Judson and the others restrained their prejudices from becoming "unhappily conspicuous." On the contrary, forty or fifty temporary residents, some of them daughters of wealth and all of them supported by parents, relatives, or patrons, would stimulate the economy in their need to be "clothed, fed and warmed."

May refuted the notion that blacks were naturally as well

as actually inferior to whites by giving a brief history lesson. He traced American culture back to Europe, and European culture to the Greeks and Romans and finally to Ethiopia and Egypt, or, "in one word—from Africa." Thousands of years ago, he wrote, blacks were "the whole civilized world of their time." He emphasized that the New England Anti-Slavery Society did not advocate or hope for intermarriage, although it was obvious God had not made such a practice impossible. Whether mixed marriages would ever take place, he delicately surmised, was a "matter which time must be left to decide." But if such marriages did occur, they would be more in keeping with the laws of God and the virtue of the nation than the "illicit intercourse" so prevalent in the South. To the charge that Prudence's followers supported immediate emancipation, May said simply, "It is true."[9]

May knew that "immediate emancipation" meant different things to different people. Its interpretation varied even among abolitionists. For May, the phrase meant that a decision to oppose slavery must be made "immediately," even if the dissolution of the hateful institution was gradual. "So long as we believe there is a wise and good Being presiding over the affairs of men," he contended, "so long we must believe it will be safe for men to do right at any moment."[10] David Lee Child, the husband of Lydia Maria Child and a Boston colleague of Garrison's, felt immediate emancipation meant the "immediate beginning" of a longer process, "an immediate inquiry to be followed by action as soon as inquiry has pointed the way."[11]

Even Garrison's definition was broad. He did not maintain that the slaves could "immediately" spring from bondage to middle-class citizenship with all its rights and obligations. That would be neither wise nor kind, since the majority of emancipated slaves would be illiterate and im-

poverished, or as he put it, "rational and injured beings."
He envisioned a period of benevolent supervision before the
ex-slaves would even be able to vote. But he staunchly
advocated they be "immediately" exempt from unjust pun-
ishment and exploitation. He demanded they be paid for
their labor and have "exclusive right to their own bodies
and those of their own children." Give them land, employment, and schools, he urged. "We shall have little to fear."[12]

Judson chose to ignore May's "Vindication Letters." Prudence informed Simeon Jocelyn, "Mr. Judson and his party
think Mr. May's letters are so very flat that they are not
worth much notice—certainly not an answer."[13] Henry
Benson, however, requested Isaac Knapp to send 150 copies
of the letters by mail stage for distribution in Providence,
where interest was high.[14]

Opening day for Prudence's school, the first Monday in
April, dawned full of hope, but when the sun went down
again, Prudence and her assistant, Almira, had only one
day scholar, Sarah Harris, and one boarder, Eliza Glasko,
from Griswold, Connecticut.[15] George Benson had written
to May that the Providence students were "not quite ready."
Two students, however, constituted enough of an invasion
to warrant another town meeting at the Masonic Hall.[16]
The resolutions this time reflected Judson's newfound dedication to the Colonization Society. They called for a petition
to be written, circulated, and delivered to the General Assembly in Hartford deploring the evil consequences of
bringing people of color from "*other towns* and other states
. . . for *any* purpose" but especially for the purpose of promoting principles and doctrines opposed to those of the
Colonization Society. The petition demanded broad social
control. Blacks were to be prevented from leaving their
towns, ostensibly to prevent interference with the "benevolent Colonization System."[17] Perhaps the authors were

inspired by the Southern system in which slaves had to show a pass when leaving their masters' plantation. It no doubt distressed Prudence to learn that Daniel Packer had defected to become one of the members of the petition committee.

Judson and his followers also voted to boycott Prudence and her family in imitation of the Non-Intercourse and Embargo Acts of the War of 1812. (Those measures had sought to wound Great Britain economically by closing American ports to British ships and refusing to export American goods to England.) Much was made of the boycott by Prudence's supporters. Henry Benson, in youthful exaggeration, wrote Garrison that no shop in the village would sell her "a morsel of food."[18] In reality, as Abraham Payne said, "all these matters were very much exaggerated . . . her teachers were never seriously disturbed or alarmed, she never really suffered for the want of water or supplies, and her pupils always had means of getting to and from her school."[19] One shopkeeper, Stephen Coit, whose son Samuel had been Prudence's student in Plainfield, would not go along with the boycott. While he was opposed to the school, he nevertheless said he would sell to anyone who wished to buy. The account books of another merchant, Edward Jenks, show that he also sold provisions to Prudence and Almira throughout 1833 and 1834. The rowdies of the town, however, sensing they would face no serious reprimands from their parents or the civil authority, yelled racial insults at Sarah and Eliza and splattered addled eggs against the sides of the house.

William Lloyd Garrison, who was keeping track of events in Canterbury, realized the situation was taking on larger dimensions than he had originally imagined. He was sailing for England at the end of April to raise money and to neutralize the influence of Elliott Cresson, the Colonization Society agent, who was already there fund-raising. Now, realizing Canterbury was also an arena in which he could battle the Colonization Society, he decided to include troubled Windham County in his farewell tour. In addition, he wanted to mend some country fences before he went away for five months.

On Friday night, April 5, Garrison spoke before a large black gathering at an "African church" in Providence. Afterward many people crowded around him, some of them weeping, to thank him and to say goodbye. "Thirty dollars was given on the spot for the mission to England," Henry Benson happily reported.[20] His father, George Benson, Sr., and his youngest sister, Helen, also attended the meeting. Dark-haired Helen, who was fondly called "peace and plenty" by her family, admitted to Garrison months later, "You had been described to me so often, my expectations I can assure you were highly raised. I was not disappointed: you were all and even more than I had imagined you to be."[21]

The following morning twenty-one-year-old Helen found an excuse to go to her brother's store, where she knew Garrison would be. She lingered unobtrusively, listening to him talk. "From that moment," she decided, "I should ever take a deep interest in [his] welfare."[22] Garrison had noticed Helen too, but it was hardly a propitious time in his life for romance. His paper was barely solvent, the state of Georgia had put a price on his head for inciting insurrection, and he was about to sail for England. Nevertheless, "If it was not 'love at first sight,' " he remembered, "it was something very like it."[23]

Garrison left later that day with George Benson for Brooklyn, having barely spoken to Helen. Samuel Joseph May had prevailed upon him to lecture at his big white meeting house on Sunday evening. Prudence and Almira rode over from Canterbury, and they all stayed at the Bensons' crowded house. Prudence forgave Garrison his indiscretions and declared that seeing him again was "a source of great joy."[24] He rejoiced to see her in good spirits and pronounced, "She is a wonderful woman."[25]

Meanwhile, Garrison's enemies were taking action of their own. When Andrew T. Judson learned that Garrison was a mere six miles away, he dispatched the sheriff of Canterbury, Roger Coit, who was the son-in-law of Daniel Packer, to Brooklyn in the middle of a thunderstorm. The mud-splattered sheriff, armed with five writs of libel from the black-lettered men, arrived an hour after Garrison had left for Hartford on his way to New York. Coit told the Bensons that the Canterburians wanted to abduct their departed guest to the South for lynching, which caused great alarm and "much sorrow" to the aged Mr. Benson and the females of his household. The disgruntled sheriff determinedly galloped after Garrison's stagecoach but could not overtake it.[26]

Foiled in this attempt, Judson decided to take matters into his own hands, and he soon left for New York himself. Garrison, however, having been warned that the writs were just a pretense to find him and abduct him to Georgia, evaded Judson. He learned that a packet boat bound for Liverpool was sailing from Philadelphia, and at the urging of friends, he caught a steamboat from New York in an attempt to catch it. He arrived in the City of Brotherly Love in the afternoon only to learn the boat had sailed that morning. He then tried to return to New York in time for a boat leaving for England on April 24. His friend Robert Purvis, the son-in-law of wealthy black Philadelphian James Forten, drove him at breakneck speed as far as Trenton, a distance of thirty miles, in three hours.[27] But it was to no avail. All the berths on the ship were taken, and he was told he would have to wait until the next sailing on May 1.

Garrison decided to hide out in the meantime in New Haven, where, at Simeon Jocelyn's prodding, he sat for a portrait by Jocelyn's artist brother Nathaniel. All that time "he was kept shut up by the artist in a room adjoining the studio, so arranged that in case of an attempt to seize him he could make a safe exit."[28]

His precautions, while melodramatic, were not paranoid. Scarcely had Arnold Buffum seen Garrison safely aboard the ship *Hibernia*, than "a lad from a lawyer's office" made inquiries as to his whereabouts. Buffum concluded that the Canterbury pursuers were close at hand, but "they happened to be a little too late."[29] After lying windbound in the harbor overnight, the *Hibernia* made for the open sea on May 2. Garrison, having brought with him no fresh lemons, Hibbard's Bilious Pills, or Barbados rum,[30] was the first one on board to be seasick.

Chapter Seven

*I*n the early spring the frogs woke up from their winter hibernation and "tried their voices each for himself, croaking hoarsely, and startling the lonely traveler at night with strange uncouth, guttural noises, and fearful mutterings."[1] The human clamor and the discord accompanying Prudence's fall from grace continued as well; and they seemed to her out of all proportion, for there were only four women walking around inside the Paine mansion, two students and two teachers.[2]

Andrew T. Judson, swelled by the success of his recent election to the Connecticut House of Representatives, was circulating his petitions against the school in sixteen towns. The petitions stated that the introduction of people of color into Connecticut from other states (although none had yet arrived) was "an evil of great magnitude" and "a calamity" that would "greatly increase upon the people the burdens of pauperism." They claimed that Connecticut had always acted benevolently toward its own black people, but should large numbers of them suddenly gather in one town, the results would be "oppressive to them and injurious to the public peace." The Brooklyn petition garnered 118 signatures, and the one in Plainfield 81.[3]

George White, the tanner who had defended Prudence at the town meeting the month before, told her that the petition composed specifically for Canterbury was different from the others. It stated that every citizen in the village abhorred slavery and would do anything consistent with the Constitution to do away with it. However, the petition went on to accuse "sundry individuals" of inviting blacks of unknown character from all over the country to come to Canterbury to be taught the inappropriate subjects of music, French, and science. The school was to be the "theater" for sentiments and doctrines that opposed the humanitarian efforts of colonization. The school's "inmates" would be taught to uphold "instantaneous and immediate emancipation" and to deride the laws and the Constitution. The Canterbury petition eventually collected 131 signatures.

Judson was also exerting pressure on Pardon to subdue his daughter, but Pardon resisted further involvement. He had already reasoned, argued, and challenged Prudence with no effect. "Of all this I informed Colonel Judson," Pardon recalled, "and concluded to withdraw from the scene, and let it terminate as it would."[4] But his neighbors did not let Pardon off so easily. One of them bluntly told him to leave town. The man said that when the lawyers, judges, and jurors were leagued against him, it would be easy to raise a mob and destroy his house. Another person confided to Pardon that someone in Brooklyn had offered to be one of twelve men willing to tear down Prudence's school first and pay for it afterward.

Pardon tried to shame the selectmen into backing off:

You are actuated by the same spirit that lighted up
the fires of Smithfield that banished Roger Williams,
the Quakers and Baptists from Boston, and particularly
the actors in the Salem Witchcraft when they tried to
kill . . . the Devil who they imagined appeared to their
inhabitants in the form of a Black man with his black
Book. I once more entreat you to stop in your mad
career before we are ruined.[5]

Ruination was precisely what Judson had in mind, and
on April 13, the day after seventeen-year-old Ann Eliza
Hammond arrived from Providence, he made his move.
That evening at about seven o'clock, Sheriff Roger Coit
delivered an official warning to Prudence based on the old
pauper law. It stated that Ann Eliza, a foreigner, must leave
the village or be fined $1.67 per week. If she did not pay
the fines, she would be sentenced and "whipped on the
naked body not exceeding ten stripes." The sheriff also
informed Prudence that the selectmen were drawing up a
similar warning for her because she was harboring the girl.
In her heart, Prudence doubted Judson would carry out a
public whipping, but the weekly fines, multiplied by all the
students she hoped to have, would destroy the school. For
the first time, Prudence seriously considered moving. She
was tempted by a letter from Arthur Tappan, which was
meant to be encouraging. He thought it best to sustain the
school where it was if it could be done without great expense, but otherwise to find another place. Samuel Joseph
May had also received a letter informing him that the population of Reading, Massachusetts, would welcome the
school.

Prudence's lapse of confidence was, however, temporary,
and the day after the sheriff's visit, she traveled to Brooklyn
to ask May whether she should pay Ann Eliza's fine or go

to court. They did not agree; she was inclined to pay, but May favored a public trial. Soon, however, May came up with an idea he hoped would get around the problem of fines altogether. Since Prudence's offense was harboring Ann Eliza, in the words of the warning, "without first paying a security which satisfied the selectmen," May procured a bond note for $10,000 signed by several responsible men in Brooklyn, including George Benson, Sr. Surely, he thought, this would protect Canterbury from any "damage" done by the pupils.

Unfortunately for her state of mind, Prudence disregarded George Benson's advice about dealing with Judson only in writing. Armed with May's written proposal, she crossed the road to deliver it personally. Judson glanced at it and then civilly inquired, "Will you have a Negro to wait upon you home?" He pointed out a drunken man by the roadside. "Here," Judson offered, "This fellow will wait upon you."[6] Judson never replied directly to Prudence or May, but in a further effort to harass the Crandall family, he asked Hezekiah Crandall to inform the gentlemen in Brooklyn that their bond was not acceptable.

Sheriff Coit, true to his word, soon returned with orders for Prudence, Almira, and Ann Eliza to appear at the "dwelling house" of Chauncey Bacon on May 2 at one o'clock, where Justice of the Peace George Middleton from Plainfield would hear the case.

The humiliation of his daughter was becoming more than Pardon could bear. One day at Andrew T. Judson's office, while Pardon was trying to be a reconciler, one of the civil authority warned him to stay away from his daughter or he would sue Pardon. "I had rather sue you than sue her," the official said.[7] Pardon replied that there was no need for any "lawsuits" because the petition committee would probably succeed in passing a law that would eliminate the school.

Although Judson appeared to agree, the summonses against Prudence were not dropped. Pardon then sought Ebenezer Sanger, a selectman, and asked him to defer legal action until after the General Assembly had met in Hartford. "Say to the selectmen from me," he pleaded humbly, "that if they have no regard for anything else, for my sake do not commence hostilities or destructive law suits, by numbering days or counting time to continue till we are stripped of our property."

But the selectmen, who had been Pardon's neighbors for twenty years, turned their backs on him. In an emotional letter to these former friends, the old Quaker declared he had no choice but to fight: "The spirit of a father that waketh for a daughter is roused. I know the consequence. I now come forward to oppose tyranny with my property at stake. My life in my hand, I enter the ship Defense. I shall reap and sow as occasion may require, and try to steer so as to avoid rocks and quicksands, and if I founder at sea we will go to the bottom together. At these thoughts my bosom heaves my tears flow and I drop my pen."[8]

The wind slowly began to shift in Prudence's direction. Six students arrived from New York, and classes began in earnest. When one of these, Ann Peterson, received a warning similar to Ann Eliza Hammond's, Samuel Joseph May hurried over from Brooklyn, prepared to comfort the terrorized girls. Instead, he found them unintimidated. Ann Eliza told him she was quite willing to undergo the ordeal of whipping if it would help sustain the school.[9] Another new arrival showed her mettle a week later. She had ridden on the stagecoach from Hartford, a journey made "miserable" by the sneers and insults of the other passengers. When she disembarked in Brooklyn, there was no one to carry her further, so the plucky girl shouldered her baggage and walked the remaining six miles.

With nine students to protect, nurture, and perhaps emulate, Prudence went on the defensive as if rallying in a
chess game. She paid Ann Eliza's fine, and lest they appear
to be cowering in their mansion, she took all the students
on an excursion to Norwich. Esther Baldwin, who went to
boarding school in Norwich, wrote to her sister Amy in
Canterbury that Prudence had been "down here among the
blacks" with a large group of "colored ladies" from New
York. She reported that Prudence actually "shook hands
with the sexton," presumably a black man, which greatly
swelled his head.[10] Amy Baldwin, who was one of Prudence's former white students, remembered her teacher
with affection, as she wrote nostalgically to Mary Clark,
another former classmate, "I hope you have not forgot going
down to . . . school to Miss Crandall, and the many pleasant
noons we have spent together under the chestnut tree study-
ing our definitions. I wish we could go to school to her
again."[11]

When Prudence returned from Norwich with her brood,
she further overcame her reluctance to "appear" in public
by writing a letter to the editor of the hostile *Windham
County Advertiser*. She restated the history of her conversion
to aiding the oppressed. She defended Samuel Joseph May
as the "warm friend and advocate" of the school and en-
dorsed all his statements to Andrew T. Judson, many of
which, she insisted, "he made upon my authority." She
affirmed her own independence and disowned any bias toward amalgamation. "The sole object, at this school," she
reiterated, "is to instruct the ignorant and fit and prepare
teachers for the people of color."

The publicity the school had received through *The Liberator* and other pamphlets began to stir some positive reactions. A meeting of the Colored People of New York
formally resolved to give education for colored youth their

"undivided support." They vowed "heartily to join any proposed feasible plan." The *Christian Secretary* of Hartford on April 20 commented that if the reception of Miss Crandall's students was "a fair specimen of the land of steady habits, Mr. Garrison and his associates had better suspend operations against the Colonization Society and lecture their neighbors on the subject of decency and common humanity."

Andrew T. Judson left for New York on April 30, but in stopping in Hartford to deposit his petitions, with their 903 signatures, he missed bagging William Lloyd Garrison. On the returning steamboat the empty-handed Judson met Prudence's brother Dr. Reuben Crandall, who was traveling from Peekskill to Canterbury. Reuben told Judson that although he bore no ill will against the black students, he was going to try to break up the school. He didn't anticipate much success with Prudence because she was so "obstinate," but he hoped at least to remove Almira from her influence. When they reached Norwich, the stagecoach was full. Sensing that there might be some advantage for himself, Judson offered to take Reuben home in his own rig.[12] Reuben's mission, however, came to nothing. He found his wayward father and his impressionable youngest sister firmly ensconced in the opposite camp.

As for Prudence, she had discovered that adversity was in some ways preferable to "days of prosperity" because it made her more aware of her dependence on God. "In the midst of this affliction," she wrote Simeon Jocelyn, "I am as happy as at any moment of my life."[13]

April came to an end. The frogs remembered how to sing in chorus, and "they filled the misty evening air" with sounds like "millions of sharp-toned sleigh-bells."[14]

Chapter Eight

*T*he most urgent business facing the Connecticut General Assembly in the spring of 1833 was the framing and passage of what became known as the "Black Law," a law that enabled local white supremacists to determine which, if any, black people could go to high school and what they could be taught. (The legislators would stand for "no pernicious principles like abolitionism," Andrew T. Judson had said.)[1]

Pardon Crandall, who had always shunned partisan politics, made one last and futile effort on his daughter's behalf before the law's passage. He wrote to the lawmakers in Hartford, entreating them to remember that "all mankind are created free and equal" and beseeching them not to grant "the prayer of any petition nor pass any act, that will entail or destroy any of the rights of the free people of this state, or other states, whether they are white or black."[2]

Andrew T. Judson's presence in Hartford annulled Pardon's appeal. Judson was among friends, and, although it was "unusual and made some talk," he was allowed to openly lobby for the bill.[3] The head of the committee appointed to draw up the law was Phillip Pearl of Hampton, Connecticut, whose daughter Hannah had been dismissed from Prudence's original school. Pearl saw fit to have his committee advised by a Hartford phrenologist who brought in "several skulls of the African race." William Jay, the son of John Jay, the first chief justice of the United States Supreme Court, later wrote about the episode. Jay, a one-time colonizationalist turned abolitionist, quoted a phrenologist who may have been the same "expert" who addressed the congressmen. After describing the lips, jaws, chin, forehead, and eye sockets of his specimens, the "scientist" concluded:

> All of these peculiarities at the same time contributing to reduce his *facial* angle almost to the level with the *BRUTE*. . . . it is . . . reasonable to suppose that the acknowledged meanness of the negro's intellect only coincides with the *shape of his head*, or in other words, that his want of capability to receive a complicated education, render it improper and impolite that he should be allowed the privileges of CITIZENSHIP in an enlightened country.[4]

Thus, the prejudices of the lawmakers were scientifically legitimized once again: black people were a subspecies of the human family, and higher education was not their right but a waste of resources.

The committee did not need much convincing. But to persuade the members even further, during their deliberations, someone imparted the erroneous information that the Maryland legislature had appropriated money to disperse their free colored population into other states as a less expensive alternative than deportation to Liberia. Panicked that a portion of these blacks would receive free passage north to Prudence's school, the legislators acted quickly.[5]

Senator Pearl summarized the consensus of the committee, albeit somewhat apologetically, for he seems to have been more liberal than most of his colleagues. Pearl cited the committee's abhorrence of the "horrid traffic" in slaves and regretted the legacy of degradation inherited by American blacks. But on the other hand, he noted, free blacks were fortunate in being exempted from the poll tax and from military service. His committee believed the white populace should "foster and sustain the benevolent efforts of individuals" in educating local black people, but he emphasized that the state of Connecticut was under no moral or political obligation to educate black people from other states. "That class of people," the report maintained, "have seldom any settled establishment in their own state or inducements to return . . . and as their last association and attachments would be here," they would tend to remain. It was widely known that "colored people in the midst of a white population . . . are an appalling source of crime and pauperism." The "immense evils" of such a situation could only be prevented by "timely prevention." Therefore, Pearl concluded, it would seem both "safe and just" to place the responsibility of accepting or rejecting the application of black individuals for residence in the hands of the civil authority and selectmen of each town.[6]

On May 24, 1833, the new statute that became the "Black Law," which superseded the old whipping law Judson had used to threaten Prudence's students, was signed into law by Samuel Ingham, speaker of the House of Representatives, Ebenezer Stoddard, president of the Senate, and Henry W. Edwards, the governor of Connecticut. The Black Law targeted anyone who set up a school, academy, or literary institution for the instruction or education of colored persons who were not inhabitants of Connecticut, and anyone else who taught or boarded such persons. The civil authority and selectmen were empowered to impose a $100 fine for the first offense, $200 for the second, and double the penalty for each offense thereafter. In restricting their right to free movement and choice of residence, the law implied that blacks were not citizens; and, in fact, blacks were not recognized as citizens in Connecticut until June 1865, and not nationally until Congress overrode President Andrew Johnson's veto of the Civil Rights Bill in April 1866.

The news that Judson had won brought a day of rejoicing to Canterbury. Men and boys shot their rifles into the air, the bells in the belfry of the Congregational Church chimed for hours, and the town cannon boomed thirteen times on the hill in back of Judson's house. As night fell and Prudence's students at last dared to look out the windows of their school, they saw dark figures dancing around blazing bonfires as people traditionally did to celebrate Thanksgiving.

Passage of the law set off a firework of debate with streamers in all directions; what was the definition of equality, the nature of freedom, the essence of justice? In this respect, at least, the abolitionists who were allied with Prudence were grateful to the lawmakers, for they hoped to push this test case to the Supreme Court if necessary. They pinned their hopes to Article IV, Section 2, of the Constitution stating that citizens in each state had the rights and privileges of citizens of other states in which they may be temporarily residing. If abolitionists could prove that black people were citizens, then the state of Connecticut could not offer education to the blacks of Connecticut but deny it to blacks from New York, Massachusetts, or Rhode Island.

One of the first reactions to the Black Law was a long letter signed "Justice" that appeared in the June 22, 1833, issue of the *Emancipator*, a New York antislavery publication. The letter systematically analyzed why the new law was unjust, inefficient, and just plain disgraceful. In the opinion of "Justice," the law was "unjust" because colored people had as much right "by nature" as whites to "whatever they can honestly acquire," be it wealth, learning, or "elegant accomplishments." The law would prove to be "inefficient," the writer contended, if its avowed object was the prevention of an undesirable increase in the black population. It prohibited only the virtuous daughters of respectable families able to pay for a private school from entering Connecticut, yet students wanting to come into the state to attend public schools could do so. Anyone wishing to "come to rove about in idleness, to lounge in grog shops, to beg, to pilfer," could also do so. The law was "disgraceful" in its intent to perpetuate injustice against an already injured mass of people. The debate that had preceded its passage had mocked the legislative purpose of consulting for the public good. At the end of the letter, the unknown author, who was obviously intimate with the situation, descended to a more personal level. The law was created, he wrote, so that the rise to intellectual superiority of the black pupils would not "mortify the pride of A. T. Judson, candidate for Congress, and Captain Richard Fenner, rum retailer on the Canterbury green."

Another dissent, in the form of an anonymous petition delivered to the General Assembly, called for the immediate repeal of the law.[7] The petition presented an argument from a class perspective. "We regard it [the Black Law] as an anti-republican law" that "widens the interval between the various ranks in society." In a truly republican society, the dissenter argued, the poor should not be made poorer, the ignorant should not be compelled to sink lower in ignorance, nor the vicious into vice. The Black Law had "a most aristocratic tendency" because "it widen[ed] the interval between the lower classes and the higher . . . not by elevating the latter, but by depressing the former."

The Hartford *Courant*, a liberal paper that would consistently condemn the new law, printed a letter signed "Canterbury" that might have flowed from the acerbic pen of William Burleigh. After criticizing Judson's role, "Canterbury" ridiculed the political posturing of his townsmen:

> It is the just boast of our present rulers to do nothing in the old way. I knew that all the Jackson members would go for the law, but I did feel a little afraid about some of the old fashion democrats and federalists—but the law breathed such a spirit of justice and love, that it went right through with acclamation. Had the old federal party thought of such a device in their day, it would have perpetuated their power forever.[8]

Two weeks after the signing of the law, Andrew T. Judson and Rufus Adams drove out to Pardon's farm and informed him that further contact with his daughter would cost him a $100 fine, which would be doubled each time he visited her. The same applied to Esther and to "Mr. May and those gentlemen from Providence." By stretching the law to include anyone who materially or philosophically supported Prudence, they hoped to isolate her from the outside world. As for Prudence, they continued, if she received any of her relatives or friends at her school, she would be "taken up the same way as for stealing a horse or for burglary. Her property will not be taken, but she will be put in jail, in close confinement, not having the liberty of the yard." As the two men were leaving, Judson casually thanked Pardon for his letter to the General Assembly. When they received it, he said, "every man clenched his

fist, and the committee sat down and doubled the penalty."
In fact, Judson added, one of the legislators promised that
if this law didn't do the job, they would pass another in a
year that would.[9]

By the end of May Prudence had thirteen students.[10]
George Benson stated in the June 15 *Liberator* that she had
eighteen or twenty, but he was probably exaggerating for
public consumption. Benson added that the pupils were
making "good proficiency" in their studies and appeared
"happy and contented." The account beseeched "colored
patrons" to send their daughters and promised they would
be protected. But despite Benson's cheery front, the school
was entering what Prudence called the "weary, weary
days."[11] The law provided the opportunity for timid souls
to withdraw from the dispute lest they appear to censure
the legislature, while for others it legitimized acts of vandalism, such as smearing manure on the granite front steps
of the school. "Troops of boys" blowing horns and beating
drums tagged after Prudence and her girls wherever they
went.[12]

Meanwhile the selectmen pressed their legal attack. One
morning in mid-June, Ashael Bacon and Ebenezer Sanger
called at the school to verify whether Prudence had students
from "abroad." Prudence politely admitted them, and they
chatted a few minutes in the front parlor. She said she had
several pupils from New York, and she introduced the girls
to the selectmen. Then on June 27, nearly a week before
the previously scheduled hearing on May 2 before Justice
Middleton, Deputy Sheriff George Cady informed Prudence and Almira that they were under arrest and escorted
them to the house of Chauncey Bacon for arraignment.

Small villages like Canterbury did not have their own
courthouse or jail. The nearest ones to Canterbury were in
Brooklyn. Local magistrates held court twice a month or,

when needed, in their own homes. The "divers signs and tokens" of such a hearing were described by a contemporary novelist:

> The horses hitched by the road-side at the gate, or under the shade of the cherry trees in the lane, standing hour after hour, stamping and whisking their tails to drive away the swarm of tormenting flies that disturbed their drowzy meditations; the little squads of men grouped about the door of the court-room at the corner of the house, or leaning across the fence, talking together in couples, discussing the case on trial, or perhaps proposing "swaps" or driving bargains, never ceasing meanwhile, to whittle diligently; the dogs lounging around the steps at their masters' feet, or romping together in the thick grass of the front dooryard; and the glimpses through the open windows of sweating spectators, sitting in their shirt-sleeves, and listening, with the interest that Anglo-Saxons ever take in judicial proceedings, to the reading of the declaration and pleadings.[13]

In this all-male atmosphere, justice of the peace Rufus Adams read the complaint against Prudence and Almira, which had been brought by Nehemiah Ensworth, whose daughter Frances had been one of Prudence's former white students. Adams informed the two women that they were bound to appear at the county court, which would sit in Brooklyn in August. He set bail for $150. One of the onlookers then pointed out that Almira was a minor and could not stand trial, so she was sent home. Prudence faced her accusers, and with all the straight-backed schoolmarm dignity she could summon, calmly replied that she did not have the bail.

Prudence had known this reckoning was coming, but so had Andrew T. Judson. Earlier that morning, Judson had dispatched a messenger to Samuel Joseph May apprising him of the arrest and the amount of bail. Judson had assumed that the gentlemen in Brooklyn, so willing to post $10,000 bond for the students, would readily supply this paltry sum for Prudence. But Prudence and May had anticipated this and had asked all their friends and supporters not to come forward with the sum.

May told the messenger he was sure there were gentlemen in Canterbury whose bond was as good as or better than his. "But are you not her friend?" stammered the messenger in amazement. Indeed he was, replied May, too good a friend to relieve her enemies of their present embarrassment. The messenger could not believe that May would actually allow the schoolteacher to enter the cell in which Oliver Watkins, the infamous wife strangler, had passed his last night on earth. But the minister assured him he would, if her persecutors were so foolish as to attempt it. The messenger rode back to Canterbury with his astounding news. Judson and Adams were furious. Calling May's bluff, they dispatched a second messenger to notify him that they were on their way to the Brooklyn jail with Prudence in tow.

Joan of Arc had no more triumphal journey than Prudence did that day. With onlookers at the side of the road and a host of the curious following, Sheriff Roger Coit led the caravan slowly through the tunnel of maples that shaded the sloping road from Canterbury to Brooklyn. Beyond the sentinel line of trees, cows grazed in the huckleberry swamps. Imprisoned themselves by low stone walls, they were unimpressed by the passing pageant. Samuel Joseph May was waiting at the jail. As he helped Prudence down from the coach, he whispered, "If you now hesitate, if you dread the gloomy place so much as to wish to be saved from it, I will give bonds for you even now." He had the money in his pocket. "Oh no," she whispered back, "I am only afraid they will *not* put me in jail."

Sheriff Coit conferred with several bystanders as if hoping for a last-minute reprieve from his painful duty of installing her in the haunted cell. One of these men sauntered over to May. It would be a "damn shame" and an "eternal disgrace" to put Miss Crandall in that wife murderer's cell, he commented. May readily agreed and urged him to prevent it by dropping the charges. "But we are not her friends," the man protested. "We don't want any more niggers coming among us." He accused May of abandoning her, but the minister said quietly, "She knows we have not deserted her."

At last, as the sun began to set, Mr. Tyler, the jailor (who was "very polite," Prudence later said), escorted her inside into a large cell reserved not for felons but for debtors. It had been newly whitewashed, and May and George Benson had brought fresh bedding from their households. When the crowd dispersed, Anna Benson was admitted to the cell, determined to stay with Prudence for the duration, "be the term long or short."

The duration was, according to plan, quite short. The next afternoon Prudence composed a letter from jail for *The Liberator*. The postscript read, "Afternoon 4 o'clock. I am this moment liberated. Mr. George Benson came forward and gave bonds for me."[14]

Chapter Nine

Oliver Watkins had strangled his wife with a whipcord. The occasion of his hanging in August 1831 had been memorable. The Reverend George Tillotson, the Congregational minister in Brooklyn, had delivered an awesome sermon: "Be ye assured, your sins will find you out." Hundreds of people had come from miles around to witness Watkins' grisly end, and afterward half of them got drunk.

The claim that she had passed a night in Watkins' cell added immensely to Prudence's martyrdom, except that she hadn't stayed there at all. Andrew T. Judson was incensed that she prevaricated about this little detail. He and Rufus Adams wrote a pamphlet, *Answers to Aspersions*, to set the record straight. It was not fair, they peevishly pointed out, to say that Watkins was occasionally taken out of his cramped cell during his last days to receive clergy and friends in the debtors' room. "Just as well might it be said by those who go into the meeting house where Watkins attended meeting some of his last Sabbaths, that *they* had been in the 'murderer's cell.' "

The story persisted, however, and soon became a minor legend far and wide. Of course, there were those who knew the jailing had been nothing more than a successful publicity stunt. The *Windham County Advertiser* criticized Prudence soundly for "ridiculously spending a night in prison without the smallest necessity of it." They warned, "She has stepped out of the hallowed precincts of female propriety and now stands on common ground, and must expect common treatment."[1] Newspapers in larger cities also carried the story. William Leete Stone, editor of the conservative New York *Commercial Advertiser* and chairman of the New York Colonization Society, portrayed her as a victim, but not sympathetically. She was, he wrote, merely "the instrument of Arnold Buffum, William Lloyd Garrison . . . she is a respectable lady, of no great capacity or education, easily led."[2] Even the national press took notice. The popular *Niles' Weekly Register*, which called immediatism "an awful tendency," was compelled to primly record, "Miss Crandall, a young lady, had been imprisoned in Connecticut because she persisted in keeping a school for 'young ladies of color' at Canterbury—contrary to law: She has been bailed out."[3]

The reactions of common people, who had little monetary or political stake in the affair, were more supportive. Mail arrived at the post office for Prudence from many places. One letter postmarked Montreal carried this definitive address: "To Miss Prudence Crandall (inhumanly and despotically imprisoned by a people calling themselves freemen)."[4] A poet from Pomfret, Connecticut, contributed a work that proclaimed, "GOD IS ON THY SIDE!"[5] At the Brown Seminary in Providence, students were assigned essays on the subject. One of them, Clarkson Macomber, who preferred collecting rock specimens, dutifully recorded in his diary that he had written a composition on "Priscilla Crandell."[6]

Edward Abdy, an English journalist and a confirmed abolitionist, toured the area in early July 1833. Abdy found the local farmers and "laboring" men more tolerant in general than the "purse-proud merchants," "flippant shop-boys," and propertied gentlemen. He arrived in Brooklyn on the stage, having ridden up top with the driver, an old fellow who wore no coat and had slippers on his feet. "For my part," the garrulous driver volunteered, "I cannot see . . . what crime there can be in trying to elevate any portion of society by education . . . if a white man will not enter my coach because I have admitted, and always will admit, a colored person into it, all I can say is, he must find some other conveyance; or I must find some other employment."[7] Samuel Joseph May escorted the English visitor to some of the nearby farms. Abdy was enchanted by the manners of the barefooted children who bowed and curtsied at the side of the road as he passed in an open carriage. One farmer told him he would "think himself disgraced if he refused to sit down at the same table with any human being who differed from him in complexion only."[8]

May also drove Abdy to Canterbury. The journalist counted nineteen students at Prudence's school. The school, he noted, was not as elite and privileged as he had heard. The basics of reading, writing, and arithmetic—laced with "religious principles"—prevailed over the "ornamental branches of education." Nor were all the students from wealthy families. The tuition of one girl from New York was being paid by a woman who had bought her own freedom from slavery and worked as a servant. Another student was the daughter of a former slave.[9] Harriet Lamson, the ward of Simeon Jocelyn, did household chores to defray her costs.

The atmosphere at the school was cheerful and intimate. "Love and union seem to bind our little circle in the bonds of sisterly affection," one student wrote.[10] "For the most part of the time," Prudence remembered, "we were our own washerwomen and kissed each other with as much freedom as though we had been all as white as snowbanks, but never for the purpose of being seen by the villagers."[11]

Abdy was only one of many visitors to the school. Hezekiah Crandall and his wife Clarissa stopped by often and so did Albert Hinckley, a village youth who had become an abolitionist. Mary and Helen Benson came from Brooklyn, Dr. Roland Green from Black Hill, and George Roberts from Providence. Roberts was the man who had conveyed the girls of that city to the school. Sometimes rowdies yelled at the guests as they entered the Paine mansion, and sometimes, on leaving, visitors found that the harness reins of their horses had been cut while they were drinking tea. The Reverend Levi Kneeland of the Packerville Baptist Church occasionally preached at the school, as did other guest clergy. One visitor recorded that the students had passed a quiet Sabbath as a "godly minister" preached twice. "I doubt not God is there," he wrote.[12]

On special occasions the students presented "mental feasts," in which they recited lessons and provided entertainment. One afternoon the four youngest students, aged ten and eleven, dressed up in their finest clothes and recited this verse:

> Four little children here you see
> In modest dress appear.
> Come listen to our song so sweet
> And our complaints you'll hear.
>
> 'Tis here we came to learn to read
> And write and cipher too.

But some in this enlightened land
Declare 'twill never do.

The morals of this favored town
Will be corrupted soon.
Therefore they strive with all their might
To drive us from our home.

Sometimes when we have walked the streets
Saluted we have been
By guns and drums and cow bells, too
And horns of polished tin.

With warnings, threats and words severe
They visit us at times
And gladly would they send us off
To Africa's burning climes.

Our teacher too they put in jail
Fast held by bars and locks!
Did ere such persecution reign
Since Paul was in the stocks?

But we forgive, forgive the men
That persecute us so
May God in mercy save their souls
From everlasting woe!

Prudence, one student wrote, took "her utmost care to pursuade [*sic*] us not to indulge in any angry feelings towards our adversaries."[13]

In mid-July Prudence fell ill with a fever that persisted throughout August. *The Liberator* laid her illness to her frightful experience in jail. Mary Burleigh, the sister of William, came over from Plainfield to assist Almira in running the school, but without Prudence at the helm, an "incident" occurred.

For some time Prudence had felt that the students who possessed certificates of membership from their own Congregational churches should be allowed to attend the church on the green if they desired. In fact, she smarted at the notion that any of her girls should be barred from church. In the first week of July she asked Samuel Hough to inquire of Dr. Andrew Harris and Deacon Ashael Bacon, members of the Congregational Church Society Committee, if she might purchase seats for her students. Dr. Harris told Hough that the students could occupy the seats in the gallery near the door, which were set aside for the colored people. Hough pointed out that there were too many students for those seats, and Ashael Bacon responded that they could extend into neighboring pews if necessary.[14]

Prudence was too ill the following Sunday to accompany the students, so she allowed twenty-year-old Almira to act as chaperone. Hannah Baldwin described to her sister the minor scandal that ensued: "Last Sabbath Almira appeared at church accompanied by twelve negroes, as many of them as could conveniently sit in the seats for blacks the rest (Almira among the numbers) sat in the pews on the front side of the church opposite the minister . . . It is said A. conducted very improperly kept those that sat with her laughing most of the time."[15]

The Society Committee, represented by Solomon Payne, Andrew Harris, and Isaac Knight, sent an indignant note to Prudence demanding to know what Almira had been doing in "pews ever occupied by white females of the parish." Solomon Payne and a few others took the precaution against a reoccurence of the incident by quickly buying the forward pews and placing their own children in them the following Sunday.

Prudence retorted in a terse note that she had obtained permission for her students to attend and a large number had wished to do so. Although she had once said she would have services only in her school, she had, quite simply, "upon mature consideration" changed her mind. Samuel Hough, the original go-between, delivered a final verbal message from the committee that the students were no longer welcome.[16] Thereafter the girls who were Congregationalists had to attend the Westminster Church two miles away.

It was not much easier attending the Packerville Baptist Church. Daniel Packer, who seems to have opposed secular instruction for blacks but not religious instruction, usually sent his carriage and driver for some of the girls on Sunday mornings. Pardon also drove some in his wagon. One Sunday after church, as Packer's carriage approached the fording place in the Quinebaug River on its way back to the school, the driver saw several rough-looking young men waiting for them. He nervously told the girls to get down from the carriage, and as they huddled on the bank, the youths seized the carriage and overturned it in the shallow water. Pardon's wagon soon caught up, but the old man did not think it wise to leave his passengers alone while he aided the driver. He forded the river quickly and sped up the hill to the school a short distance beyond, where he dropped off his passengers. Then he returned for the stranded students. When all the girls were safe, he and Hezekiah went back and pulled Mr. Packer's carriage out of the river.[17] Soon after this incident Daniel Packer announced that he was taking his wife and daughter on an extended trip to Saratoga and Niagara. Daniel Packer, Jr., publicly declared that neither Prudence nor her scholars would be allowed inside the meeting house while his father was away.[18]

It was also during this time that a rock smashed a north window of the school's first-floor parlor. The incident occurred at night. Almira had just left the room. The rock was "about the size of my hand and about an inch and a half in thickness," Almira told George Benson. It was thrown with such force that it tore through the curtain and strewed glass across the room.[19]

Samuel Joseph May was perplexed about how to deal with such episodes. Village officials averted their eyes. The local press dismissed such harassment as "boyish folly" and attributed vandalism to blacks "belonging in the neighborhood."[20]

May realized just how far his leadership and moral influence had eroded when he attended the annual meeting in July of the Windham County Colonization Society, which he had founded. Many men from Canterbury attended, including Andrew T. Judson and Dr. Andrew Harris. When the annual report was read, May found himself alone in opposing a statement to the effect that the practicality of ending slavery by colonization had been demonstrated. May had facts at his disposal to show that in 1820 there were 1,538,038 slaves, but by 1830 their numbers had grown to 2,009,304.[21] Moreover, because of an expanding market for cotton, the demand for slaves in the deep South had risen sharply along with the price plantation owners were willing to pay for them. In 1830 a prime field hand went for $400. By 1832 the price hit $500, and it kept rising until 1837, when a healthy male slave could cost $1,100.[22] But May's facts made no difference, and he was overruled.

The next item of business was the appointment of agents to organize auxiliary branches of the society. Although Judson had been associated with the Colonization Society only a short time, his friends appointed him the agent for Canterbury and secretary of the county. They also made him the substitute for the orator at the next quarterly meeting and primary speaker for the meeting after that in six months. (Previously the society had met once a year, but with the crisis in Canterbury, the members voted to convene every three months.)

As the meeting progressed, May introduced a resolution that the black men and women who were to go as instructors to Africa ought first to be instructed themselves, but Judson insisted that what May meant by instruction was indoctrination in abolitionist principles. When May tried to rebut this, Dr. Harris interrupted and said May had no right to speak. Judson's motion prevailed. After the meeting May felt he was becoming an object of general distrust and worried that he was losing for Prudence whatever support she had.[23]

In New York Arthur Tappan was following developments in Canterbury in the metropolitan papers. Tappan had met May years ago in Boston when, as a youth, he had been a clerk in the hardware department of the mercantile firm of Sewall and Salisbury. For a brief time he had boarded with the May family. Tappan wrote to May expressing his joy in learning that he was espousing Prudence's cause. He knew May could not afford to bear the expenses of the contest, and he offered to be his "banker." He instructed May to keep accounts accurately, spare no necessary expense, employ the best legal counsel, and inform him whenever he needed more money.[24] May replied with a long and grateful letter in which he described the antagonism of the local press. Even a printer, whose shop May had assisted in establishing, had said he dared not print anything favorable to the school or he'd be ruined.[25]

Much to May's surprise, three or four days later, there was a knock at the door of his study and Lucretia admitted Arthur Tappan. He had come, he said, to assess the situation for himself. The two men talked for several hours, and then Tappan rode over to Canterbury. There he met Prudence's students and spoke to each of them. He examined the rock, which Prudence was displaying upon the mantelpiece, and the broken window. When he returned to Brooklyn, Tappan told May that the state of affairs was "even worse than I supposed." But the solution, he said, was obvious: "You must start a newspaper as soon as possible."

It so happened that a press in Brooklyn had recently been abandoned. "We must have it," Tappan announced. The two men found the owner and rented it on the spot for a year. Then Tappan placed the lease in May's hands, boarded the stage, and was gone. By the next morning the euphoria of Tappan's visit had evaporated, and May realized that in addition to his other responsibilities he was now the proprietor of a printing office. Casting about in his mind for someone who might help him, he recalled reading an article in the *Genius of Temperance* written by twenty-three-year-old Charles Burleigh, the brother of William and Mary.

That very morning he rode over to the Burleigh farm in Plainfield. It was a hot, sultry day in the midst of haying season. May was told at the house that Charles was in the field with his father. May insisted on the urgency of his business, and finally someone went to retrieve Charles. The young man walked wearily up to the house. He sported a four-day's growth of beard, his shirt-sleeves were rolled up, and his trousers were "the worse for wear." But when May made his proposition, the young man's "eyes kindled as if eager for the conflict."[26] May arranged for a substitute laborer to join Mr. Burleigh, and the following Monday Charles was working at the press in Brooklyn.

The editorship of the paper bent young Burleigh's career in a new direction. Although he eventually passed the bar— brilliantly, it was said—he became an apostle of antislavery rather than a lawyer. (In later life he looked like a figure out of the Bible with his long flowing hair and beard. He roamed the countryside carrying antislavery pamphlets stuck on the end of his walking stick, and was much sought after by artists as a model for Jesus Christ.)

Burleigh produced the first issue of *The Unionist* two weeks after becoming its editor, on August 1, 1833. The paper appeared every Thursday thereafter for nearly two years. It pledged itself to no party and promised to accept articles on both sides of the school question unless they were of "a scurrilous or abusive character." Judson and Adams' *Answers to Aspersions* appeared in the second issue. Alongside it was a piece called "The Spirit of Reform," in which the author, probably Burleigh, proclaimed, "It is best that we should follow the many in all ways which are indifferent; perhaps it is best that we should follow them in some ways which are inconvenient; but we must not follow them to do evil."

With the advent of *The Unionist*, the Crandall affair became a genuine debate that was discussed whenever people gathered. Edward Abdy, having had a pleasant stay in Canterbury, left for Hartford on August 9. This time he sat inside the coach with several loquacious men who were condemning Prudence. After listening in silence for as long as he could bear, Abdy interjected that as a European it seemed to him "much ado about nothing." What sense did it make, he asked, to allow black and white children of the humbler classes to be educated together and not black and white children of the wealthier classes? If the carpenter's and mason's child escaped unscathed, it was likely the lawyer need not fear.[27] When he finished there was, for a short while, silence on the subject.

Chapter Ten

*T*he gulf between Prudence and her gentlemen enemies widened. By late summer 1833, the advantage seemed to be turning toward Prudence like a welcome tide, although it would later recede once again to the other shore.

In Boston, Lydia Maria Child dedicated her new book, *An Appeal in Favor of That Class of Americans Called Africans*, to Samuel Joseph May "for his Earnest and Disinterested Efforts in an Unpopular But Most Righteous Cause," namely, Prudence's school. It was the first antislavery work of book length to be published in the country. When he heard of the honor, May said, "Now, indeed, I *must* go forward, I can never draw back."[2]

With Arthur Tappan's money, May hired three of the finest lawyers in Connecticut to defend Prudence in her upcoming trial: William Wolcott Ellsworth, Calvin Goddard, and Henry Strong, all of them opposed to the Black Law. Of the three, Ellsworth was the most renowned. A graduate of Yale, he was the son of Oliver Ellsworth, who had succeeded John Marshall as second chief justice of the

United States Supreme Court, and was married to lexicographer Noah Webster's oldest daughter. He was tall and dignified, "like an embodiment of a typical Yankee, equally able to trade horses, make a political speech, and offer prayer."[3] At the time of Prudence's trial Ellsworth was a U.S. congressman. Later, in 1838, he was elected governor of Connecticut.

Prudence's defense team faced special prosecuting attorney Chauncey Fitch Cleveland (who succeeded Ellsworth as governor of Connecticut), Andrew T. Judson (who, despite his best efforts, never became governor), and Ichabod Bulkley.[4] The day before the trial was to begin, however, the celebrated Chauncey Cleveland fell ill and requested to be excused. The court replaced Cleveland with the lieutenant governor state's attorney, a man named Stoddard, but when he too became suddenly indisposed, Johnathan Welch, a lawyer from Brooklyn, was hastily chosen, probably because of his availability and his stamina rather than his legal acumen.

Prudence was charged with instructing and boarding students who were not inhabitants of Connecticut without the prior consent of the civil authority and selectmen of her village. The prosecution needed to prove only one of these two offenses—instructing or boarding—for conviction, and as the occupation of landlady had not yet been outlawed, they intended to prove she was an illegitimate and illegal teacher.

A week before the trial, the prosecution ordered Deputy Sheriff Cady to deliver summonses to some of the students to appear as prosecution witnesses. When Cady arrived at Prudence's door, one student, Mary Elizabeth Wiles, begged to be excused because her mother was ill and she had to go home. Cady told her it wasn't his job to excuse her, but he would inform the public prosecutor of the situation. Prudence, who was just recovering her strength after weeks of fever, snapped that she didn't see the need for witnesses anyway because she intended to confess she had broken the law. With that she closed the door in the deputy's face.[5] Her lawyers had explained to her that the jury could decide upon the character of the law as well as the conduct of the accused. The defense strategy, therefore, would be not to deny her guilt but to prove the "wickedness" of the law.[6]

The trial began on August 22, 1833. Once again Prudence traveled the sloping road to Brooklyn through fields and meadows "thickly dotted with white farmhouses, orchards, and clumps of walnut and shade-trees."[7] She passed the cemetery at the edge of town, then Samuel Joseph May's meeting house with its belfry that looked like a windmill, and finally arrived at the door of the new white courthouse. Nothing as exciting had occurred in Brooklyn since the trial of Oliver Watkins two years earlier, and the courthouse was packed with spectators despite the oppressive heat. In the middle of the sea of somber, frocked gentlemen there sat one very tall individual who wore a conspicuously bright blue stock that was "knotted with care."[8] He was the Reverend Calvin Philleo, a widowed Baptist preacher from Ithaca, New York. Philleo had preached occasionally in Levi Kneeland's church in Packerville, and he was familiar with events in Canterbury. He had decided to marry Prudence and was looking forward to meeting her.

Three judges oversaw the crowded courtroom. The associate judges were local magistrates by the names of Griffin and Chase. The presiding chief judge, Joseph K. Eaton, hailed from Plainfield. He had been president of the Windham County Bank when Andrew Judson, Rufus Adams, and would-be prosecuting attorney Chauncey Cleveland were members of the Board of Directors. He had also served with Judson as a director of the Windham County Mutual Fire Insurance Company. Edward Abdy, who was admittedly on Prudence's side, thought that Judge Eaton evinced "a marked spirit of hostility" toward the defense throughout the trial.[9] Trial accounts show he allowed the prosecution lawyers to refer to Prudence disrespectfully as "Prudy." Had his neutrality been questioned, Eaton would have been compelled to reveal that he had been a member of Senator Pearl's committee, which had formulated the Black Law and had advocated its passage on the floor of the House.[10]

During the impaneling of the jury, the defense objected to one juror from Canterbury who had signed a petition against the school. He was dismissed, but a second man, who had voted for the Black Law in the legislature, was ordered to serve.

A correspondent for the Hartford *Courant*, a paper friendly to Prudence's cause, left a sketch of the proceedings.[11] The prosecution called selectman Ashael Bacon as its first witness. Bacon recounted his visit to the school in June to investigate whether there were students from abroad staying there. Deputy Sheriff Cady next told the court that he had spoken to students when he had delivered the summonses to the school.

Prosecutor Welch then called Ann Peterson, one of the New York students, but William Ellsworth immediately rose and objected that the witness need not answer questions that might implicate her in a crime. Andrew T. Judson said that the girl was not being charged with a crime and therefore had to testify because the legislature had expressly enacted that the pupils should be witnesses. Ellsworth replied that that was precisely the issue, whether the legislature possessed the power to make a witness give potentially damaging evidence. The bench ruled in favor of the prosecution, but Ellsworth said Miss Peterson had been advised to remain silent. He wished the court to understand that the counsel had no wish to "embarrass the trial," but they conscientiously believed the rights of the witness were such that she could not be compelled to testify.

Welch, nevertheless, proceeded to interrogate the girl. When had she come to Canterbury, he asked? Did Miss Crandall keep a school for colored girls who were not inhabitants of the state? Had the defendant instructed any person of color other than herself since the tenth of June last? The teenager refused to answer on the grounds that she might incriminate herself, and Welch eventually let her go. He called two more students, Catherine Ann Weldon and Ann Eliza Hammond, but they also refused to cooperate. The frustrated prosecutor dismissed them with the threat that he might charge them with contempt if they didn't change their minds.

Welch then called Jacob Gould, a white man, who said he knew Ann Eliza Hammond and her family in Providence. He testified that her father, Thomas Hammond, had been pretty well off when he died. Next, the Reverend Levi Kneeland of Packerville took the stand, but he refused to admit if any of the students present in the courtroom had attended his church. When asked if he had eaten at Miss Crandall's table during the time that the school was in session, he replied that the court had no business to know. Welch moved to have him committed to jail for contempt, and he was taken from the courtroom.

The next witness, Eliza Parkis, a laundress, testified that she sometimes helped with the washing and other chores so that the students could concentrate on their studies. She was acquainted with Ann Eliza Hammond and had once slept overnight in a room with Theodosia De Grass, who was from New York. She said she had never seen any of the girls being instructed in the schoolroom, although she had seen them wandering throughout the house reading books. Dr. Roland Green of Black Hill testified that he had often been to the school as a physician and as a friend. He had heard some of the girls recite lessons in grammar and geography, and it had been his pleasure, he said, to welcome some of them to his home.

The stifling day wore on. Welch had established that some of the girls were not Connecticut inhabitants. He had disclosed that they were reading books and reciting poems, but he had found no one who would say Prudence was the actual teacher.

After several hours, Levi Kneeland returned to the courtroom at his own request. He had been advised that he could not be implicated, and therefore, with all due respect, he was willing to talk. To Welch's annoyance, however, Kneeland had little to say. He had twice visited the school, but he had trouble remembering particular faces. In fact, he could not identify anyone in the courtroom as a student. He had taken meals at the school and had listened to recitations. He thought Miss Crandall had told him some students were from New York, Providence, and New Haven, but he wasn't sure. After this frustrating testimony, Welch decided he needed more witnesses and dispatched Deputy Cady to fetch Eliza Glasko, a student from Connecticut who had stayed behind in Canterbury.

Meanwhile, Welch called Albert Hinckley, a young abolitionist convert. Hinckley admitted that he had been to the school several times, but he didn't know if he'd been in the schoolroom as he didn't know which room *was* the schoolroom. He never saw Miss Crandall engaged in instruction. He never conversed with her on the subject of the residence of her pupils, and he didn't know if any of the colored ladies in the courtroom were from the school.

Witness after witness exhibited similar amnesiac symptoms. Hezekiah Crandall said he knew his sister kept a school for colored girls, and he recognized Ann Eliza Hammond and possibly Ann Peterson. He knew Amelia Wilder by sight and by name, but he didn't see her present. He had never been in the schoolroom and had never heard any pupils recite. James B. Chandler, the next witness, couldn't remember "with certainty" when he had visited the school, and so he was excused. George Roberts acknowledged that he had driven Ann Eliza Hammond to Canterbury five months earlier, but didn't know if she boarded there.

When court adjourned for the day, Prudence was still a free woman. She walked her students to the Benson house, which was just down the road from the courthouse. Prudence had christened the place "Friendship Valley," and there they stayed the night.

The second day went better for prosecutor Welch. The first witness, Eliza Glasko, told Welch that even though she came from Connecticut, she feared she would be accused of abetting Miss Crandall because she paid to support the school. Therefore she would not answer any questions. Welch moved she be held in contempt. A mittimus was prepared, which stated she should be taken to "the common jail in Brooklyn . . . there to remain at her own case until she shall give evidence." But as Eliza was led through the crowd, William Ellsworth rose and announced that although his advice to the girl not to testify had been dictated "by an imperious sense of professional duty," now, rather than see her committed, he would encourage her to answer the questions. Eliza returned to the stand and admitted she was a member of the school. She identified Ann Eliza Hammond from Providence and pointed out two of the New York girls.

Finally, Mary Benson of Brooklyn was called. She said

she thought the school was "very interesting." She also said what Welch had been waiting two long days to hear: she had seen Prudence teaching geography and arithmetic. Welch had his case.

Because the indisposed Chauncey Cleveland was unavailable to deliver the summation for the prosecution, and Johnathan Welch was only a local stand-in, the honor fell to Andrew T. Judson. Judson assured the jury that the law in question did not prevent colored children from attending district elementary schools or even higher schools. In fact, he boasted, the blacks of Connecticut enjoyed the benefits of a $1,800,000 school fund, which was both ample and generous. Nevertheless, he maintained, towns had a well-established right to decide who should be allowed to become inhabitants by residence within their limits. Therefore it was not fair or even safe to allow someone, without the consent of officials, to open a school and invite any class of pupils she might please from other states.

Judson pointed out that many states, Northern and Southern, regarded colored people as the kind of population that required special legislation. Tanners, taverners, surveyors, doctors, and manufacturers were liable to similar scrutiny, he said, and that was only right and reasonable.

The passage in the United States Constitution referring to equal rights and privileges for all citizens in the various states did not apply to this situation, he asserted. Citizenship was defined by suffrage, and since only "free white males" could vote, black people were obviously not citizens. The privilege of being a free man was higher than the right to be educated, and if blacks could not even be free, Judson reasoned, why should they be educated? He assured the jury that he did not wish to oppress anyone. He heartily wished all the slaves could be emancipated immediately, but only if it could be done without destroying the Constitution and desolating the land. That, unfortunately, did not seem possible.

Johnathan Welch spoke briefly, and then defenders Henry Strong and William Ellsworth had their turn. Ellsworth began his closing remarks with the admission that it was no secret Miss Crandall kept a school for colored girls, but each member of the jury had to determine not only if a law had been broken but if that law was constitutional. In other words, was Miss Crandall protected by a higher power? The question was simply, could the legislature of Connecticut pass a law prohibiting the citizens of other states from coming to Connecticut to pursue the acquisition of knowledge in a way open to Connecticut's own citizens?

To Ellsworth's mind, black people were already citizens. In the Revolutionary War black soldiers had died for their country, and their names were inscribed on the pension rolls. Furthermore, colored men could appeal the laws for protection of their rights in every state; could they do this if they weren't citizens? "I scout the idea," he argued passionately, "that a man born here is not a citizen because his father was black while I am a citizen because mine was white."

It remained for Judge Eaton to instruct the jury, and it puzzled Samuel Joseph May that his opinion on the constitutionality of the law, upon which the entire case rested, was rendered "somewhat timidly." But then, as village chronicler Abraham Payne put it, Eaton was an "amiable and excellent man whose intellect had never been much disturbed by the investigation of historical or constitutional questions."[12]

The correspondent for the Hartford *Courant* had to leave before the jury returned their verdict, but he felt that it was "the almost universal opinion" of the spectators that the jury would never convict her. "The current was turning and setting with *great force* in her favor," he wrote.

After deliberating for several hours, the jurors returned and reported they could not reach an accord. Judge Eaton instructed them on several points and sent them back. Again they returned and again they were sent back. Finally the foreman of the jury told Judge Eaton they were irreconcilably split, with seven for conviction and five for acquittal. Eaton reluctantly dismissed them and continued the case to the next term of the county court in December.

The jury consisted of local men, and nearly half of them, it seemed, agreed with William Ellsworth, supported Prudence, or simply disliked the elegant Andrew T. Judson. It had become painfully clear to Judson that his would not be an easy victory. Preexisting antagonisms complicated what Judson had once assumed to be an obvious issue that all gentlemen could agree upon. His coalition was far from homogenous. Not all the men were Democrats. Some, like Judson, were Masons, but others were anti-Masons. The Reverend George White and Daniel Frost, Jr., were prominent temperance men, while Richard Fenner was a liquor retailer.

Moreover, Judson's racist zeal offended some people who favored a superficially harmonious status quo over a radical change of social policy toward blacks. Connecticut, "the land of steady habits," had historically preferred a policy of benign gradualism. Most citizens opposed agitation either for or against slavery, but they were sympathetic to noncontentious, nonexpensive expressions of goodwill toward blacks such as they perceived the Colonization Society to be.[13]

Judson's unrelenting harshness toward Prudence, a "lady" by most standards, may have produced a backlash.

Her new students had turned out to be intelligent, well mannered, and tastefully dressed. Edward Abdy believed that most of them had "better claims to grace and beauty" than the majority of "belles and matrons of the district."[14]

Still, some of the village women were contemptuous of the show the Crandall girls had put on. When Almira was asked how she had endured the night her sister was in jail, she demurely replied that she had prayed. "I well remember," wrote Abraham Payne, "the indignation of some pious, but not beautiful females, because 'this impenitent little thing' pretended to have been praying all night."[15]

Other women, however, rallied to Prudence's defense. The August 17, 1833, *Liberator* printed a piece from the *Female Advocate* that called Judson "this modern Nero, this heartless being, unworthy the name of man." The lady editors urged their readers to emulate the biblical example of Esther, who by cleverness and courage saved her people from destruction at the hands of the vile Haman.

The melodramatic image of Judson as villain was touted for all it was worth by Prudence's admirers. A letter to Judson from a man in Pittsburgh, Pennsylvania, was published in the *Norwich Courier*. Although Judson argued that it showed what kind of people Prudence's school was attracting, he was greatly embarrassed by it. "I will be in Canterbury in three weeks," the feisty author wrote, "and you may prepare yourself for me, for I mean to beat you under the earth, if I can lay my hands on you. If not I will take a shot at you. You poor dead dog."[16] Esther Baldwin, who read the letter, informed her sister Hannah that Judson felt "very agitated about it."[17]

There were other letters too. One from New Bedford, Massachusetts, proposed a Yankee deal. Since Britain, France, and Germany espoused liberty and equal rights, the correspondent offered to take Judson abroad on exhibition in a cage. He guaranteed at least $5,000 for two and a half years and promised "a colored person shall every morning clean out your den, provide your food, and give you that attendance which is commonly given to that wise and elegant creature, which with the exception of the tail, most nearly resembles the human form."[18]

The Reverend Nathaniel Paul, a black fund-raiser for the Wilburforce Colony in Canada, wrote to Judson from London. He "praised" Judson's actions, which were "so patriotic, so republican, so Christian like in their nature" that word of them "should not be confined to one nation or continent but . . . the WORLD should know them and learn and profit thereby." Paul volunteered to spread the word: "Yes sir, Britons shall know that there are men in America, and whole towns of them too, who are not so destitute of true heroism but that they can assail a helpless woman, surround her house by night, break her windows, and drag her to prison, for the treasonable act of teaching females of color to read!!!" Before he signed it "Respectfully yours," he assured Judson, "I shall make no charge for the service I may render you."[19]

Nathaniel Paul added to Judson's worries in a more fundamental way: he loaned William Lloyd Garrison—penniless as always—the sum of $200 so the editor could return to America from England.

Chapter Eleven

*W*illiam Lloyd Garrison had triumphed in England. He had won every debating duel with Colonization Society agent Elliott Cresson. In his own immodest summation, Garrison declared that he had exposed the scurrilous character of the Colonization Society "expeditiously, comprehensively, and effectually."[1]

Garrison's triumph, however, only served to make him and his followers more hateful than ever to conservatives at home. *Niles' Weekly Register* had begun printing bizarre stories about black people, insinuating that the slave insurrection in Cuba or the rape of a nine-year-old girl by a black man in Hartford were problems that would never have surfaced if the abolitionists hadn't stirred them up. William Leete Stone of the New York *Commercial Advertiser* branded Garrison, the consummate agitator, as the "misguided young gentleman who had just returned from England, whither he has recently been for the sole purpose, as it would seem, of traducing the people and institutions of his own country." The paper warned, "He would do well to consider that his course of conduct in England has kindled a spirit of hostility towards him at home."[2]

The colonizationists could no longer ignore Garrison, even though by choice and necessity he confined his mischief largely to New England. Garrison's campaign against the colonizationists was gaining steam at a time the society was weakening because of furious infighting over leadership and finances. As R. R. Gurley, secretary of the society, delicately put it, "The calls on [the society's] bounty far exceeded the funds at its disposal."[3] By the end of 1833, the colonizationists faced a $46,000 deficit.[4] The abolitionists, on the other hand, were thriving. From four local societies in 1832, there were now forty-seven societies in ten states.[5] The colonizationists viewed the formation in October 1833 of a New York antislavery chapter with much alarm because such an organization could draw upon Arthur Tappan's fortune.[6]

On October 2 the New York chapter was scheduled to hold an organizational meeting in Clinton Hall, but upon learning that anti-abolitionist demonstrators would disrupt them, they secretly altered their plans and procured the lecture room of the Chatham Street Chapel with the help of Lewis Tappan, brother of Arthur, who was a trustee.[7] So when 1,500 angry anti-abolitionists gathered at Clinton Hall that night, they found it locked and deserted. William Lloyd Garrison wandered unrecognized through the crowd, as puzzled as the next man. He had arrived in New York from England only three days earlier and had not been informed of the change.

Somewhat later that evening, as the group celebrated their supposed rout of the abolitionists at Tammany Hall, someone shouted out that the abolitionists were at that very moment meeting at Chatham Chapel. The mob rushed to the chapel but found their way barred by a heavy iron gate.

Inside, about fifty abolitionists hastily prayed, passed resolutions, elected officers, and ran out the back door. When
the anti-abolitionists learned their quarry had once again
escaped, they conducted a mock meeting of their own, forcing an old black man, whom they dubbed Arthur Tappan,
to make a speech. Then they voted for "immediate emancipation and immediate amalgamation."

Reverberations from this ugly evening were still strong
when Prudence's second trial began less than a week later.
Andrew T. Judson had been very busy after his July defeat,
and had managed to move the trial up from December to
October. Prudence received only six days' notice of the
change, and it caught her lawyers and her supporters off
guard. Samuel Joseph May, believing he had a respite of
several months, had taken his family on a lecture tour. Henry
Benson wrote to him, "As Miss Crandall's trial comes on
this week, we think it advisable that you should be there
as soon as possible. . . . The movements of the Canterbury
people were rather sudden and matters are not in the situation in which they should be."[8] But May could not return
in time; he advised the lawyers that if the case went against
them, they should appeal to the Court of Errors.[9]

On September 26 Judson had arranged to harass Prudence by having her rearrested. Bond was set for $150, but
this time Richard Fenner and William Lester leaped forward
to pay it before she could send herself to jail again. Judson
and Fenner were also compiling new "evidence" against
Prudence. Fenner submitted a statement to the effect that
Prudence had solicited letters of introduction from him to
gentlemen in Boston under false pretenses. The two men
also persuaded Mary Barber, a servant in the Jedidiah Shephard house when Sarah Harris had worked there, to submit a version of Sarah's acceptance into the school that
differed from Prudence's. According to Mary, they said,

Sarah never asked Prudence if she could attend the school. Instead, the teacher invited her to enter for a period of nine months as preparation for teaching. Mary claimed Sarah told her "she should never thought of going if Miss Crandall had not *proposed* it to her, and she had concluded to go."[10]

Judson had reason to be optimistic about the second trial. The chief justice would be the venerable David Daggett, who was known to favor the Black Law. Daggett, a former mayor of New Haven, had strenuously opposed that town's school for black youths back in 1831. He was also the vice-president of the Hartford Colonization Society.

Daggett's judicial history was disheartening to Prudence's supporters. In a highly publicized case in 1812, when he had been Connecticut attorney general, Daggett had indicted a Baptist minister named Joshua Bradley for being "a person of evil disposition" who had "tried to impose himself upon many of the citizens of . . . Wallingford, North Haven, East Haven, and Branford . . . as a preacher of the gospel . . . and thereby seduce and draw away from their respective pastors and ecclesiastical societies to which belong many of the aforesaid citizens." Bradley was acquitted, but the case demonstrated Daggett's attitude toward "strangers" or "foreigners" with divergent opinions.[11] In 1831 the judge ruled on a case concerning black "paupers" accused of draining the charitable resources of towns. The plight of freed slaves who were infirm or penniless had come up in the courts many times since the end of the eighteenth century. Who was responsible for the welfare of such individuals, the towns with their statutes providing for the support of "all poor and impotent persons" or the former owners of the slaves? Daggett ruled in favor of the towns in a decision that stated that towns were obliged to support former slaves only when the master of the ex-slave was impoverished as well.[12]

Daggett had definite opinions on the constitutionality of the Black Law, and unlike Judge Eaton, he was not timid in delivering them. When Prudence's trial began, the defense entered a plea of not guilty, and both sides basically proceeded to restate the points they had made in the first trial. After the lawyers had given their summations, Judge Daggett, who was every inch a magistrate with his aristocratic "Roman" face, his expensive clothes, and his scrupulously civil manner, began an elaborate instruction to the jury. His words were all the more impressive delivered in his "powerful voice," which ranged "through the whole scale, from a subdued yet distinct whisper" to something like "a trumpet call."[13]

Daggett first urged the jury to put aside any feelings they might have about the "popularity or unpopularity" of the law in question, for they must "pass upon the facts." Yet he reminded them that the court had the right to give its opinion, and it was his opinion that to call slaves, Indians, or free blacks "citizens" would be a perversion of the term as it was used in the United States Constitution. Such persons were not styled as citizens, he maintained, when the Constitution fixed the basis for representation as "free persons" and excluded indentured servants and Indians. Furthermore, at that time, every state except Massachusetts tolerated slaves, and they were not citizens. He pointed out to the jury that free Negroes were not considered citizens in any of the state constitutions, either. Then, knowing full well that William Ellsworth was the son-in-law of Noah Webster, Daggett quoted Webster's definition of "citizen" to demonstrate that blacks did not fit it. Finally, he leaned forward and told the jury with solemnity, "I am bound by my duty, to say, they are not citizens."

As almost an afterthought, Daggett told the jury that even if blacks *were* citizens, he was not sure the Black Law would be unconstitutional because legislatures may regulate schools. Education was a fundamental right, but the law did not prohibit schools: "It places them under the care of the civil authority and the selectmen and why is this not a very suitable regulation?"

The two other magistrates in the case, Judges Bissell and Williams, did not agree with Judge Daggett that black people were not citizens, but they were intimidated into silence. The minutes of their consultations with Daggett were recorded by Bissell but not published until after his death many years later. At the time of the Dred Scott Decision in 1857, when the Supreme Court decided definitively, if not eternally, that black people were not citizens, Judge Williams, who was by then eighty years old, wrote to his old friend Judge Bissell for advice on "whether there ought to be any delicacy in saying what were our opinions on the subject [of black citizenship in 1833], though no judicial opinions were given. For myself, I must say I did not then doubt, nor since have doubted that our respected friend was wrong in his charge to the jury."[14]

Yet Daggett's charge to the jury prevailed, and the jurors found Prudence guilty. The defense immediately filed a motion in arrest of judgment on two technical points: that the superior court had no jurisdiction over the offenses charged and that the particular information in the formal charge was insufficient.

Because of the appeal, Prudence was not sentenced. She returned to Canterbury and managed to function as if nothing unusual had happened. That in itself was shocking to some people, who thought the chastisement of public condemnation would shame her into submission. The *Windham County Advertiser* was astonished that the number of students was not falling, but rising. They erroneously reported that the Paine mansion contained "more than thirty wenches who are sent from all quarters of the globe."[15] Mr. Holbrook, the editor, pointed out that "the peaceable and undisturbed manner . . . in which the instructress has of late been permitted to go on with her school, in violation of the law," was sorely trying to the "forbearance" of the good people of Canterbury.

The "good people" of Canterbury kept up their petty sniping. One morning in late August 1833, in the middle of a drought, Mariah had pulled up the bucket from the well in the front yard and found the water contaminated with manure. Neighbor Richard Fenner's well was near the road and had ever been available for the use of travelers, but Fenner forbade anyone from the school to draw one drop. Pardon Crandall carted barrels of water from his farm two miles away until the drought subsided and the students could use a well located in the basement of the school. In other incidents, a visiting minister who called at the school was refused the privilege of preaching in the Congregational Church on the green. And Dr. Andrew Harris, when called across the road to attend a student's sudden illness, declared as he escaped, "You need not send for me again—I shall not come if you do!"[16] A man of his word, Dr. Harris did refuse to come on a subsequent occasion and boasted of it.

Then in late October, Prudence did something so outrageous it seemed to justify the townspeople's persecution: she entertained William Lloyd Garrison one afternoon in Canterbury. She showed him the infamous stone on her mantel, and he advised her to treasure it and not have the window repaired. In retaliation for Garrison's affront, the men who had been "libeled" six months earlier in *The Liberator* sent Sheriff Coit to Brooklyn to deliver libel papers to Garrison at the Bensons' house. To make sure he would be there, the sheriff waited until after midnight before pounding on the door. Garrison was furious and vowed to fight back. "I shall readily comply with their polite and urgent invitation to appear at the Windham County Court," he wrote. "As they have generously given me *precept upon precept*, I shall give them in return *line upon line* (in *The Liberator*) a little and *there* (in the court room) a great deal."[17]

The *Brooklyn Advertiser* snidely commented that now Garrison and the "Canterbury heroine" might have the "pleasure" of standing together before the same tribunal: "There will doubtless be great mutual sympathy, in as much as they will both be arraigned for alleged defense of the same (as they pretend) holy cause." The press, eager to soil Prudence's reputation, insinuated a romance between her and Garrison. The sometimes irrational emotions of love, it seemed, were the only possible excuse they could think of for Prudence's loyalty to abolitionism. But they were wrong. Garrison was falling in love, it was true, but with Helen Benson and not with Prudence.

In late November he casually planted a hint of his intentions within a long letter to George Benson: "What news from Canterbury? I long to get there once more, but more particularly under the hospitable roof of your father. I confess, in addition to the other delightful attractions which are there found, the soft blue eyes and pleasant countenance of Miss Ellen are by no means impotent or unattractive."[18] It was the last time he got her name wrong.

As for Prudence, whose sense of vulnerability after the trial may explain her lapse of judgment, love or one of its crueler semblances took her in too. The tall man with the blue cravat declared himself. He was Calvin Philleo, a forty-six-year-old Baptist minister who had just left a three-year ministry in Pawtucket, Rhode Island, and was living in Ithaca, New York.[19] He was a widower of two years' duration and the father of a married daughter, a sickly eigh-

teen-year-old daughter, and a gifted twelve-year-old son.
The boy, Calvin Wheeler, went to school in Suffield, Connecticut, where his father had preached before going to
Rhode Island. As the Suffield stagecoach passed near Canterbury, Philleo had heard of Prudence and had attended
her first trial. He was diligently looking for a new wife,
preferably one with property.

When Calvin Wheeler grew up, he wrote a novel in which
he described the sensory delights of Thanksgiving in a village much like Canterbury. From every kitchen chimney,
he wrote, rose "wreaths of smoke" so that the frosty air "was
full of . . . the delicious odors of the oven and the spit."
There were roasted turkeys on "broad pewter platters," pies
"skillfully compounded of pumpkins, mince-meat or apples," and "round-bellied puddings speckled with plums
and unctuous with suet."[20] The Thanksgiving of 1833 at
Prudence's school may have been more meager than this,
but there was gaiety in abundance. On November 28 the
entire school attended the double wedding of Sarah Harris
to George Fayerweather III, a blacksmith from Kingston,
Rhode Island, and Mariah Davis to Sarah's brother, Charles
Harris. Mariah and Charles Harris set up housekeeping in
a small house next to the school, where Mariah worked as
before. In early December there was another wedding, that
of George Benson to Catherine Stetson of Waltham, Massachusetts. Lucretia May, left behind once more with the
children, wrote to her husband, who was with Garrison in
Philadelphia for the founding of the American Anti-Slavery
Society, that "Cousin" Helen had gone to Waltham for the
ceremony. "I wonder if the wedding will be as comical as
the courtship has been," she commented sourly. "To equal
it in privacy they must be married down cellar in the dead
of night. But each to his own taste."[21]

But this merry holiday spirit was not to last. The *Wind-*

ham County Advertiser, apparently oblivious to the season of good cheer, printed an editorial on December 19 that ominously announced, "TO ALL WHOME IT MAY CONCERN: From what we learn we have good reason to believe that a determination had been formed to BREAK UP the Negro school in Canterbury by some means or other in less than two months."

Chapter Twelve

*T*he "junto at Canterbury," as William Lloyd Garrison called them, sent an anonymous petition to the Connecticut General Assembly shortly after Prudence's second trial, asserting the rights of white citizens to defend themselves from black encroachments. They urged self-respecting white men to adopt "all measures which are necessary for self-preservation."

Free black people, the petition's authors stated, were so newly sprung from the "barbarism of slavery" that they had few artificial wants and were ignorant of the decencies of life and "improvident" of the future. They worked for next to nothing, thus forcing white wage earners to enter almshouses or else leave for the "western wilds." Thousands of "our most valuable citizens," they claimed, had been banished by the "influx of black porters, black truckmen, black sawyers, black merchants, and black laborers of every description." The poorer classes were most affected, but "the time is at hand, when those who sit in high places and roll in luxury, must look to their own security."[1] These were not idle ramblings; those who felt threatened were quite prepared to do, as they put it, whatever was "necessary" to preserve their way of life.

Thus one of the most vicious episodes in the short history of Miss Crandall's Female Seminary began on the frosty morning of January 28, 1834, when the Norwich stage-coach stopped in Canterbury and a young black man, laden with bundles, stepped out. Frederick Olney, the *Liberator* agent for Norwich, was visiting his friends Mariah and Charles Harris at the school.[2]

Prudence admitted the young man, who was well known to her, and escorted him to the "keeping room," an informal parlor or common room on the second floor, located at the front of the house in the northeast corner. The room had been strung with evergreen festoons for the holidays, and there was a cheery fire in the fireplace. Olney sat down in front of the blaze in his overcoat, shivering from the cold. Presently he remarked that the clock on the mantel was beating irregularly. Prudence laughed and said she hadn't noticed. When Olney asked her if the Harrises were at home, Prudence replied that they were in the kitchen, and the young man made his way downstairs.

Maria Robinson, a student, was sewing when Olney came back upstairs a short while later and asked for a piece of paper. He said he had promised a lady in New York that he would write her as soon as he had seen her little daughter at the school. He wrote the letter, sealed it, and left the room.

After the midday dinner, Olney returned again to the keeping room to tinker with the faulty clock. A number of girls passed in and out of the room, chatting and laughing. One of them, Amy Fenner, was the first person to notice smoke. "What's the matter?" she anxiously asked Olney. He crossed the room and put his ear to the wall. "I can hear it roaring," he shouted. "Quick, I need an axe!" The girl was too terrified to respond. Olney ran from the room, down the stairs, and out the front door. At the corner of the house, between two clapboards above one of the large front windows of the first floor, he saw a tiny lick of flame.

By now the smell of smoke was pervasive. Maria Robinson, frantic that the sewing she had left by the hearth had caught a spark, tried to enter the room but recoiled from the billowing smoke. She too ran outside. "Is the chimney on fire?" she cried. "No," Olney told her. "Run. Run and ring the fire bell!"

Across the street in Dr. Andrew Harris' house, a visitor named David Morgan paused at the parlor window to watch a strange sight. The headmistress of the school he had heard so much about was struggling around the corner of her house lugging a tub of water. A black man took it from her and dashed it against the side of the building. Then another black man (Charles Harris) ran up with an axe, and the two men began hacking at the clapboards. Knowing something to be terribly amiss, David Morgan ran across the street to offer his assistance.

Richard Fenner was in his store when he heard the fire bell and the cries of "Fire!" When he arrived on the scene, he barged into the house and asked Prudence if the trouble was in the cellar. "No," she told him angrily, "my house has been set on fire!" Ralph Robinson, the district schoolteacher, came at a run when he heard the bell, his excited students pounding after him. Chauncey Bacon was in Jenk's store when he heard the commotion. A boy in the crowd outside the fence told him what was happening, and he ran home for his axe. When he returned a few minutes later, Bacon joined a group of men who were hacking at walls and prying up hearths in a futile effort to locate the source of the fire. Bacon struck a number of holes through the plaster of a wall in the first-floor parlor, but found nothing. Then he checked the cellar, the attic, and finally the keeping room, where Richard Fenner was taking up the floorboards. For some reason, Bacon then returned to the parlor directly beneath the keeping room, and for the first time saw a small blaze high up in the corner of the room. He charged back up the stairs and yelled that the whole floor of the keeping room must come up. The men there set about this task with vigor and soon uncovered the fire within the wall.

Ebenezer Sanger arrived late, just in time to observe Frederick Olney informing Captain Horace Bacon that he could stop cutting up the mopboards because the fire was out. The crowd outside began to dissipate. A few of the schoolboys hung around in case a miracle should occur and the fire start up again. Upstairs, Frederick Olney put a comforting arm around one of the frightened students and teasingly asked the rest if they had cried. The girls smiled reluctantly. "Such a one!" they said. Olney told them in a fatherly way that they should never be scared before they were hurt.

Frederick Olney was the hero of the day, but the times were too troubled for that to be anything but an affront to the white men. Several days after the mysterious fire, Olney was in a barber shop in Norwich when two Canterbury gentlemen, James Cary and Horace Bacon, entered. The spirited conversation in the shop centered on the fire. One man insisted it must have started from the inside of the house, but Olney disagreed. "I know as much about it as anyone," he boasted. "I suppose you do," murmured Horace Bacon. Olney then recounted to the group how he had been fixing the clock when smoke began to fill the room. At first he thought the evergreen garlands had caught fire or that a spark had ignited the carpet. Then he heard the roar inside the wall, and when he ran outside he saw flames spouting through a crack between the sill of the window and the molding above, about seven feet off the ground. He had shown the spot to Delano Baker, Ebenezer Sanger, and Richard Fenner after the fact. "Here gentlemen of the jury," he had said, "is where the fire began." When Olney finished his story, James Cary informed him that he was under arrest for arson.

Judge Rufus Adams set the trial for March. The authorities in Canterbury looked no further for suspects, and rumors flew that Prudence had ordered the fire for publicity. George Benson, Jr., immediately sent word that he wished to appear as a character witness for Olney.[3] Henry Benson wrote to Garrison's partner, Isaac Knapp, "I have known him [Olney] *for a longtime* and I believe him to be a very fine man and entirely innocent of the crime charged against him."[4] As an afterthought, he added, "I presume you have heard that Miss Crandall is engaged to a Baptist minister."

Four days after Henry Benson's letter reached Boston, another arrived for Garrison from Helen Benson carrying the same news, sorrow over Frederick Olney's arrest and astonishment over Prudence's engagement. Garrison had arranged to see Helen Benson a month earlier in Providence, where she was staying after her brother George's wedding. He urged her to start a friendly correspondence with him, and he wrote her on his return to Boston that he was depending upon her to start a female antislavery society in Providence.

Helen waited one month to the day before replying. She expressed doubts about sustaining "a correspondence with one whose talents and attainments" were so superior to her own. She delicately told him that a female antislavery society at the present would not be possible, because ever since his last speech in Providence, "never have I seen a lady who felt willing to have the subject mentioned in company." She

Close-up of Prudence Crandall, based on the portrait by
Francis Alexander. *Courtesy of the Prudence Crandall
Museum, Canterbury, Connecticut.*

Prudence Crandall's mother, Esther
Carpenter Crandall. *Courtesy of the
Prudence Crandall Museum.*

Hezekiah Crandall. *Courtesy of the
Prudence Crandall Museum.*

Prudence Crandall Museum, site of the Canterbury Female Seminary, Canterbury, Connecticut.

Advertisement for Prudence Crandall's boarding school in *The Liberator*, March 2, 1833. *Courtesy of the Prudence Crandall Museum.*

Early sketch showing the Congregational Church on the Green and the Paine mansion. *Courtesy of the Prudence Crandall Museum.*

Congregational
Church on the Green.
*Courtesy of the
Prudence Crandall
Museum.*

Samuel Joseph May. *Courtesy of the Cornell University Library.*

Sarah Harris Fayerweather. *Courtesy of the Prudence Crandall Museum.*

Portrait of Andrew T. Judson. *Courtesy of the Prudence Crandall Museum.*

William Lloyd Garrison, age 71, April 1876. *Courtesy of the Sophia Smith Collection, Smith College.*

Helen Benson Garrison. *Courtesy of the Sophia Smith Collection, Smith College.*

Packerville Baptist Church, attended by Prudence Crandall. *Courtesy of the Prudence Crandall Museum.*

Troy Grove, Illinois. *Courtesy of the Prudence Crandall Museum.*

William Lloyd Garrison, age 35, from a daguerreotype by
T. B. Shaw. *Courtesy of the Sophia Smith Collection, Smith
College.*

Wendell Phillips Garrison, age 40,
June 1880. *Courtesy of the Sophia
Smith Collection, Smith College.*

Francis Garrison Jackson, 1886.
*Courtesy of the Sophia Smith Collec-
tion, Smith College.*

Prudence Crandall in
1874, age 71, before
she moved to Kansas.
*Courtesy of the
Prudence Crandall
Museum.*

Prudence Crandall's grave
in Elk Falls, Kansas.
*Courtesy of the Prudence
Crandall Museum.*

agreed there was "not a shadow of a doubt" that the fire in Canterbury was "the work of an incendiary."[5]

Garrison wrote back as soon as he read her letter. He praised her communication for its "frankness," its "lack of affectation," and "its contemplative spirit." He was sorry the ladies of Providence had found his allusions to the rape of black women in bad taste. Their modesty was nothing more than "rank prudery" and "heartless refinement." As for "the persecuted, the dauntless, the heroic Prudence Crandall," she had his full admiration and sympathy.[6] But her engagement baffled him as much as anyone. The strange, lanky minister had materialized and then disappeared like a wandering magician, taking with him, as if by sleight of hand, the heart of his friend, a heart that had seemed invulnerable to all assaults.

Garrison had no opportunity, however, to bring up the topic when he came to Brooklyn for Frederick Olney's trial in early March. He was far more preoccupied with his own romance. As he drove Helen over to Canterbury (love making him bold, for he distrusted horses), he tried to tell her that he loved her, but his "tongue was tied," and he unhappily decided to express his feelings in writing instead.[7]

Garrison was deeply moved by the "quietude of spirit" and the "domestic order" that prevailed at the Benson farm even though Prudence and all her students were staying there during the trial. "Some families under such circumstances," he wrote to Helen's father, "would have been thrown into utter confusion—and bustle, bustle, nothing but bustle, and running to and fro, would have been the consequence."[8] Having grown up fatherless and needy, Garrison considered the Bensons the ideal family. He was, in a sense, courting them all, and their home was for him, as it was for Prudence, a sanctuary.

Garrison had to leave Brooklyn before Olney's trial was

over, but he heard more than enough. The prosecution witnesses theorized that the fire had started inside the house and insinuated that Prudence knew it. Ebenezer Sanger supposed someone had gotten down on his or her knees and thrust a lighted taper through a crack under the mopboard. Vine Robinson, an inspector for the fire insurance company, hypothesized that a match had been stuck through the crack between the mopboard and the floor and pushed along until it fell about two inches onto the upper sill of the ground floor window below. Ralph Hutchinson, another insurance examiner, essentially agreed but thought the fire could have begun as well outside the house, where there was a clapboard "burnt to a coal." Hutchinson suggested the fire might have been introduced at a spot where he noticed mortar had been removed from under the sill. David Morgan, the visitor at Dr. Harris' house, said he and Richard Fenner had picked off some mortar from the spot after the fire to examine it further, but he had noticed then that some of the mortar had been removed earlier.

As his stagecoach left Brooklyn, the lovesick Garrison felt his "heart [grow] liquid as water" at the thought of leaving all the people he cared about behind. He was escorting Lucretia May part of the way to Boston; the other riders did not know their identities, for they buzzed uninhibitedly about Prudence's school. At one halting place, a rider climbed on who had, Garrison observed, "evidently rejected the doctrine of total abstinence." The fellow was "horrified" at the thought of intermarriage between blacks and whites and wouldn't leave the subject until Lucretia stifled him by tartly commenting that she would personally prefer a virtuous and sober colored man for a husband over an intemperate white man. At another tavern station, two more "anti-temperance" men entered the coach. They were for letting the school "go ahead," although one of them said he'd never abide a "nigger" marrying his sister, and what he didn't understand was why some people were trying to keep the blacks from going to "Siberia."[9]

Garrison had to wait nearly a week for the news that the jury, after deliberating fifteen minutes, acquitted Frederick Olney of arson.

Chapter Thirteen

*I*t should have been a happy time for Prudence. Frederick Olney had been acquitted. Then, in April, Andrew T. Judson lost his reelection bid for the state legislature. Prudence stood, *The Liberator* exulted, "upon a pinnacle of honor higher than the pyramids."[1] She was engaged to be married.

In reality, the trials that had passed had drained and exhausted her. Judson's defeat at the state level only opened the door for him to be elected representative to the Congress of the United States a few months later. And as for the betrothal, it seemed Prudence had pledged herself to a man that her friends knew better than she did, and their joy for her was mitigated by the fear that she had been won by the force of his personality rather than by the strength of his character.

A string of unpleasant rumors followed Calvin Philleo. Helen Benson and William Lloyd Garrison, who would never like the man, tried to keep Prudence from becoming entangled, but they had little success. The possibility that Prudence might "marry ill" came up in nearly every letter that traveled between the two during the spring of 1834, and since Garrison's proposal to Helen in March, there had been many letters.

Calvin Philleo was one of nine sons born to Enoch and Sarah Philleo, impoverished farm folk in the backwoods of upstate New York. He grew up in a "rude log hut" that was "barren of any refinement."[2] Despite their humble circumstances, Enoch Philleo gave his sons exalted names such as Milton, Bonaparte, Jefferson, and Darias (for a Persian king). Two other sons were named Martin and Luther. Biblically speaking, some of the brothers thrived on fertile land, and some had a thornier time. Luther Philleo, who was a "genius," made violins, and Bonaparte became a respected doctor with progressive political ideals. But another brother who took up medicine, Addison, never finished his medical studies. He and two other students suddenly left the Fairfield Medical College after being accused of grave robbing.

Enoch Philleo indoctrinated his boys with the conviction that they were the proud descendants of victims of Huguenot persecution. He abused his Scottish wife for her Baptist beliefs; throughout his life, Calvin would refer to Baptists as a "persecuted people."[3] Calvin's character was made up of these elements, a personal identification with persecution combined with a grand sense of his own superiority.

While Calvin was apprenticed to a blacksmith, he underwent a religious experience that led to his conversion to his mother's faith. He soon discovered he had some talent as an exhorter, which was greatly enhanced by a fine speaking and singing voice described as "one of a thousand."[4] His children thought he could have been an opera singer. When Prudence first heard him pray, she said, "A man who can make a prayer like that must be a good man."[5] The inspired blacksmith prepared himself for the ministry at Hamilton College and took up his vocation in Amenia, New York, where he preached his brothers' regiment off to the War of 1812.

In 1825 Philleo took a church in Suffield, Connecticut, where he introduced a Sabbath school for children. One church member, a child at the time, remembered that the school was an "innovation not in harmony with the feeling of the majority of the church members."[6] The opposition of his flock to this and other "innovations" mattered little to Calvin Philleo, for he felt his decisions had divine sanction. Congregations should submit to the authority of their ministers, just as wives should submit to their husbands, children to their elders, citizens to their governments, and Christians to the Almighty. That was the natural order. Philleo could not abide the individualism of the Quakers or the tolerance of the Unitarians. The "argument if it may be called argument," he once sermonized, "is that it is no matter what mode we adopt, if only we mean well, if only we are sincere. An angel would not dare think and talk thus; such a course would exclude an angel from heaven! God does not deal in non-essentials."[7]

After the overbearing minister was dismissed from Suffield, he took up his ministry in Pawtucket, Rhode Island, a town north of Providence. A Universalist minister in Pawtucket, Jacob Frieze, left an acrimonious record of his encounters with the new Baptist minister. It must be noted that Frieze may have resented Philleo's raiding the pool of common rural folk who were their potential congregants. Frieze's little church was in dire straits at the time.[8] The veracity of Frieze's accusations cannot be known, but if they were not true, they were at least pervasive. When Prudence asked Helen Benson if she had ever heard of Calvin Philleo when he had lived in Pawtucket, Helen reluctantly answered yes. "She then questioned me so closely as to what I had heard," Helen wrote to Garrison, "that I was absolutely obliged to tell her."[9]

When Philleo arrived in Pawtucket, the area was nearly exhausted from revivalist fever. An indefatigable Free-Will Baptist named Ray Potter had been working over the town for a decade, subjecting the people to "prayer meetings, conference meetings, church meetings, meetings for preaching, and other meetings without names . . . sometimes seven in a day; attended at all hours . . . from sunrise to midnight."[10] (Potter later went to jail for an illicit affair with one of his female parishioners and ended his life as a successful cardboard manufacturer.)

Although Philleo was more traditional then Potter, Jacob Frieze lumped the two together. The Universalists, a small sect with beliefs similar to the Unitarians', embraced the concept of universal salvation granted by a merciful deity. Their emphasis on the goodness rather than the depravity of mankind put them at odds with the Baptists from the start.

Frieze denounced the style as well as the religious tenets of the Baptists. Their aggressive proselytizing engendered "continual bickerings" among friends and within families. Even in their own churches, Frieze contended, chaos reigned: "There you will find members quarrelling among themselves—members quarrelling with their Pastor—Pastors quarrelling with each other—and some who have only ceased to quarrel with each other because they have ceased to speak together."[11]

The minister accused the Baptists of ensnaring converts by paralyzing them with fear and annihilating their reason. These revivalists, he said, insist all people are in danger of roasting on a spit in hell unless they give themselves up to God, but then they learn that God has already damned "one half, three quarters, even nineteen twentieths of them to all eternity." Such "preposterous absurdities," Frieze argued, literally drove people out of their senses. With salvation restricted to so few, Frieze thought Baptist revivalism was undemocratic. It "constricted the human heart," so that converts became "haughty and overbearing." The ministers themselves "look with a Pharisaical contempt on all they consider sinners."

Frieze specifically singled out the behavior of the new-comer Calvin Philleo in at least one sermon and an open letter. He wrote: "You have given the people of this village reason to suppose that you considered them a set of un-principled scoundrels. You have stated . . . that you feared *'they would shave your horse's tail and mane'* and otherwise insult you."[12] Frieze also cited Philleo's reference to the people of Pawtucket as "a poor crippled race, unable to raise a dollar." In reality, Frieze said, they simply had neither the ability nor the desire to fill his "pockets with cash."

Yet it was not Philleo's greed but his alleged relationships with women that drew Frieze's most bitter invective; in one letter, he accused Philleo of "thrust[ing] yourself unbidden, into . . . families, and drag[ging] them to the floor with you, to listen to the ebulitions of your fanaticism." There was a footnote to Frieze's letter: "I understand you have promised to call on every family in the place. Some of the MEN, I among the number, would like to be at home at the time. Or can you more readily convert the FEMALES *souls?*— You understand me. J. F."[13]

These accusations unfortunately coincided with Philleo's blatant wife hunting. His wife, Elizabeth, had died in 1831, and their oldest daughter, Emeline, had married soon after. The minister was desperate to find a new mother for his two younger children. He had even gone so far as to ad-vertise for one.[14]

One prospective mate withdrew after hearing "various reports" about him. Another woman, a milliner, told Philleo to leave her shop after he declared he would propose on his next visit; the milliner was already married. Prudence, who was flattered that the minister proposed to her at their first meeting, had no way of knowing this was simply the style of a man in a hurry. Helen Benson tried to warn her. "I felt a weight off my mind by so doing," she wrote to Garrison, "though I do not think any thing I said made the difference to her for 'love' you know heightens every virtue and I found in her estimate he was almost a perfect being."[15] He could make Prudence believe "black was white if he chose," she concluded in despair.[16]

Prudence's contrariness was nothing new. She was, after all, a "stiff-necked" Crandall. She often acted on impulse, and an impulse once taken, if challenged, became intractable. There were also practical matters that Prudence, if no one else, had considered. She was unmarried at thirty-one, and her livelihood was threatened. How many more proposals would there be, and how many more schools if this one failed? Her own solitude was all the more painful to contemplate because she suspected her friends Helen Benson and William Lloyd Garrison were in love. In addition, both Sarah Harris Fayerweather and Mariah Davis Harris were expecting babies.

Of these things Prudence said little. Her friends did not know if she regretted her pledge to Philleo but refused out of pride to admit it. Perhaps, they surmised, she did not believe the stories about him, or if she did, perhaps she thought she could reform him. Prudence "received all I said very kindly," Helen reported to Garrison, "and observed, though she had given him her heart . . . still she had so *perfect* a control of *herself*, she could at any moment withdraw her affections."[17]

In early April, Garrison wrote to Prudence asking her to come to Boston and sit for a portrait commissioned by the New England Anti-Slavery Society. Calvin Philleo had been expected in Canterbury for weeks, but he had not yet come. Prudence, restless in the cage of a long winter, eagerly sprang at the opportunity to escape. She looked, Helen thought, "unusually handsome this spring."[18]

Prudence's portrait, by Francis Alexander, a well-known Boston society painter, was conventional in many ways. The classical pillar on the left and the drapery in the background were standards props. The subject herself consented to wear a modish though somber dress with huge sleeves padded with down-filled cushions—they were called "imbecile sleeves." But there Prudence's concession to fashion ended; she refused to be "beautiful." Her brown hair was drawn back in the plainest and most functional of styles. There were no curls, no frothy little white bonnet. There were no rings on her fingers, no brooches on her bodice (although wearing up to seven at a time was the rage). Light streams in from the left side of the picture, illuminating her long pale face with its enigmatic smile that is both wistful and triumphant. It is the light alone, an unintentional Quaker metaphor, that makes her lovely.

Prudence was a celebrity in Boston. Nightly, Garrison escorted her to banquets and fetes given in her honor by abolitionists. She was showered with gifts. On these out-ings, Garrison took the opportunity to lecture her on folly. He warned her to ignore flattery, to "bend like a reed" before exaltation but stand "lofty and unyielding as the oak" when principles were involved.[19] After she left Boston, Garrison confidently informed Helen, "Prudence has wholly given up Mr. Philleo."[20]

Prudence did seem humbled. She divested herself of many of the gifts she had received in Boston. She gave a valuable seal to Helen Benson, and her portrait eventually ended up in Samuel Joseph May's parlor. In the wake of an eight-day revival meeting at the Packerville Baptist Church, she became reacquainted with the doctrines that sin was self-love and virtue was disinterested benevolence. She began to visit all the black families in the area "to impress upon them the importance of imbibing correct principles and setting a good example for their children."[21]

And Prudence confirmed to Helen Benson that even though she had not "a single proof" of the allegations against Philleo, the romance was finished. "Only think, Helen," she said sadly, "I am expecting him every day." Helen lamely comforted her with the thought that time would probably disclose the truth. "I am resigned to it," Prudence answered.[22]

April passed into May. The "alders and osiers . . . hung out their tasseled catkins," and the leaves of the birch trees quivered "even in the faintest breeze," revealing "their delicate silver linings to the sun." In the "moist lowlands" the "bright-eyed blossums of the cowslip shone out like stars from among its dark green leaves."[23] Prudence still waited.

The affair between Prudence and the elusive minister had become common gossip. Close friends regularly discussed her off-and-on-again intentions. "Dear Brother," Henry Benson began a letter to his brother George, "Prudence has come to a firm determination of marrying Mr. ———— (I forget his name)."[24] Even Samuel Joseph May indulged in the pastime. As he was returning from one of his journeys, a "gentleman" on the coach asked directions to Canterbury. May told Helen Benson he was sure Philleo had come, but he was mistaken.

Finally, at the end of May, Calvin Philleo arrived, "somewhat tardy," Garrison sarcastically observed.[25] Prudence immediately confronted her betrothed with the stories she had heard. His facility with words did not fail him, and he explained himself satisfactorily. Prudence took him around and was "extremely anxious to have her friends think well of him."[26] None of them did. Dr. Roland Green, who had traveled on the boat with Philleo, told his son who told Helen who told Garrison that he found the minister "very disagreeable, and took a very great dislike to him."[27]

The couple traveled to Brooklyn on a Saturday. May was out of town once again, but the Bensons received them for tea. After they left, Helen Benson immediately sat down to send Garrison "the particulars" as he had requested. "I must say," she began, "I was rather agreeably disappointed in his appearance, he was a much meeker looking man than I anticipated." Nevertheless, she suspected him because "he will not let you look him in the face but holds his head down a good deal . . . seldom [gives] you a chance to look at his eyes which strongly indicates guilt."[28] She could not shake off her prejudice against him. "I was as polite as I could be to him," she wrote, "invited him to tarry with us the night but he declined to my joy." She refused to go hear him preach on Sunday, although her mother went and was "exceedingly gratified with the sermon."[29]

Two weeks later Philleo left for Boston. Prudence wrote anxiously ahead to Garrison, praising her fiancé and, between the lines, begging him to suspend judgment. For his part, Garrison told George Benson, he would not condemn Philleo because he had "never heard any special and vital allegations brought against him."[30] He did not, however, approve of Philleo's plan to increase the number of scholars at Prudence's school to one hundred, especially as the legislature "to its everlasting disgrace" had adjourned without repealing the Black Law.[31] Garrison admitted to Helen Benson that he was as perplexed about the real nature of the minister as she was. He thought if Prudence married him, she would be wise to give up the school. Yet, puzzling as Philleo was, Garrison concluded, "He certainly appears to be a good man."[32]

As soon as Calvin Philleo left Canterbury, Prudence flew to Samuel Joseph May "in great tribulation." The visit could not have pleased Lucretia May, who jealously hoarded every second her husband spent at home. She had recently informed him that his congregation was falling away as a result of his neglect: "I deeply lament that you should have considered it your duty to give your attention so much to other subjects."[33] But May comforted his friend. He knew her own sorrows made her reluctant to send the widower away disappointed. She would marry him, May already knew, "out of pity if nothing more."[34]

Chapter Fourteen

*H*ezekiah Niles, editor of *Niles' Weekly Register*, had been alerting the public to the alarming rise of murders, assaults, and swindles being perpetuated by "foreigners." "A great proportion of the thieves and pickpockets," he warned, "are young Englishmen, well-dressed, and having the appearance of gentlemen."[1] The rascals were even said to be operating in the gallery of the United States Senate.[2]

While these "foreign paupers and foreign rogues" were plaguing innocent individuals, something even more sinister was thought to be happening to the nation.[3] The British, in order to regain their lost empire, were creating chaos by promoting amalgamation between blacks and whites. By late 1834, members of the Philadelphia Colonization Society clearly perceived a diabolical link between English and American abolitionism. "Can we doubt of the existence of a well-defined object, a settled and systematic design?" they asked.[4] The English had, after all, brought slavery to America in the first place. There seemed to be ample evidence that English money and organization was now behind the success of the American fanatics. Arthur Tappan and his associates had timed the founding of the American Anti-Slavery Society to coincide with British emancipation, which, Hezekiah Niles knew from reliable sources, had totally ruined the West Indies.[5] And hadn't William Lloyd Garrison gotten the English to renounce the Colonization Society, and now wasn't he bragging that George Thompson and Charles Stuart, the infamous British agitators, were coming to America?

The British connection, in part, kindled four days of rioting in New York City on July 4, 1834. While the initial targets of anger were Chatham Hall, where a mixed black and white audience had attended an antislavery meeting, and the homes of Arthur Tappan and other leaders, another target was the Bowery Theater. The Bowery's stage manager, an Englishman, had gotten into a fist fight with a butcher and had reputedly cursed, "Damn the Yankees, they are a damn set of jack-asses and fit to be gulled."[6] In reporting the attack, Hezekiah Niles explained that the manager was punished for being "disrespectful to the American character."[7]

The American character, or essence, was not to be found in a sentimental notion of the "melting pot." Quite the opposite: racial and ethnic blending was decidedly Un-American and represented, in the coarsest expression of the day, "mongrelization." After more than a week of turmoil, the New York office of the American Anti-Slavery Society was compelled to publish a disclaimer in the papers that began, "We entirely disclaim any desire to promote or encourage intermarriages between white and colored persons."

Canterburians were not so provincial that they knew nothing of "British plots" and the collusions of abolitionists on both sides of the Atlantic. They could see the cancer spreading. Plainfield had an antislavery society with forty-three male and female members. By early July there would be a society in Brooklyn, and the ladies there were organizing a separate society of their own. Furthermore, William Lloyd Garrison, that all too frequent visitor, relayed a "transatlantic tribute" to Prudence in the June 14 *Liberator* from "Female Friends" in Glasgow, Scotland. The Scottish ladies were sending an ornate plate "in testimony of their high admiration of that ardent benevolence, heroic fortitude, and unflinching steadfastness in the midst of wanton and unequalled persecution." The plate was to lie on display in the shop window of Mr. Alexander Mitchell, a jeweler on Argyle Street in Glasgow, until it could be entrusted to George Thompson to carry to America.

Intermarriage had never occurred in Canterbury, but it was perceived as a genuine possibility given the frequent references to the subject. H. B. Robbins, one of Prudence's former white students, wrote (not quite accurately) to another classmate, Hannah Pearl, that "Miss Crandall is going to be married to a Methodist minister so Lucy told me yesterday he is a white man and is that not strange how she should have him."[8] William Burleigh, the younger brother of Charles, who had become junior editor of *The Unionist* and a teacher at Prudence's school, also alluded to the subject. One night as he was returning home at twilight, rotten eggs landed on him "like grape shot from a seventy-four." Burleigh was so furious he predicted in print that the parents of the bullies would live to see their "offspring dangling from the gallows." He also added that these same parents need have no fear of their sons' marrying any of Miss Crandall's pupils because none of the students would ever have them.[9]

After the enormous dimensions of the threat of amalgamation had been pointed out to them by national leaders and journalists, the Canterburians became more devout than ever in their attempts to frighten the school out of existence. One night someone hurled a rock weighing nearly two pounds through a window of a first-floor bedroom at the school. The rock barely missed a student and took with it ten panes of glass and part of the window sash. An even grimmer warning against race mixing was found in the front yard one morning: a black and white cat with its throat cut, impaled upon a fence post.

There was little Prudence and her band could do against such attacks. It never occurred to them to station someone with a shotgun at an upper window to discourage vandals and arsonists. Prudence's pacifism was rooted not only in the Quakerism of her youth, but in the revivalist belief in the potential for good in all people if only they came to see the light. In her righteousness, she need do no more than be an example. Indeed, she dare not do more, for all her upbringing forbade doing evil that good might come of it.

She was, along with Samuel Joseph May, the Bensons, and others, a follower of Garrison's theories on nonviolence, which he called nonresistance. Garrison's views were also religious in nature, based on an absolute refusal to compromise with sin, but they had their pragmatic side too. He dealt from a position of weakness. It was his strategy and his talent to so enrage his enemies with invective that they discredited themselves as rational and fair-minded people in retaliation. For this reason, Garrison's critics condemned him and his followers for igniting the fears and challenging the honor of decent men who in ordinary circumstances would never smash church windows or beat black men with brickbats. They blamed the abolitionists, in their irresponsible drive to undo civilization, for unleasing passions that were better left repressed. Thus the blame for the upsurge in violence in the society was laid at the feet of the abolitionists, not the white supremacists. "Does it not appear that the character of our people has suffered a considerable change for the worse?" Hezekiah Niles lamented. "We fear the moral sense of right and wrong has been rendered less sensitive than it was—that a spirit of *force*, in certain cases, has begotten it in others."[10]

The third and final trial of Prudence Crandall began in this crisis atmosphere in the Supreme Court of Errors in Brooklyn, Connecticut, on July 26, 1834. The attending judges were Samuel Church, Clark Bissell, Thomas Williams, and Chief Justice David Daggett.[11]

Once again, with infinite patience, Prudence's lawyer William Ellsworth argued that the students were not "foreigners" or "aliens" so radically different from other people that they merited special treatment. The students posed no threat to anyone, Ellsworth reiterated. They were not slaves or paupers. They were the daughters of respectable, even wealthy, parents. Having nowhere else to go, "they retired to a place by themselves" and sought out a "virtuous and competent teacher" so that their lives would be happier and more useful.

The Black Law, Ellsworth continued, forbade citizens from other states to go to school in Connecticut because they did not have a legal residence there. Yet, although the law was prompted by racism, the problem it posed was less one of color than how much power the legislature was allowed to execute. If it was a crime to teach, feed, and entertain such citizens, then it might be made equally criminal to sell them a farm or rent them a house. Yet the pupils were human beings born in the United States, and they owed the same obligations to the state as white citizens did. If allegiance was due from our colored population, Ellsworth maintained, its correlative was due from the government, namely protection and equal laws: "He [a colored person] is not a citizen to obey, and an alien to demand protection."

Ellsworth condemned the "unhappy hour" such a travesty became the law. It was a "wanton and uncalled for attack upon our black population" and caused anguish among black citizens, many of whom were "exasper[ated] to madness" by it. It made Connecticut "an ally in the unholy cause of slavery itself."

Andrew T. Judson, in his arguments before the court, upheld the legislature's prerogatives. The state had the right to regulate its own schools in its own way, independent of the question of citizenship, he argued. In addition, as "literary corporations" were empowered to admit or exclude students at will, so the state had the same right. The object of the law was to regulate schools for colored persons coming from other "governments" by putting them under the jurisdiction of a Board of Visitors. If the keepers of such schools, like Miss Crandall, would not submit to such regulation, then they must be excluded as "a dangerous and destructive population."

Judson again asserted that blacks were not citizens and were never meant to be by the framers of the Constitution: "It matters little what may be the opinion of a few madmen or enthusiasts now." He was obsessed with the peril facing not only Connecticut but the nation. He beseeched the judges not to surrender the country "to another race of men." "I would appeal to this court—to every American citizen and say that America is ours—it belongs to a race of white men, the descendants of those who first redeemed it from the wilderness. The American name and character have been handed down to this generation and it is our duty to preserve that character and perpetuate that name."

Judge Williams, who was to render the final decision, chose to do it well away from Brooklyn, in Hartford. "It was an open secret," wrote Abraham Payne, "that his associates, unwilling to overrule the Chief Justice [Daggett], discovered a defect in the warrant."[12] The original warrant for her arrest charged Prudence "with harboring and boarding colored persons, not inhabitants of this state, without license, for the purpose of being instructed." This implied, according to Judge Williams, that the boarding house had no license, but the warrant did not specify that the school itself had no license. The object of the legislation was to regulate unlicensed schools, but because the information in the case omitted to say the school was not licensed, it contained a "fatal flaw." Williams dismissed the case on the technicality of insufficient information.

The abolitionists were crushed. Now they could not take the case to the Supreme Court and have the question of the citizenship of black people decided for decades to come. Furthermore, without the repudiation of the Black Law, Prudence and her students hung in a dangerous limbo. Opponents still believed the school to be illegal. Only now they had exhausted all legal means to stop it. It was as if they had lost while playing according to the rules, and she had won by cheating.

Prudence made a sudden decision after the trial. In mid-August Garrison wrote to his "blooming rose" in Brooklyn that he had had a visit in Boston from Calvin Philleo, his daughter Elizabeth, and Prudence Crandall, who, he said teasingly, existed no more. Instead there was "Mrs. Philleo, who has taken her place, and resembles her in all things precisely. . . . The bride looked smilingly—the bridegroom manifested a complacent spirit—and the young miss betrayed symptoms of hilarity. . . . And so, my dear," he concluded, "they have got the start of us by almost a month!"[13]

The enemies of the school had not relented even on Prudence's wedding day, August 12, 1834. Her ally Reverend Levi Kneeland was dying, and Prudence had turned to Reverend Otis Whiton, the new minister at the Congregational Church on the green. Whiton agreed to publish the bans and perform a private ceremony in the school, but on the morning of the wedding he sent a note saying he could not come "under existing circumstances." The minister had received an envelope containing a substantial donation to the church and a note requesting him not to perform the wedding.[14] So the tiny wedding party drove over to Brooklyn, where Reverend Tillotson of the Congregational Church married them. The couple immediately left on a wedding trip, which included Boston and Philadelphia.

In Boston, Philleo preached twice in a black meeting house. He was at his charismatic best, and again Garrison confessed to Helen Benson, "I am more and more puzzled to determine accurately his real character. He may be an eccentric man—a covetous man—and occasionally an erring man in trivial matters, but I cannot think he is habitually a bad man." Nevertheless, Garrison could not bring himself to congratulate the couple. Instead, he wished them every happiness and invited them out to see the cottage he had rented for Helen. When the newlyweds left Boston, he felt with Pindar, "O matrimony! thou are like to Jeremiah's figs. The good were very good—the bad too sour to give the pigs."[15]

During the Philleos' stay in Philadelphia, the Quaker abolitionist Lucretia Mott arranged for Prudence to meet "about fifty families of our most respectable colored people, and engaged a sufficient number to warrant her beginning here."[16] But if Prudence and Calvin had thought of escaping Canterbury for the placidity of the City of Brotherly Love, they changed their minds, for that city soon had a race riot to rival New York's. During three wild days of rioting, the homes of over forty black people were assailed. Many blacks fled into New Jersey. At least one man was killed trying to swim across the Schuylkill River to safety. Included in the carnage was an Ursuline convent, burned by men who painted their faces to look like Indians in mimicry of the Boston Tea Party. They dragged three pianofortes and a harp from the building and burned them in a bonfire. In contrast to the response to the fire in Canterbury, the Philadelphia *Atlas* condemned "attacking a convent of women, a seminary for the instruction of young females, and turning them out of their beds, half-naked in the hurry of their flight and half dead with confusion and terror."[17]

Upon their return to Canterbury, Prudence and Calvin met the flamboyant Englishman Charles Stuart, who delivered piles of gifts to them from the British Isles. A Baxter's Bible and two volumes of Cruden's *Concordance*, "beautifully bound in russia," came from the Ladies of Edinburgh as a "mark of respect" for Prudence's "Christian courage." There were also two lovely Staffordshire plates made specially for Prudence, decorated with pictures of black people on the border, many letters, "trifles" for the students, a sampler, a pincushion, a pen wiper, and a lithograph of Daniel O'Connell, the champion of Ireland.[18]

Prudence's wary neighbors soon observed another Englishman entering the school, as Edward Abdy returned once more. He had just been shown around New Haven by Simeon Jocelyn. The blacks there, he noted, carried clubs and hammers to defend themselves after dark.

Prudence was not at home when Abdy called, nor was Almira, but William Burleigh received him. On the parlor mantel, Abdy saw the most recent stone, twice as large as the one he had seen on his first visit. It rested next to a long pole and part of the window sash that had been broken by it. The glass in two of the four windows of the room was shattered. There were still twenty students in the house.

On the morning of September 4, 1834, on a day that threatened to storm, Samuel Joseph May married Helen Benson to a very nervous William Lloyd Garrison in Brooklyn. After a large wedding breakfast, the couple left for Boston, not knowing that they would never again visit Prudence's school.

On September 9, a daughter was born to Sarah Harris Fayerweather, and was named Prudence Crandall Fayerweather. Late that night, a band of men crept up to the school and surrounded it. At a signal, they began to yell and beat the walls and doors and windows with lead pipes and timbers. They tore out two windows, including the sashes and ninety panes of glass, in one sitting room alone.[19] They also smashed a window in a bedroom at the back of the house where two students were sleeping. One of the girls was so traumatized she coughed up "a pint of blood."[20] Some of the men entered the house and overturned furniture, leaving much of the ground floor uninhabitable.[21]

The neighbors did nothing. The authorities were mute. Samuel Joseph May came immediately; when he saw the mess, his heart fell. "It seemed foolish," he concluded "to repair [the house] only to be destroyed again."[22]

For the first time, Prudence was so beside herself she could not appear in public. Her pupils, May soon learned, were afraid "to remain another night under her roof." Calvin Philleo put notices in *The Unionist* and *The Liberator* stating that the house was for sale and offered a $50 reward for the apprehension of the perpetrators. Loyal William Kinne immediately offered to rent the house until it was sold, which it was, two months later, to James Aspenwall.

Prudence asked May to tell the students the school was closing. She was not present when he did so. "The words almost blistered my lips," May remembered. "My heart glowed with indignation. I felt ashamed of Canterbury, ashamed of Connecticut, ashamed of my country."[23] It was over.

The Later Years

Chapter Fifteen

*C*alvin Philleo took his new wife to a remote farm in upstate New York, and there he kept her while the fires of hatred burned elsewhere. The year 1835 was a time, Simeon Jocelyn wrote, when "men's faces gathered darkness."[1] Lewis Tappan remembered it well. He and his fellow activists were "continuously watched," followed by "droves of boys," and occasionally hissed at in the streets. Their wives were "insulted by passers-by" and their children "shunned at school." In short, "they were considered and treated as disturbers of the public peace and as outlaws in the community."[2] It was the year William Lloyd Garrison was captured by a mob in Boston and dragged through the streets by a rope while Helen, several months pregnant with their first child, watched helplessly.

Yet against "wind and tide," the abolitionists were founding new societies, dispatching lecturing agents to provincial areas, and, most important—owing to revolutionary changes in the printing industry—distributing thousands of petitions, publications, and illustrations throughout the country.[3]

The American Anti-Slavery Society alone published four journals, which were sent gratuitously to "responsible citizens" throughout the country. In addition, the New York office produced souvenirs such as handkerchiefs, neckties, medals, children's primers, and candy wrappers blazoned with vivid illustrations and pithy slogans. This propaganda storm stunned the South like a sudden and unseasonable northern blizzard, and the reaction was swift and furious.[4] On July 29, 1835, a mob in Charleston, South Carolina, attacked the post office and burned the abolitionist publications in a giant bonfire along with effigies of William Lloyd Garrison and Arthur Tappan. The *Richmond Enquirer* of August 27 declared, "We shall hereafter consider the propagation amongst us of incendiary doctrines as an actual *levying of war* upon us." The *Richmond Whig* urged hanging for those responsible. Enormous sums of money of up to $50,000 were offered for the capture, dead or alive, of prominent abolitionists. Garrison wrote his brother-in-law George Benson that he had heard of an offer of $3,000 for Arthur Tappan's ears alone.[5]

Southern postmasters appealed for repressive measures, and from the pinnacle of government in Washington, D.C., President Andrew Jackson responded: "Until Congress meets, and makes some arrangements by law, on this subject, we can do nothing more than direct that those inflammatory papers be delivered to none but who will demand them as subscribers; and in every instance the Postmaster ought to take the names down, and have them exposed through the publik journals as subscribers to this wicked plan of exciting the Negroes to insurrection and massacre."[6]

The citizens of Washington feared "insurrection and massacre" because the slave population of the nation's capital roughly outnumbered the free black population two to one. Their most lucrative business, besides politics, was slave trading. English journalist Edward Abdy noted, "The farmers in the neighborhood of Washington breed slaves, as our graziers breed cattle, for the market."[7] As manufacturing and farming did not thrive in the immediate area around the capital, slaves were routinely hired out by their rural masters to fill service jobs in hotels and restaurants. This practice left much of the large free black population unsettled and unemployed. As a consequence, the Colonization Society of Washington flourished.

Thus it was, to the wrong place at the wrong time, that Dr. Reuben Crandall came to Washington, D.C., in the spring of 1835, thereby setting off a series of tragedies for the Crandall family.[8]

Reuben had not meant to move to the South. For seven years he had practiced medicine and lectured on chemistry in Peekskill, New York, but in the fall of 1834 the head of the household in which he had lived compatibly for several years left Peekskill to relocate his business in Georgetown, Virginia. This entrepreneur, Mr. Austin, planned to return for his wife and children in the spring, but he was unable to do so because of compelling business reasons. Mrs. Austin had been ill much of the winter with "bleeding from the lungs." For this reason and because his children were "poor travelers," Mr. Austin beseeched his personal physician and friend to accompany his family in his place. Reuben was a reluctant samaritan, but he finally consented.

While she was closing down the house in Peekskill, Mrs. Austin gave her untidy bachelor boarder a large box for his myriad papers, which were "lying about as waste paper in the garret." These were mostly abolitionist pamphlets and newspapers from Boston, New York, Baltimore, and Washington, all several years old. On some of these Reuben had written "Read and Circulate," but this, despite his good intentions, he had failed to do. Reuben, who was addicted to collecting all nature of things, put the materials into the box.

The Austin entourage arrived in Washington in the spring of 1835, when the city was blooming with a far wider variety of flowers and trees than Reuben had ever seen in the North. When he was offered the position of lecturer on botany at a seminary in adjacent Alexandria, Virginia, he accepted. But by the time he had settled his affairs in Peekskill and returned to Washington, it was too late to begin the course, and it was decided he should wait until after summer vacation.

Reuben rented a small office in Georgetown from a man named Jacob Oyster. By mid-July, when post offices across the South were being attacked by citizen mobs, Reuben was roaming the fields, filling his tin specimen box with weeds and flowers. Every evening he pressed his samples between the pages of the old "waste paper" newspapers and spread them out in the yard behind his office to dry.

One day Reuben's landlord, Jacob Oyster, brought the lurid news that a local slave, John Arthur Bowen, had tried to murder his mistress with an axe.[9] The intended victim was Mrs. Anna Thornton, the widow of the designer of the United States capitol. "I found him [Reuben] in the yard," Oyster later recounted, "and asked him if he had heard the news. He said no. I then told him, and said we had nobody to blame but the New Yorkers and their aid-de-camps; and I told him the boy said . . . he had been excited by these New York publications. He turned round and said 'I do not approve of putting them in circulation, the excitement is too high already.'"

One day in early August—perhaps it was raining—Reuben belatedly unpacked the box Mrs. Austin had provided him in Peekskill. Oyster, who was present, saw some of the abolitionist newspapers and pamphlets "put in between the books, as if for packing." He did not mention them and neither did the doctor. Unfortunately, in the midst of the confusion of unpacking, another neighbor named Henry King came in and casually picked up one of the pamphlets with "Read and Circulate" written on it. "The latitude is too far south for these things . . . they won't do here," King said, but added, "By your leave I will take this and read it over." Reuben nodded his assent, but it was King's impression that "he would rather I would not take it."

King took the pamphlet to a nearby shop where he read an article describing the whippings of a sixty-year-old black man and young black mother. Shocked and offended, King threw the paper aside. Another man picked up the discarded item—William Robinson, who had recently received an unwelcome mailing from the American Anti-Slavery Society. Suspicious of the coincidental appearance of the loathsome propaganda in the neighborhood and the arrival of the doctor from New York, Robinson determined to find out if the words "Read and Circulate" on the pamphlet were in the doctor's handwriting. He took the pamphlet to a Dr. Cruikshank, who had a prospectus written by Reuben. Convinced that the handwriting on both specimens was identical, Robinson hastened to the office of District Attorney for the District of Columbia, Francis Scott Key.

Key, who was a founder of the Colonization Society (as well as author of "The Star-Spangled Banner"), was a flamboyant figure with a string of legal victories to his credit. In 1807, at the age of twenty-seven, he had successfully defended Aaron Burr's coconspirators against treason. Years later, he got Sam Houston off the hook for caning Representative Stanberry of Ohio, an act committed in public on the floor of Congress. Key was under pressure to do something about the current antislavery agitation and he welcomed a scapegoat, particularly one who was conveniently related to a bona fide abolitionist. Although Key allegedly admitted to some of his "confidential friends" that there was no evidence that could convict the doctor, he issued a warrant for Reuben's arrest on the exotic charge of seditious libel, which meant the dissemination of propaganda intended to incite the slaves and free blacks of the area to insurrection.[10]

On the evening of August 10, 1835, Constables H. B. Robertson and M. Jeffers confronted Reuben at his office and demanded to see his printing press. Reuben replied he had no idea what they were talking about, but invited them to look over the premises. The constables soon discovered the "seditious" wastepaper in Reuben's trunk. As they carried him away to jail in a hack, the astounded doctor appeared shaken but spoke freely, even compulsively. He said he was innocent, but he would not deny his convictions; he was an antislavery man.

Francis Scott Key demanded the death penalty and opposed bail because, he said, "the abolition society, being rich, would pay any sum rather than have the prisoner punished." The court, however, set a sum of $2,000. When Key moved to have this amount raised to $15,000, the court settled for $5,000.[11] This was an impossible sum for Reuben to raise, and he spent the next eight months in jail.

The news of Reuben's arrest dismayed his family. Almira, who was newly married to a schoolteacher and living in New York City, sent the news to Prudence on the remote twenty-acre farm in Boonville, New York, where Calvin had taken her. Almira worried that Reuben's character, if not his actions, would condemn him: "I tremble for him. I fear his life will be the sacrifice. . . . I know that when he fully engages in anything, he will carry it through, if he is engaged in the anti-slavery cause, I think he will sacrifice his life before he will give up one iota of his principles."[12]

Prudence might have been on the moon for all the help she was able to send her family. Two of her stepchildren, Calvin Wheeler and Elizabeth, were in delicate health, and her husband had been unfit for steady work for some time as a result of a condition called "overwork of the brain."[13] Calvin had been attempting to establish libraries for Baptist ministers at the same time he forbade his wife to read books. He had preached occasionally, but he began to have lapses of memory in the pulpit. These instances gave way to seizures that "greatly impaired his judgement." He had taken to wandering far from home, leaving an untidy trail of debts in his wake.

"Our whole land is sick," Pardon wrote to Reuben early in the new year of 1836. He was afraid and helpless, as were other friends and relatives, to aid his son: "If I should come to your assistance, I should be taken by Lynch Law and perhaps be tied up by the neck without a judge or jury."[14] Why, he begged to know, weren't Reuben's lawyers doing more to move the case along?

Reuben wrote back that his counsel thought the prejudice against him was so great on account of the abolition debates taking place in Congress that they should wait a term before going to trial. At the end of the letter he told his father not to attempt to visit him. "I am the same as dead to the world. . . . There is nothing you can do for me here."[15]

Reuben's trial began on April 15, 1836. His was the first case of seditious libel ever brought before the court.[16] The "libels" were chosen from materials confiscated at his office and ranged from an appeal against slavery penned by the Quaker poet John Greenleaf Whittier to a woodcut print showing a white man whipping some black children. The latter was presented by the prosecution as "not fit and proper to be seen and represented."

Francis Scott Key, like Andrew T. Judson, saw a grand historical significance in his case and magnified the charge of illegal publication and distribution into the crime of the century, committed not only against the inhabitants of Georgetown, but against an entire anxious nation: "It is a case to try the question of whether our institutions have any means of legal defence against a set of men of most horrid principles, whose means of attack upon us are insurrection, tumult, and violence."

Key tried to convince the jurors that Reuben knowingly "published," or made available, deceitful materials that were calculated to provoke insurrection and that he did so in his capacity as agent for the "opulent and extensive" American Anti-Slavery Society. He tried to link Reuben to the Northern-based postal campaign that had caused so much local hysteria, and insisted that Reuben's possession of abolitionist documents was prima facie evidence that he had been the one circulating them. "I say that a man who keeps a doctor's shop," Key argued, "and lays such libels on his counter before the eyes of everybody, and in the face of day, has published the libel to every individual who comes into the shop, just as much as if he should pull it out of his pocket and offer it to them." He added that drying flowers between abolitionist newspapers in the backyard was another obvious ploy to expose them to the public. If interlopers like Crandall were allowed to come and circulate such papers, Key warned the jury, then the protection of life and property in the South was at an end.

The defense lawyers, Mr. Bradley and Mr. Coxe, tried to defuse Key's emotional arguments with levity, logic, and reason. The "libels" were not intended to excite sedition in the black population, they reassured the jury, because they were not even addressed to the black population, but to educated and respectable white male citizens.[17] How could the materials be incendiary, they asked, when their language was no more stimulating than Sunday sermons from the pulpit or orations in the halls of Congress? Even if they were seditious, mere possession, after all, was no crime; for, like arsenic in the hands of an apothecary or gunpowder "properly kept, under necessary restrictions," a man might keep questionable papers "in his possession with perfect innocence because he is criminal only according to the use he makes of them." Mr. Key, they argued, had been unable to find any other evidence of Reuben's clandestine activities other than the accidental "circulating" of one pamphlet to Mr. King. If he had, they assured the court, the attorney general would have made it known "though it had been sunk ten fathoms deep in the filthiest well, or burned to impalpable powder."

Indeed, "no insurrection had been produced, no human being injured," the defense contended, except for Dr. Crandall himself, rudely snatched from society while "he was innocently occupied in professional pursuits and quietly pursuing the even tenor of his ways." This travesty was compounded, they continued, by the prosecution's refusal to accept written depositions in lieu of personal testimony from the prisoner's friends and family in the North, who were afraid to come to Washington.

Yet, ironically, one Northerner did testify in Reuben's behalf: the Honorable Andrew T. Judson, who was serving a term in the House of Representatives.[18] Judson related his chance meeting with the doctor on the steamboat in the spring of 1833 as he was returning to Canterbury after filing the legislative petitions against Prudence's school: "I told him the difficulty we had had with his sister. He said he was going to break up the school. He said he didn't know as he could, because Prudence was a very obstinate girl; but he had another sister, younger, then engaged in it, that he could at all events get her away. . . . I always understood he used his whole influence to break up the school as much as any other individual, and appeared to be as zealous to effect that object."

The defense obviously regarded Reuben as a gentleman with a shared liberal sensibility, a judicious professional man who "had always avowed himself to be opposed to slavery, yet . . . has always been as firmly opposed to excitement." The jury seemed to agree. After retiring for less than an hour to consider the evidence, which Reuben called "the most confused mess you ever saw," they returned a verdict of not guilty.[19]

William Lloyd Garrison had been following the trial in the North. In July, during a stopover on a speaking tour, he jotted a note to Helen filled mostly with tender inquiries about his infant son George Thompson Garrison. But he also added, "Some of the time I sat upon a rock and read portions of the trial of Dr. Crandall—a trial which ought to make stones speak, and rocks cry out."[20] Garrison did what he could; he wrote a piece for *The Liberator* in which he attacked Key for imprisoning Reuben, declaring, "The tyranny of Nero was no worse than this."

Reuben returned to New York and published an extended version of the trial transcript in the hope that its sale would "release him from the embarrassments," financial and otherwise, that the trial had caused him. He also hoped to regain his health, for during his eight-month imprisonment he had developed an "irritating cough."

Chapter Sixteen

*I*n the Canterbury cemetery, angels of death, granite, moon-faced visages with outstretched wings, perched on gravestones as if they had just alighted to take another soul. An angel of death seemed now to hover over the Crandall family, waiting to carry them off one by one.

Almira became ill in New York, and her husband, John Rand, brought her home to Canterbury. Hezekiah's wife, Clarissa, was also unwell. Reuben's "irritating cough" grew worse, and he too sought solace under his parents' roof. When he arrived, he found Almira near death. There was little to be done except rock her back and forth to relieve her pain. A recent letter from Prudence in Boonville, New York, indicated that she had no knowledge of her sister's grave condition. As Prudence had been "improperly neglected," Reuben informed her that "the disease is so complicated, it is difficult to say which organ is diseased or which organ is the most so. Her suffering is extreme, beyond your imagination to conceive."

Reuben urged Prudence to come to Canterbury and stay

until the end. Mary Burleigh, the sister of Charles and William, had been at the house for weeks as a nurse and companion, but had gone home to rest. Their mother, Esther, was exhausted and seldom got to bed before midnight. "Our house is a thorofare now," Reuben wrote, "hired men upon the farm, hired girls in the house, watchers every night, friends calling by night and day, all of which makes a deal of labor for somebody." Despite her suffering, Almira seemed "perfectly resigned and happy." She begged Reuben to tell Prudence, "I would have answered her letter if I had the strength. Tell her I want her to forgive me all the trouble I ever caused her, and that I can truly forgive her everything."[1] A month later, on August 18, 1837, at the age of twenty-four, Almira died without seeing her sister again.

Reuben, now gravely ill, decided to go to Jamaica where he hoped the climate would strengthen his lungs. Esther and Pardon begged him not to go, but as John Rand wrote them from New York, "go he would, if he had not five dollars when he got there."[2] Reuben arrived in Kingston, Jamaica, after a calm voyage of thirteen days during which his bread and the milk from the cow on board the ship spoiled in the tropical heat. He soon realized he had made a fatal mistake; the coastal weather was too hot for consumptives, the highlands were too cold, and he could not afford "to keep to sea." He collapsed in a boarding house where he lived on "goats' milk and graham crackers." He asked his father or Hezekiah to send him some winter pears or "Dr. Baldwin's sweet apples . . . I miss my sweet apples and pears very much."[3]

On January 20, 1838, a missionary, D. S. Ingrasham, wrote Pardon that his youngest son was dead. His last wish had been that his father "repent quickly" and "turn to God and return to the Church." His last message to his mother was to tell her "she has been the best of mothers that ever lived."[4]

In grief and despair, Pardon wrote Prudence that he was leaving Connecticut forever: "I have swapped away my farm in Canterbury for six hundred acres of land in the state of Illinois. I shall settle my affairs as soon as I can and go into the wilderness to seek any assylom [*sic*] or hiding place from the turmoils and contentions of this world and find a place to lay my weary and decrepit bones."[5]

Like his ancestor John Crandall, Pardon turned toward the wilderness. He went alone across New York State and into Pennsylvania, where he followed the Ohio River until it flowed into the Mississippi. Then he traveled upriver to Rockwell's Landing in La Salle County in the northern part of Illinois. Twelve miles from the river, amid prairie grass that sometimes grew taller than a man, was a cluster of buildings known as Troy Grove.[6]

There were only three hundred folks in Troy Grove. Most of the New Englanders who had come to Illinois flocked to the Galena lead mines farther west. Eighty miles east, Chicago was as yet an undeveloped outpost on marshy land near the great lake. The state was divided politically and culturally in half, with Scotsmen from Virginia and trappers and hunters from Kentucky inhabiting the southern half of the state.

Pardon boarded with the Webster family while he supervised the erection of a primitive log cabin and the digging of a well. His nearest neighbors were the Root family, also from Windham County. William Hickok, an abolitionist from Vermont, owned the general store. His son James became a lawman before he was twenty-one, and once killed, as legend had it, four men in sixty seconds. He became known as "Wild Bill."

There had been a long spell of malaria, or "ague," in the area, with river towns like Rockwell's Landing, La Salle, and Peru the hardest hit. A newspaper correspondent wrote back East that in the town of La Salle he had seen a cemetery with three hundred graves that had never been rained on.[7] In the spring of 1838, excessive flooding soaked the bottom lands for months. Then extreme heat dried the topsoil into a crust. As farmers split the brittle earth with their plows, swarms of disease-carrying mosquitoes escaped into the air.[8] Pardon soon caught the fever and made his way back to his family in Canterbury, a broken man.

The angel of death continued to hover over the household. On July 8, 1838, Hezekiah's wife, Clarissa, gave birth to her sixth child in eleven years; they named the infant after her fragile mother. Eleven days later Pardon died. On the morning of his funeral, Clarissa sat up in bed with great effort and reached for one of her children. Suddenly she fell back upon the pillow, dead of a heart seizure. Clarissa's sister, Nancy Cornell, came down from Black Hill to help the bereaved household, and it appeared after several months that she and Hezekiah might marry, but then she too died.

Throughout all this turmoil, Prudence remained in Boonville, nursing her consumptive daughter Elizabeth and shielding her stepson, Calvin Wheeler, from the brutal scrutiny of his father, who behaved half the time like a child and the other half like a jailer. Money was very scarce. George Benson, Jr., who had moved from Providence to the farm in Brooklyn after the death of his father and younger brother Henry within months of each other in 1837, discussed Prudence's financial difficulties with Samuel Joseph May: "She will no doubt pay you the remainder with interest so soon as she can. She had paid all her old debts excepting the ballance [*sic*] due you, and I suppose she has done it without the knowledge of her husband who is an unprincipled man."[9]

Prudence finally persuaded Calvin to leave the remote Boonville farm and return to Canterbury around 1840. Calvin bought a homestead from former deputy sheriff George Cady about a mile from Prudence's old school in the part of Canterbury called the North Society. The Philleos rejoined the Packerville Baptist Church.

In the five years Prudence had been away, much had changed. The Windham County Anti-Slavery Society was strong and active. The Black Law had been repealed in 1838. Phillip Pearl, chairman of the committee that had written the law, had converted to abolitionism and claimed he "could weep tears of blood" for his part in the affair of Prudence's school.[10] In the same legislative session that repealed the Black Law, Connecticut lawmakers voted against the annexation of Texas, against the slave trade in the District of Columbia, and for the right to petition Congress against slavery. Yet, in the same year, there was a serious race riot in Hartford, and the conditions of black people in Connecticut had improved little.

Andrew T. Judson no longer lived in the village. President Andrew Jackson had appointed him United States Circuit Judge for the District of Connecticut. The *Norwich Courier* of July 6, 1836, which had praised him in his prosecuting days, accused him of "intriguing" for the judgeship. "Mr. Judson has been either in or a candidate for office ever since he was of age and he joins any party that will gratify his ambitions." In his new position, they predicted, "he will look and sing small."

In 1839, however, Judge Judson made a famous ruling. The previous spring a Spanish vessel called the *Amistad* had carried a cargo of slaves from Africa to Cuba in violation of Spanish law. In Havana, two Cubans bought forty of the

slaves and embarked with them for Puerto Principe. During
the voyage, Joseph Cinquez, one of the Africans, led a mutiny and forced the Cubans to navigate the ship out of Ca-
ribbean waters all the way up the eastern coast to Long
Island. There a United States brig took the ship into custody
and escorted it to rest in the New Haven, Connecticut,
harbor.

The Spanish minister and President Martin Van Buren's
State Department wanted to ship the Africans back to Cuba
to stand trial for mutiny and for the murder of the ship's
captain, but New York abolitionists took up the cause and
claimed the black men were not Spanish subjects, but native
Africans. Judge Judson conducted a hearing after which
he released the men from the New Haven jail where they
had been taken during the dispute. "These poor men shall
not sigh for Africa in vain," he said. The United States
Supreme Court upheld Judson's decision to return the men
to their native land, where Judson had always thought they
and all their displaced countrymen belonged in the first
place.[11]

Charles Burleigh had left Canterbury for Boston to work
in the *Liberator* office. Samuel Joseph and Lucretia May
had left Brooklyn in 1836 for a parish in South Scituate,
Massachusetts, taking Prudence's portrait with them. In
the fall of 1842, May accepted the directorship of the Lexington Normal School for Teachers. He had decided to
dedicate himself "body and soul" to his first love, education.
"I have crossed the Rubicon," he wrote in his acceptance
letter to educator Horace Mann: "I dread nothing save the
question between myself and the Board respecting the admission of a colored girl. That, however, may never arise.
I think it never will arise. If it should, I hope I shall be
directed into the right course."[12]

Prudence's students too had gone their separate and diverse ways. Sarah Harris Fayerweather was living in Kingston, Rhode Island, where her husband owned a blacksmith shop with his brother. Elizabeth Smith returned to Providence and eventually taught school in that city. Harriet Rosetta Lamson, Simeon Jocelyn's ward, had died at the age of eighteen.

Another student, Julia Williams, continued her education at the Noyes Academy in Canaan, New Hampshire, a school that welcomed black students of both sexes. There she met an intense young man named Henry Highland Garnet, the acknowledged leader of the black students even though he had a crippled leg and was in constant pain. Integrated education at Noyes was short-lived, however. On August 10, 1835, three hundred armed men with ninety yokes of oxen dragged the main school building off its foundations to a swamp a half mile away, a task that took two days to accomplish. Fourteen black male students, taking directions from Henry Garnet, closed themselves inside their dormitory and molded bullets. Garnet actually fired a double-barreled shotgun from a window in self-defense and lived to tell about it. Julia Williams went from the Noyes Academy to the Oneida Institute, a manual labor school in Whitesboro, New York. In 1842 she married Henry Highland Garnet.

Garnet's militancy grew in the wake of Northern urban race riots, the entrenchment of slavery in the South, and the battles over its extension into the West. At a Convention of Colored Citizens at Buffalo, New York, in 1843, he appealed to the slaves: "Heaven, as with a voice of thunder, calls on you to arise from the dust. Let your motto be resistance, resistance, resistance!"

The issue of resistance, or rather "nonresistance," was one of the factors blamed by Lewis Tappan for the split among white abolitionists in the early 1840s, but other reasons included "women's rights," "denunciation of the clergy," "personal ambitions," "unavoidable sectarian affinities and prejudices," and "political action."[13] The Tappan brothers and their followers broke away from the American Anti-Slavery Society and formed their own organization, the American and Foreign Anti-Slavery Society. Arthur Tappan and William Lloyd Garrison did not speak to each other again for twenty years.

Prudence's personal life was so demanding that she was unable to participate in the larger disarray of organized politics. Calvin often disappeared for long periods of time. When Calvin Wheeler turned seventeen in 1839, he qualified as an able-bodied seaman, although he was frail and rather short, and sought refuge from his father on the wide sea. He made several voyages to the West Indies and collected wonderful tales to tell his stepcousins.

The health of his sister Elizabeth deteriorated so alarmingly that Prudence sent her to her uncle Bonaparte Philleo, a doctor in upstate New York. There for a while she seemed to rally until she "took cold" at a funeral; she died shortly thereafter. Calvin was not at home when news of his daughter's death arrived in Canterbury, and so could not accompany his grieving wife to Little Falls, New York. When he did show up there, he had an epileptic seizure and fell unconscious into the fireplace. (The family attributes to William Lloyd Garrison a comment that "in an absent minded moment [Prudence] fished him out.")[14] He badly burned one side of his face. There was "a tremendous inflamation of *every* part of the burnt flesh," Prudence wrote home. "Leeches were applied to the parts affected, cupping and bleeding were resorted to and in fine everything to reduce the system and prevent mortification." They used "barrels of ice water" to relieve the pain. Calvin sat upright in a chair without sleep for three nights and days. The sight of his left eye was "lost beyond recovery," and he was permanently disfigured.[15] When Calvin recovered somewhat, however, he resumed alternately bullying and ignoring Prudence and fighting with his brother-in-law Hezekiah.

Meanwhile, the land in Illinois lay fallow. The title had gone to Esther at Pardon's death, and she intended to pass it on to her two remaining children. Prudence and Hezekiah decided that it was one piece of land Calvin would never get his hands on, that it would be a Crandall sanctuary if they should need it.

In 1841 Hezekiah traveled to Illinois for two months to plow some of the land and plant wheat. He fixed up the house that Pardon had begun to build and made arrangements for a fence to be added. In August 1842, when Hezekiah's second wife, Almyra Burgess, was about to have a baby, Prudence left Canterbury for Illinois with thirteen-year-old Obediah, Hezekiah's son, in tow. She was forty years old and she was leaving her husband.

By November, Hezekiah, her coconspirator, was jubilant with their achievement: "You and O. have done wonders for the time. Just look back and see what has been done since you left Canterbury—1500 miles to travel—done a large haying—got in 50 acres of wheat, made many repairs etc. This proves what you can do."

From across the miles, back in Connecticut, Hezekiah oversaw their "Crandall homestead." He ordered Prudence to get staves cut at the mill and use them to elevate the corn house. That way when the rats climbed up to get the corn, "they are exposed to cats." Prudence and her nephew should sow the remaining ground with oats before the next wheat harvest. They must cover the potatoes with horse dung to keep them from freezing, and they should stow the plow in Mr. Root's barn for the winter to "prevent rotting." His "dear Obediah" must take advantage of his aunt's presence to study: "When you write see that you spell your words right." He must wear his greatcoat when he went out riding or to meeting. If he got a dog, it should be the "best kind— a sheppard dog." "The move of the cow and the horse was a good one," Hezekiah wrote approvingly to Prudence, "but you ought not to have told Philleo as he will be out and claim the whole lot. You may depend on his coming. He has rented his farm for some years and is in York state this winter."[16]

In their second year in Illinois, Prudence and Obediah managed to start construction of a large house that eventually rose to two and a half stories and became a boarding school. As Hezekiah had forewarned, Calvin did come west, but finding that Prudence once more "had command of her premises," he purchased a small piece of land from New Englander Benoran Briggs and left again.

Calvin Wheeler, who had turned from seafaring to the law, and his sister Emeline were driven by their father's reckless habits to petition the probate court to declare that Calvin was insane and wholly incompetent to manage his estate in Canterbury. The court appointed Calvin Wheeler and Roswell Ensworth, a selectman, conservators of Calvin's affairs. By this legal maneuver Calvin's children hoped to save their "dear mother" from embarrassment and their father from total ruin. Calvin responded with suspicion and anger and would not cooperate.

By the fall of 1844, Calvin was acting rather unbalanced, and the Packerville Baptist Church committee met to decide whether to allow him to remain a member. He escaped to Boonville, where he wrote his son several rambling, defensive letters; his plans were desperate delusions in which Prudence was cast in the dual role of villain and savior. "Mr. Pardon Bennett will hire my farm next season. Your mother will open a boarding school on the premises.—In order to have any credit I must be settled—your mother must be home."[17] He was soon off to Pawtucket where, he bragged to his children, he was much beloved by everyone. He still believed his destiny hinged on Prudence, who "should return to stop the talk of her leaving me and also to inspire confidence in the public mind. I could have no credit while she is West." He was fifty-seven years old, skinny as a "penknife," disfigured, and quarrelsome. In his confused mind, cosmic malevolent forces thrashed at him, but he remained defiant: "I will never give up—I will stand firm to the helm till the storm abates. I never yet knew a storm but was followed by a calm. . . . If you should see mother before I return give her my best regards and tell her every man to his past."[18]

Esther Crandall came out to Illinois with little Clarissa Crandall, who was a timid, sickly child with spinal problems.[19] Once when Prudence had been asked why she married her husband, she had replied, "Someone had to take care of him."[20] Now that Obediah had family with him, she felt compelled to return to her husband in his need.

On November 16, 1844, having recrossed half a continent alone, she scrawled a hasty note to Calvin Wheeler from the farmhouse in Canterbury: "I arrived here last night. If you know where your father is I wish you would inform him that I am in the homestead south chamber with a good warm fire waiting to see him or you or any other good friends that may please to call."[21]

The reunion between Prudence and Calvin did not prove to be a success, nor did Prudence remain for long in the East. The couple soon left Canterbury for Providence, where Prudence organized literacy classes for black adults in the "phonotypic" method, using a chart with forty-two characters that represented the sounds of spoken language. "I view this reform as a great leveler, by which the condition of the human family is to be normally and intellectually raised," she optimistically stated.[22] Calvin came and went as he pleased while Prudence worked. Soon Emeline reported to her brother that their father was "up to his old tricks" and was renting his farm.

Worried about her stepmother's well-being, Emeline sent two of her children to Providence to find Prudence, but the landlady informed them "that mother had been obliged to give up the house as the only way of getting rid of father. This woman spoke of father with the greatest dislike and said his abuse of mother was beyond conception."[23]

Prudence had gone to Boston, where William Lloyd Garrison kindly printed an advertisement for her phonotypic classes in *The Liberator*. The Garrisons were now struggling to support five children.[24] Prudence taught in a church when it was not otherwise in use, from six to seven in the morning and at three in the afternoon. Unfortunately, Prudence's "novel experiment," as Garrison tactfully put it, did not succeed any better than her reunion with Calvin. She decided to go west again and asked her husband if he wanted to accompany her. Calvin agreed, but changed his mind at the last minute because he had an inspiration of how to make a fortune with "a sort of fence with turned wooden posts." He had written to Washington for a patent and had casually remarked to Emeline that if she wished "to enter into partnership on the fence account to just advance 30 dollars."[25]

By now Prudence was almost destitute. She told Emeline that when her funds ran out she planned to sell her clothes. Calvin received a letter from her written on a canal boat bound for Buffalo. She was on her way back to Illinois to live her life, and this time she did not return.

Chapter Seventeen

Many Eastern women who trekked westward at mid-century, leaving behind their fine china, their rosewood pianos, and their feather beds, did so reluctantly.[1] Prudence was not one of these women.

Deep down in the Puritan consciousness, the wilderness represented chaos. It was the domain of dark and wild creatures, even of the devil himself.[2] Yet it was not the mythologized wild creatures of the West, the Indians, that most women feared; they dreaded loneliness, disease, poverty, and growing old early. But these prospects held no terror for Prudence.[3] She did not merely endure going west. Neither did she, like a proper lady faced with something unpleasant, transcend it. She reveled in her frontier experience like a man.[4] The wilderness was not the place where she lost her soul. It was the refuge in which she reclaimed it.

Had she stayed in the East, she might have sought an alternative to life with Calvin in one of the utopian communities like that of the Shakers, which valued the equality of women. "How Aunt would have shone at Brooks Farm!"

declared one of Prudence's grandnieces. "She would have been a match for Margaret Fuller!"[5]

Other abolitionists, including George Benson, had tried the utopian route in their quest for a better society. After selling the family farm, "Friendship Valley," in 1841, Benson and several associates had invested in an abandoned silk factory and five hundred acres of land on the Connecticut River. They called their experiment in harmonious communal living the Northampton Association of Education and Industry, but the community, numbering 125, was better known as Bensonville. Unfortunately, it did not survive past 1846.[6]

Prudence's life was bound tight by necessity, and her choices were few. She could not depend on Calvin, but on the other hand, a great number of her relatives seemed to depend on her. She resumed what she did best, teaching.

Prudence called her house on the prairie the Philleo Academy, and for years it was the only school around.[7] Some of her students boarded with her. Their parents paid tuition with food and supplies, but even so, sometimes they had only "potatoes thickened with milk" to eat. Her motto was "Make it do." She tinted the sheets and pillowcases yellow so they would not show the dirt. In that way, she did not waste soap in frequent washing. She taught "thrift" along with reading, geography, arithmetic, and good manners.[8]

Prudence was called "strong-minded" by the local folk because she wore her hair cut short and advocated phonotypic spelling reform, temperance, and women's rights, but she had their respect.[9] "Our children would have grown up fools if it hadn't been for Mrs. Philleo," one farmer declared.[10]

For a while in the 1850s she wore the notorious Bloomer outfit. Amelia Bloomer, an Eastern temperance lecturer and editor, had advised her women readers that one way to demonstrate the independence of their sex was to adopt part of the traditional male costume, namely the trousers part. The Bloomer "dress" sported a skirt that reached halfway between the knees and the ankles. Underneath this skirt, loose trousers tapered to the ankle where they were secured with an elastic band. A number of women's rights advocates in the East tried the outfit, though it was exceedingly rare to do so in Illinois. A male friend of the doughty activist Elizabeth Cady Stanton summed up the opinion of most men when he remarked on her black satin creation, "I have seen scarecrows that did credit to farmers' boys' ingenuity, but never one better calculated to scare all birds, beasts, and human beings."[11] Prudence did not wear the Bloomer dress for long, and no one else did either.

One by one Hezekiah's children by his first marriage to Clarissa Cornell joined their brother and sister Obediah and Clarissa at their aunt's.[12] Nineteen-year-old Reuben came west on foot during the early days of the gold rush. He had $47 in his pocket when he left Canterbury and $27 left when he reached Troy Grove. With this he purchased a mean-tempered blooded mare from a grateful farmer and in time raised $1,500 worth of livestock. Eventually he and Obediah built twin red brick farmhouses within sight of each other across the field from Prudence, who often went to Obediah's at lunchtime and, perched on a high stool at the head of the table, lectured the farmhands on women's rights as they ate.

Calvin's children, Emeline and Calvin Wheeler, remained in the East, but Calvin came out to Illinois to reclaim his wife in 1847. He was very uncomfortable to find so many "stiff-necked" Crandalls in the same place. It galled him to be accepted through his wife's "mere suffrage." "I feel displeased with myself that I should have come out here," he wrote to Calvin Wheeler. "I shall never crouch to the Crandal[ls]."[13] He returned to New England, but soon he no longer had property there to drag Prudence back to even if she had been willing to go.

Calvin had apparently fallen behind in mortgage payments on the Boonville farm to a Mr. Loomis of Suffield, Connecticut. In 1852 the property was auctioned, against Calvin's will, for $1,000 when it was easily worth four times that much. The messy affair embarrassed Calvin Wheeler. "You should remember," he mildly reproached his father, "that I live in Suffield and am dependent for a living from the people of Suffield."[14] Calvin Wheeler had been unsuccessful in keeping his father "from being cheated out of everything" and he felt great concern for the old man's plight.[15] He had married Elizabeth Pease Norton of Suffield, and they were planning to buy a big house. "Get mother in from Illinois," he urged his father, "and join fortunes with me and make one family—one home—in [this] village." He assured his "dear jealous suspicious father" that he need not lay out "one cent" of his own money: "My proposition is only you get your own in a safe place— cease your wanderings—get your wife—my dear good kind gentle mother—and settle down with me and my dear little wife—your daughter—in a happy quiet New England home . . . till the end of your days."[16]

But Calvin would have none of it. He blamed Calvin Wheeler's meddling for the ruin of his fortunes, and to accept "mere suffrage" under his son's roof was more distasteful than accepting it under his wife's. He wrapped his cloak of gloom tightly about him and stalked back to Illinois.

There, he and Prudence worked out a sort of uneasy accommodation. They slept in separate bedrooms, and although they took meals together at the same table, Calvin provided his own food. He took to wandering again and speculating in land, but when he was in his wife's house, virtually as a guest, he found devious ways to assert his authority.

It was his habit to pray after, and not before, meals. He would sink to his knees in the doorway that separated the dining room from the kitchen. His droning prayers usually took the nature of a directive to the Almighty to seize his enemies by the scruff of the neck and the seat of the pants and dangle them over hellfire until they reeked of brimstone. Meanwhile, the hired girl, unable to pass into the dining room from the kitchen in order to clear the table, had to go out the back door, walk down the porch, and enter the front door. She made this trip about a half dozen times for an average meal; Calvin's prayers could be depended upon to continue until the table was cleared.[17]

Time had not made him more merciful toward "lesser" or weaker beings. On leaving the house, he carried his cane upside down so he could hook kittens with it and fling them out of his way as he crossed the porch.[18] He was not always sensitive to people to whom he was indebted, either.

Calvin preached sporadically in nearby Mendota, a town that had sprung up like a weed patch two and a half miles from Troy Grove in 1853 at the junction of the Illinois Central Railroad and the Chicago, Burlington, and Quincy Line. Once he addressed a Methodist congregation in the absence of their beloved pastor, a slow, easygoing man. Calvin offended his listeners by preaching a hellfire sermon in which he made an uncharitable analogy: a quiet, slow-moving man never has any effect on a crowd, he said, while a man riding on horseback and whooping it up stirs the crowd to action.[19]

But Calvin did not preach regularly, for his obsession with acquiring property took hold of him once again. The first land he bought was in Nauvoo, Illinois. Joseph Smith, the Mormon leader, had taken his followers there in 1839 after they had been driven out of Missouri. "Nauvoo," Smith said, was Hebrew for "beautiful place." Before a decade had passed, twenty thousand of the faithful had gathered, and there amid scandal and extravagance they so offended their neighbors that Smith was jailed and murdered by a mob with painted faces. Forced to flee westward again, the Mormons left behind a ghost town of shops and houses—some still filled with fine furniture.[20] One of those who walked in the back door, so to speak, as the Mormons fled out the front was Calvin Philleo.

Calvin's other property was near Cordova in Rock Island County. Cordova was situated near the site of a blockhouse erected by soldiers near Rock Island, an island in the Mississippi River, during the Black Hawk War in the early 1830s. Once, the Sauk Indians had gathered berries and nuts there. "It was our garden such as white people have near their big villages," their chief, Black Hawk, had said.[21] The place was indeed so beautiful that the white men fabricated a war and took it away from them. "I see the strength of the white man," Black Hawk said much later. "They are many, very many. The Indians are but few. They are not cowards, they are brave, but they are few."[22]

Calvin knew of Cordova because his brother Addison had played a significant role in the Black Hawk War. In Galena, Illinois, Addison, who practiced journalism as well as medicine, published the *Galenian*, a newspaper whose standard was "Let Us Support the Interest of Our Own Country, and She Will Support Ours." When the conflict began, Addison's paper raged for a "war of extermination until there shall be no Indian (with his scalp on) left in the north part of Illinois."[23] The doctor rode out with the troops and soon had the opportunity to practice what he preached. He scalped two Indians himself, one of whom was still alive at the time. As the old Indian groaned, according to eyewitnesses, Addison said, "If you don't like being scalped with a dull knife, why don't you keep a better one?"[24] He was thereafter known as the "scalping editor."

Calvin continued to covet Prudence's property and once or twice came close to getting it. One of Emeline's sons, LeBaron, had come to live in Troy Grove because his mother could no longer afford to send him to boarding school. LeBaron showed real promise as a gentleman farmer. He liked to lie upon his bed on Sunday afternoons, "with boots on the white spread," reading Shakespeare. He was also a great help to Prudence, and although cash was scarce, they had wheat, oats, potatoes, "fat hogs in the pen and plenty of chickens."[25] "I am very pleased with LeBarron [*sic*]," she wrote Calvin Wheeler. "He reminds me of you often."[26]

Prudence and LeBaron decided to buy a span of horses, "Grandmother one and I the other," the boy explained to his uncle Calvin Wheeler. Prudence borrowed $200. "Now times wasn't hard when this bargain was made," LeBaron wrote, "but now they are adamant." The youth could not come up with his half of the money, and he asked Calvin Wheeler to loan him the sum to relieve Prudence from paying an exorbitant 25 percent interest on the loan. When Calvin found out about LeBaron's letter, he was angry. He had a scheme of his own, as he explained to Emeline: "I offered to purchase a team and the necessary tools, and, of course, own them and thus manage the farm jointly and have a part of the crop. But this did not take. 'She is wiser than seven men who can render a reason!' "[27]

Emeline, whom Prudence called "the dearest stepdaughter that ever any one had," sided, as always, with her stepmother.[28] While she hesitated to advise Prudence ("Father would get possession of any letter I might send her"), she told Calvin Wheeler in emphatic terms that she thought the time was long overdue for Prudence to divorce their errant father, who was no more than a "squatter" on her property.

> Letting go the question as to individual wrong and right in regard to father, it is a fact and has been for the last fifteen years that mother's life has been rendered wretched and to a degree which is wonderful. Why she has not sunk under it e'er now is a mystery, and if the poor heart stricken woman whose life has been one long sacrifice wishes to be legally free from her tormenter it is a coward and a villain who will seek to hold her hand.[29]

Despite Emeline's blessing in the matter, Prudence did not divorce Calvin because he was as dependent upon her, in his own convoluted way, as were her nieces and nephews. But, like Emeline, she approved of divorce for other women. In 1855 Calvin Wheeler wrote a popular romance called *Twice Married: A Tale of Connecticut Life*. After receiving a copy of the book, in 1857, Prudence wrote her stepson about a Mrs. Vogel, who had spent several weeks with her. The story of this woman's marriage and divorce from "a brutal husband a Baptist minister" would make, she assured him, a fine novel: "I sincerely think you could make thousands of dollars out of the affair."[30]

Emeline, a widow, had been one of the first assistants to Samuel Gridley Howe, the director of the pioneering Perkins Institute for the Blind in South Boston. Her courtship by Charles K. Whipple, William Lloyd Garrison's assistant at *The Liberator*, had been a torturous affair. Emeline, who was by her own admittance of a "volcanic nature," refused him in 1848, but he had never withdrawn his proposal, and five years later she consented. She was soon drawn into abolitionist circles and became intimate with many of Prudence's old allies.

Garrison's nonresistance, which had once seemed such a lofty ideal, now struck many abolitionists as an inadequate and ineffective response to the brutal realities of "Bloody Kansas," where a minor war was being waged over the extension of the "peculiar institution" into the Kansas territory.[31] Illinois too was splitting apart over the issue of slavery. In 1848, despite opposition from the northern counties, the legislature incorporated an anti-immigration provision into its constitution to prevent the state, as Democratic senator Stephen Douglas put it, from becoming "an asylum for all the old and decrepit and broken-down Negroes that may emigrate or be sent to it."[32]

The Illinois provision seemed to anticipate the passage two years later of the Fugitive Slave Law. This law provided that any claimant with affidavit "proof" could take possession of any black person if he could convince a special federal commissioner of his claim that the black person was a runaway slave. The commissioner in each case received a $10 fee if he resigned the black person to captivity and a $5 fee if he ordered his or her release. The black person in question had no recourse to a judicial trial or hearing.

Chicago's response to this law was to hold a mass meeting in the city hall, which passed resolutions declaring, "We recognize no obligations of a moral and legal value resting on us as citizens to assist or countenance the execution of this law." The large and well-organized black community of the city formed a vigilante committee to be on the constant lookout for kidnappers.[33]

The outrageous law caused open rebellion in other areas of the north also. In Syracuse, New York, Samuel Joseph May, who had once said, "The spirit of nonresistance is the highest attainment of the soul," "coerced" a sheriff to release a slave named Jerry McHenry who was being held for extradition.[34] "If anyone is to be hurt in this fray," the conscience-stricken minister told his comrades, "I hope it may be one of our own party."[35] As it turned out, no one was seriously injured in the jailbreak. McHenry eventually got to Canada, and the authorities found it inexpedient to press charges against the men who helped him because the general populace hailed them as heroes.

Prudence and Obediah were the most outspoken abolitionists in the Crandall family. It is possible and even likely that, along with the Hickoks, they occasionally aided slaves trying to reach Chicago, the terminus of various tracks of the Underground Railroad, one spur of which ran through Troy Grove. The Dred Scott Decision of 1857 was all the more unbearable to them because Chief Justice Roger Taney cited *Crandall vs. the State of Connecticut* in his historic ruling that black people were not citizens. The decision guaranteed that Southerners could take slaves as property into the West. Taney, a colonizationist, said the Northern states had abolished slavery because it was unprofitable to them, not because they viewed black people as anything other than "inferior beings." Every state, North and South, he wrote, prohibited interracial marriage. Several liberal Northern states that had shown an early hostility to the slave trade and might be expected to have lenient laws relating to race had passed laws of convenience to the white race and refused to elevate the blacks. He cited the Black Law to show that even Connecticut regarded black people as "altogether unfit to associate with the white race, either in social or political relations; and so far inferior that they had no rights which the white man was bound to respect."

In the midst of this political turmoil, Calvin Wheeler, who had been in ill health for some time, died at the age of thirty-six. Nearly ten years had passed since he had last seen Prudence. "When I married, Calvin was a little boy," she wrote his widow Elizabeth. "I loved him dearly and always did."[36]

The death of this beloved stepson had, in its way, as profound an effect on Prudence as anything that had ever happened to her. After all the other deaths, she could not accept his, not with her intellect, not with her heart.

Shortly after Calvin Wheeler's death, the Baptist Church to which she belonged expelled her for heretical beliefs but gave her a letter testifying to the purity of her life and character. The belief from which she would not recant was that no soul could ever be lost.

Chapter Eighteen

*P*rudence began to write poems in which she was no longer earthbound and finite.

> I love to wait the flowing tide
> And see the ships o'er ocean ride
> I love in spirit just to fly
> Beyond the stars that gem the sky.[1]

The prairie sometimes seemed to her as flat and vast as the sea upon which Calvin Wheeler had sailed away, and the boundary between the solid land and the ephemeral sky seemed, especially at night, as if it did not exist.

"He is not dead," she wrote Calvin Wheeler's widow, Elizabeth. "When you visit [the] ground that covers his perishing remains do you never feel the presence of that precious jewel, whose dust crumbles at your feet, comforting your sad heart? I do not doubt his spirit presence is with you, and that you could with certainty realize it—if only you knew how to."[2]

Prudence had found a way to keep Calvin Wheeler with her; she had become a spiritualist. Spiritualists believed each mortal body sheltered a spirit that was sometimes called the soul, or the conscience, or, in Quaker terminology, the "inner light." This light never went out. At death it found its ultimate home in the spirit world, which lay beyond the natural world. Spiritualists believed the spirits regularly visited and influenced the human beings left behind.

There was no hell in the spirit world, only progressions of lovely heavens, all of them described by spiritualist mediums as cooler, sweeter smelling, and more sparkling than anything in Illinois.[3] Calvin Wheeler was safe there, and, from the sense of peace Prudence felt when his presence made itself known to her, he was happy. She began signing her poems "Hope."

In the late 1850s when Prudence turned to it, spiritualism was a broad movement, the seeds of which had come from many sources: from pseudo-scientific European theories, from the rarified intellectualism of transcendentalism, from general religious discontent, and from psychic needs to escape loneliness, economic hardship, and marital abuse. For some believers spiritualism was a religion, for others a science. In both cases it helped to make the universe seem less mysterious and arbitrary.

It is generally agreed that the American debut of spiritualism occurred in 1848 at the home of the Fox sisters in upstate New York. Although the girls later admitted they made their famous rapping noises by cracking their toe joints against the floor, many who heard them believed the noises came from beyond. This openness of mind to such possibilities, like the opening of a secret door, ushered in the era of the spirits.

Eminences such as Horace Greeley, William Cullen Bryant, James Fenimore Cooper, John Roebling, and

Judge John W. Edmund of the New York Court of Appeals were believers. The author Nathaniel Hawthorne saw demonstrations of spirit existence that he believed were genuine, but all in all he thought messages from the other side were more trivial than profound and did not pursue them.[4]

A number of abolitionists, including Lydia Maria Child, Harriet Beecher Stowe, and LeRoy Sunderland, became spiritualists. William Lloyd Garrison first commented on the phenomenon as early as 1854. In 1867 he attended a séance led by a twelve-year-old girl and reported, among other things, bells ringing, pocketbooks levitating, and ladies' bosoms unbuttoning.[5] Several years later, writing to a friend, he said his "curiosity was fully gratified" concerning spiritualism. He admitted that many mediums were "unprincipled," much of the literature was "utterly worthless," and many followers simply indulged their "morbid love for the ridiculous." Nevertheless, he felt that "this is no more to the disparagement of Spiritualism itself than the follies and extravagances of professed Christians are to Christianity, or the unprincipled acts of Democratic partisans are to genuine Democracy."[6]

Spiritualism did not require of Prudence a conversion or a leap of faith. She had been ripening toward it all her life. The Quakers of her childhood had always revered the "inner light." Later the revivalists in Windham County had instilled in her the notion that salvation, or everlasting life, was available to every willing heart. The spirit at work during the revivals had produced swooning and babbling in tongues, but the spiritualists could also point to physical "evidence" such as automatic writing and floating objects, even though the aim of spiritualism was not to arouse religious emotions but to calm passions by making the unknown rational and understandable.[7]

Prudence had also been influenced by the lonely theological stand of Samuel Joseph May, the only Unitarian
minister in the state of Connecticut when she first met him.
Unitarians were religious liberals. To them, all ideas could
be expressed and none were totally wrong. They believed
human beings were made in God's image and therefore
could not be hopelessly depraved. Spiritualists believed similarly that human beings were part of God, made of spiritual
stuff. In both views, Jesus was the most divine of human
beings, but he was not a divinity himself. At the end of her
life Prudence described herself as a "Unitarian Spiritualist."
She said she stood with "those who deny that the God of
nature was ever born of a woman and that Jesus of Nazareth
with all his living words and mighty deeds never performed
an original act."[8]

Spiritualism was also compatible with Prudence's political views. It offered the possibility that people could progress toward perfection. The journey through the circles of
heaven was a personal journey, and no sex, no class, no race,
no chosen few had the advantage.

Such individualism had always been the style of the early
abolitionists whose purpose had been to tell the truth and
to witness it in their lives. Their "fanaticism" was, in part,
their refusal to relax their righteous stance for even a moment because they had assumed the responsibility of being
perfect so that others could emulate them. Through them,
society would thus be changed, not by the collective violent
overthrow of institutions, but by the mass improvement of
individual character, one person at a time.

Prudence was particularly drawn to spiritualism because
of the prominence of women mediums. She admired Emma
Hardinge, a famous medium, and hung the former actress's
portrait on her wall in Cordova.[9] Other women's rights

advocates such as Elizabeth Cady Stanton, Susan B. Anthony, and Frances Willard also leaned toward spiritualism although they did not advocate it in public.[10]

Prudence's spiritualism was also a reaction and a subtle resistance to the theological and marital oppression of her husband. In spiritualism, misery came not from the original sin of Eve, which separated humankind from God, but from "obstructions to the process of nature."[11] For Prudence, God was a force but not an avenging father figure, and if there was no male deity, then it followed that there was no need to respect his earthly representatives, male ministers. She also rejected Calvin's tenets of predestination, the Last Judgment, and a fiery hell. Her favorite expression was "God is love."

As might be expected, Calvin's contempt for spiritualism grew proportionately along with his wife's devotion to it. And yet, as a measure of spiritualism's ability to comfort, he too seemed consoled by it after Calvin Wheeler's death. Near the end of the Civil War, when he was feeling gloomy over his "bleeding, bleeding, yes bleeding guilty country," Calvin wrote a long letter to his daughter-in-law Elizabeth, advising her "not to mourn over the dead": "He [Calvin Wheeler] once said that if the world was his—he would give it all to know beyond a doubt that he should have a conscious existence after the death of the body. Now he knows—not only that he is immortal but he knows where and how you are—and how you feel. You will soon meet on the shores of immortality. And you will know each other."[12]

At the outbreak of the war Prudence had moved to Mendota, partly, Emeline felt, to get rid of Calvin. The town had grown rapidly. There were several large hotels, a sawmill, a drugstore, and a meat market. The Baptist Church even had its own organ built by a Mr. Tewksbury in his kitchen. The first saloon had been run out of a wagon, but now, to the disgust of most of the women, there were at least a dozen permanent establishments. It was said of Mendota that when the surveyors laid out the town, they got so drunk that some of the blocks were two feet wider at one end of town than they were at the other.[13] With the growth of its population, the town council allocated substantial funds for two large public schools, one for the German children and another across the railroad tracks for the Irish children. There was no longer a need for the Philleo Academy.

La Salle County had given Abraham Lincoln a majority of 1,000 in the 1860 election despite the warnings of Senator Stephen Douglas that a Republican triumph would find the Western prairie covered with black settlements.[14] For his part, Lincoln, while opposed to the extension of slavery and its attendant brutalities, favored black colonization to Central America. "Anything that argues me into . . . social and political equality with the negro," he said at the time, "is but a specious and fantastic arrangement of words, by which a man can prove a horse chestnut to be a chestnut horse."[15]

On April 12, 1861, the *Mendota Reporter* trumpeted, "We rejoice to know that we have no traitors or rebel sympathizers in Mendota." War fever infected the town. A company of one hundred men drilled to the fife and drum up and down the main street and then boarded a train for Springfield and glory. The black men of Mendota were not asked to serve their country until the end of the war. Then seven blacks started out with a recruiting officer for Joliet to be mustered into the army in much the same way that black men in the South were finally being armed. When they reached La Salle, however, a gang of Copperheads attacked them and drove them from the city. Walking back to Mendota, they nearly froze to death.[16]

Prudence, like William Lloyd Garrison, arranged her nonresistance principles to regard the war, in part at least, as an antislavery campaign. Emeline's husband, Charles Whipple, sent her a box of materials from Boston containing, among other things, pamphlets defending the success of emancipation in the West Indies. "You said 'send them broadcast and give them to soldiers,' " she wrote him. "This I am endeavoring to do." While the other ladies of Mendota knitted scarves and sent their winter blankets to the front, Prudence established herself in the front room of a shoemaker's shop owned by James Pilkington, an Englishman engaged in the Underground Railroad. The present occupant of the shop was a Mr. Ashton, one of sixty Illinois volunteers who had ridden with John Brown in Kansas. "They both have hearts as great as Big Thunder," Prudence claimed. "I think you would laugh to see me perform the duty of giving." Dressed in men's trousers and overcoat, she stopped people on the street and asked them if they lived in the country, and if they did, she gave them copies of the West Indies pamphlet to distribute.[17]

Before the war was over, Prudence and Calvin moved to his 140-acre property on the banks of the Mississippi River about twelve miles west of Cordova. Calvin, the Yankee trader, sold the property to Prudence for $2,000—"much lower than to any one else," he crowed to Elizabeth—and then moved into town while "Mrs. P." took care of building him "a nice comfortable" house.[18]

Calvin loved the area of Cordova, calling it "a quiet,— moral—I may say religious community."[19] A young Boston traveler, quite a romantic, was given leave to roam about their property in 1867, and the impressions he sketched for

The Christian Register confirmed Calvin's opinion that it was a spot of "perfect beauty." Filtered through his Eastern sensibility, the young man's description spoke of the "tropical luxuriance" of the verdant islands in the river and a group of cattle standing in the water as "a perfect Gainsborough." He observed that the turtledoves with their "ashes-of-roses" plumage would make valued pets, and he mistook the light from the night train to Chicago for a "fire on the prairie."[20]

Away from the rest of the Crandalls, Calvin seemed to mellow. He wanted little more than to sit on his porch in the early evening and watch the cows wander up from the bottom land with tinkling bells around their necks. And for once he had his wife all to himself.

He wrote loving paternal letters to his daughter-in-law in Suffield, Connecticut, and sent profuse greetings through her to all the people he had ever known there. Emeline was pleased her father was behaving, and she wrote Elizabeth, "Do not for a moment doubt that Father expressed his sincere feeling for you. No man ever loved his children more than he has sometimes done, and no person was ever more demonstrative in his feelings than he. If he was always up to his best moments life would have been a very different thing to some who have suffered from his eccentricities and characteristics."[21]

The Indian summer of Calvin's life did not last long. Esther Crandall, now in her eighties, came to live with the Philleos part of the time. The frail old woman sat for hours with a shawl over her lap gazing at the boats going up and down the Mississippi River. Calvin, who was only four years younger, treated her civilly, for, as he reported to Elizabeth, "she did not come out for nothing—to use her words—she says she is going to lay out her money here."[22]

Unfortunately, the strain of taking care of the two old

people made Prudence ill, and, unable to manage the farm as well, she began to sell off her cows, calves, and hogs. Finally she made arrangements to sell the beloved farm itself for $3,500, "very cheap."[23] She took Esther and Calvin back to Troy Grove in 1869, where they moved into the old part of Obediah's house. Calvin had a room of his own where he spent much of his time reading by the fireplace. Obediah brought him his food. He wanted only bread, milk, cornbread, and apples.[24] The old man pined for Cordova. He was a pathetic creature now, wearing a black patch over his blind eye, doddering about the neighborhood in an old flowered dressing gown that flapped about his skinny legs. Children ran away from him.[25]

Esther's health continued to fail. For a while she could still eat by herself, "her eating apron under her chin just like a child," if the "victuals" were cut up very small. But soon she had to be drawn from room to room in her rocking chair.

A letter from Sarah Harris Fayerweather caught up with Prudence in Troy Grove. Sarah's husband had died, but before the war their home in Kingston, Rhode Island, had been an antislavery center visited by many abolitionists, including Frederick Douglass and the Garrisons. Sarah had helped many fugitive slaves by hiding them, gathering clothes for disguises, and giving first aid.[26]

Once at an abolitionist convention in Boston she had met Emeline. They had talked for hours about the Canterbury days. As Emeline told her sister-in-law Elizabeth, "I do not know when I have enjoyed an afternoon better than in this woman's society. She is very intelligent and ladylike, well informed in every moment relative to the removal of slavery and converses very well."[27] One of Sarah's daughters was going south to work among the black people devastated by the war. Her sister Mary, who had also been at Canterbury, was already in Louisiana teaching with her husband, Mr. Williams.

Sarah filled Prudence in on all the people they had known. Amy Fenner had become Mrs. Parker, and Ann Eliza Hammond, who Prudence believed had died, was planning to go to England. One sad piece of news was already known to Prudence. Their good friend Samuel Joseph May had died in Syracuse, New York. On the day before his death, the president of the newly founded Cornell University, Andrew D. White, visited May's bedside and told him that a generous patron had offered the university a very liberal gift on the condition that women should have the same opportunities as men at the institution. May told him that if that happened, he would like the university to have the portrait of Prudence, which he had cherished for so many years.[28]

Sarah remembered Esther well and requested a lock of her hair and sent her a kiss. One day not long after Prudence received the letter, in 1872, Esther did not recognize her daughter and sobbed that "her heart was bursting for her Prude was drowned."[29] She died soon after, and was buried in Troy Grove near her grandson Reuben. But she was not really gone for Prudence. "Not long since," she wrote Obediah a few months later, "I saw my dear mother's face shining with light—and I said 'My precious mother' and as soon as I could say it she was gone.—You will doubtless call it illusion, a phantom but to me it is reality and I enjoy it. I saw her with my spiritual eyes not with the physical eyes for I have both as well as any other human being."[30]

Prudence took Calvin back to Cordova. Fortunately the sale of the farm had fallen through, and they rented out the bottom of the house to a family who worked the farm. The rye crop came in well that fall and the buckwheat too. Her team was "excellent" and the "plowboy not to be beat." "I am as happy as a clam in salt water," she wrote Obediah, "for I shall have a house to live in and own the manure on the farm and keep straw or sell it just as I please."[31]

Then one day her niece Clarissa appeared on her doorstep with three small children, Lucy, Willie, and Rena. The country was foundering in a severe depression, and Clarissa's husband had left her to prospect for gold in Colorado. Calvin resented the prattling and pounding of the children, and Clarissa and Prudence held séances, which he positively could not abide. His nightly prayers grew tyrannously long. "Any neighborhood, blessed Lord," he intoned, "any neighborhood that will be led around by an old squash-head and that's my wife Lord, and Clarissa, Lord, sits on the fence!"[32]

During the last year of his life, Calvin suffered a series of strokes that left him paralyzed and bedridden. On January 5, 1874, Prudence was released into widowhood:

> Come ye bitter cups of sorrow
> Ye can never my peace destroy
> I'm on a voyage of endless pleasure
> and will banish angry strife
> On times current I am floating
> Ever budding into life.[33]

Chapter Nineteen

*P*rudence spent another year in Cordova. Little Lucy and Rena went daily to school. Their mother Clarissa recovered sufficiently from her depression at being abandoned by her husband to do housework and mending. The family had twelve calves to feed day and night. On alternating Sundays they held services at LeBaron's farm, where he lived with his wife and two daughters. Her life was ordered and secure, but this was not a condition that Prudence, now seventy-three years old, necessarily savored.

In 1876, a watershed year in her life, Obediah and his wife Myra went east for the centennial celebration and returned with the news that Hezekiah, recently widowed for the third time, was finally selling out and coming west. Soon after Hezekiah arrived, a man named Hammant from a remote place called Elk Falls, Kansas, convinced Prudence and her brother of a wonderful deal. He had a 160-acre farm there he was willing to swap for their place in Cordova. The two old people were "ripe for adventure," as Rena put it, and accepted his offer sight unseen.[1]

Everyone had heard of Kansas. It was "Ho for Kansas" and "Kansas the Beautiful." The state motto, "Ad Astra per Aspera," meant "To the stars through the wilderness." Drought, grasshoppers, and tornadoes had not deterred thousands of farmers, immigrants, and disappointed gold-seekers from settling there. By then the buffalo were gone, and even the days of the cattle drives in western Kansas were numbered. A new invention, barbed wire, would soon make the plains impassable for the huge herds, and the railroads would extend into Texas, making the drives unnecessary. As if to mark the end of an era, Wild Bill Hickok of Troy Grove, once the sheriff of Abilene, Kansas, the wildest cow town of them all, was shot in the back while playing cards in a saloon in Deadwood in the Dakota territory.

The old life was almost over for the Indians as well. In 1833, when Prudence was fighting for her school, President Andrew Jackson had told Congress that Indians had neither the intelligence, the industry, the morals, nor the desire for improvement that would lead to favorable changes in their condition. He favored their removal beyond the boundaries of the United States. In 1876, when Prudence and Hezekiah decided to move to Kansas, the plains Indians were making their last stand on the Little Bighorn in Montana against the whites, who Black Hawk had said so many years ago were "many, very many."

The following spring, Prudence, Hezekiah, Clarissa, and the three children boarded a train that carried them across Missouri into southeastern Kansas. There the land was reputedly fair, with timber and plenty of stone. They traveled the last thirty-five miles in a stagecoach that lurched first one way and then the other over the rough roads. Hezekiah, hanging on for dear life, kept shouting, "We're gone!" When they reached Elk Falls, "a crude Kansas town," at nightfall, they hired a rig to carry them out to the farm about a mile away. Rena remembered, through her child's eyes, that the house was small and poor. Her mother was so exhausted that "Aunt Prudence" made up the beds on the floor.

Only half of the 160 acres was under cultivation with broom corn. The first thing Prudence and Hezekiah bought was an ox to plow the rest. They planted corn and sugarcane and started a vegetable garden. Then they bought some chickens and "made do" until the crops came in. They ate cornbread and molasses, potatoes and milk. One of Hezekiah's daughters, Esther, feared they would starve, but Rena did not remember ever being hungry. Prudence, to save money, cut her dresses from single pieces of coarse black cotton and tied them at the waist with string. Oblivious to the dictates of fashion, she cheerfully told Rena, "Stand still, and you will see the same styles return after a course of years."[2]

In November Prudence wrote her niece Huldah, "I never spent a more pleasant summer than this has been in all the seventy-four years of my life." The grasshoppers were no problem. The family made eighteen gallons of sorghum ("the best I ever saw," said Prudence) and had potatoes, pumpkins, turnips, and, to Prudence's great joy, two hundred peach trees. "We think they will bear next year. One little tree bore thirteen peaches this year," she bragged.[3]

It was a time of renewing old friendships. Sarah Harris Fayerweather came to visit for several weeks. In her old age she was a distinguished and dignified woman: "She was tall, fine looking and had a voice of peculiar sweetness. Her favorite attitude was sitting erect with clasped hands, while her steady gaze seemed to pierce far below the surface of things. She made a beautiful picture with abundant gray hair framing an almost colorless ivory face whose smile redeemed it from severity."[4] Rena wondered how the two old ladies could sit together so long and still find things to talk about.

Prudence also heard from another old friend. "Thank God you still live," she wrote to William Lloyd Garrison on March 20, 1879. He had sent her a copy of *American Traveler* in which he had an article, a copy of the memorial he had written for Helen, who had died in 1876 after years of invalidism, and a pamphlet of the eulogies presented at her funeral. Prudence wrote back that although she had many "dear friends" under glass—"I mean their pictures"— she hesitated to cut out Helen's likeness for fear of injuring the pamphlet.[5] She inquired after George Benson, apparently unaware that he had moved to Lawrence, Kansas, in 1860 and had spent his last years as a representative in the state legislature. It was a brief, chatty letter. She did not know Garrison was ill.

The old abolitionist had spent the summer of 1877 in England and had said farewell to his old comrade George Thompson. He was living alone in his house, Rock Ledge, in Roxbury, near Boston, holding séances in which he wrote down messages from Helen for their children.[6]

Garrison answered Prudence's letter as soon as he received it, enclosing another picture of Helen. She then sensed his loneliness and pain, for when she wrote back, exactly one month before he died, she told him she was going to frame pictures of the couple together and hang them apart from all the others, "however much I may love them for it would be too much like allowing unholy hands to touch you."[7]

Hungry for news, she inquired after his grandchildren. She said she knew "it is impossible for you not to be interested in the woman suffrage question for it comes under your ban of *Liberty* for *all*." She wondered if he was acquainted with Mrs. Julia Ward Howe, who was such an advocate of peace.[8] Finally, she asked Garrison if he could explain something important about which she had heard. She had read that some "colored persons" were going to make a settlement in the Indian territory about thirty miles south of her farm. "I almost wish I could go with them," she wrote. "My health is very good and if I should continue to enjoy the same till they get settled I am sure I shall visit them some time."[9]

For some reason Prudence did not send the letter for nearly three weeks. By that time she had added a postscript: "I have heard that the colored people from the South are by scores coming in to Kansas—but I heard of none near us—but quite a number have been sent to Topeka."

These people were called Exodusters; they were former slaves who had simply walked away from the old plantations in the river parishes and counties of Louisiana and Mississippi in the early spring of 1879. At first small groups left, then hundreds and then thousands of people. They carried their few belongings with them, and all they knew was that they were going to John Brown's Kansas.

There were already several stable black communities in Kansas. Organizers like "Pap" Singleton from Tennessee and Henry Adams of Louisiana had planned orderly, well-prepared expeditions since 1869. The Singleton Colony was near Baxter Springs in Cherokee County in southeastern Kansas. Nicodemus in Grahman County had been founded mainly by Kentuckians in 1877.

But the emigration of 1879 was different in that it was largely spontaneous, uncoordinated, and unorganized. Some whites blamed the railroads for sending their agents into the Southern countryside to lure ignorant black people to Kansas land that had to be opened within a limited time or returned to the government. Railroad agents had distributed chromolithographs of a mythical Kansas that did not exist. One such lithograph entitled "A Freedman's Home" appeared in a Vicksburg, Mississippi, newspaper and depicted a vine-covered cottage at sunset. Through an open window, the daughter of the house can be seen playing a grand piano. A cook is working in the kitchen, and hired hands are leading fat livestock into the sturdy, ample barn.[10]

The reasons for the mass exodus from the South were in reality far less positive. By 1879 every black Republican government that had been set up after the war had fallen. The slave system had been smashed, but the revolution was incomplete. Southern whites were forcing black people back down into a caste of menial laborers, and the separation of the races, lacking now the intimacy of slavery, had widened further.

The key to power in the South remained land ownership. The few blacks who had purchased land from ruined planters after the war had lost it under various pretexts such as back taxes. On land still held by whites, blacks were paying exorbitant rents. They were forced to borrow money at outrageous interest rates, cheated at company stores, and overcharged for ginning their cotton. Most black families could accumulate nothing.[11]

Some black editors extended the blame for this situation to the Northern abolitionists. One black paper, *Peace Advocate* of Washington, D.C., proclaimed: "Old abolitionists ever since the war have been appealed to in behalf of the Negro's landless condition to furnish the capitol required to secure homesteads for the freedman, but in vain."[12]

Another sorrow of the blacks was the lack of schools and black teachers. This was due to deliberate misappropriations in some cases, but more basically to the fact that the South was attempting to maintain two separate school systems with funds for only one.[13]

Terror reigned in the South. Thousands of blacks who protested injustice were raped, maimed, whipped, or lynched. William Lloyd Garrison, observing the exodus from his vantage point in the North, understood what lay behind it. In the *New York Daily Herald* on April 24, 1879, he wrote: "Self-prompted as a movement it tells its own story of years of unrequited toil, merciless exactions and persistent brutality of treatment; of blasted hopes and broken spirits in their several localities where the victims were born and raised, and to which they tenaciously clung until longer endurance became impossible."

Southern reactions were divided. On the one hand, many whites were glad to see the ragged men, the women with kerchiefs round their heads, and the barefoot children departing. Some planters thought they could easily replace the "niggers" with imported Chinese "coolies." But as thousands of blacks walked away and the impracticability of the Chinese solution became apparent, they tried to staunch the flow. General Thomas Conway of Mississippi reported to President Rutherford Hayes that "every river landing is blockaded by white enemies of the colored exodus; some of whom are mounted and armed, as if we are at war."[14]

Black leaders were also divided. Henry Highland Garnet expressed unqualified enthusiasm. He lauded the exodus for being a black initiative undertaken without paternalistic help or leadership.[15] Frederick Douglass opposed it. "The business of this nation," he bitterly pointed out, "is to protect its citizens where they are, not to transplant them where they will not need protection."[16] If blacks were compelled to leave the South, he said, then the late Confederacy had won.

The fraternity of black newspaper editors, while generally supporting the movement, had initial doubts. The editors of the *Christian Record* of Philadelphia "opposed seeing the

poor and the inexperienced of any class huddled together."
Editor William Eagleson agreed in the May 3, 1879, issue
of the Topeka *Colored Citizen* that it would be far better if
the young, the healthy, and the financially secure emigrated
first. Soon, however, the black newspapers united in their
support of the movement.[17]

The citizens of Kansas also manifested a confusion of
reactions. Like an echo from the past, the May issue of *The
Western Homestead* magazine, published in Leavenworth,
predicted "the wandering refugees" would become public
paupers. Furthermore, because of their "disregard of all
sanitary laws," Kansans believed the poor people would
introduce yellow fever into the larger population.[18] Yet
when the first Exodusters, having been refused entrance to
Kansas City, landed at Wyandotte, located just west of the
junction of the Kansas and Mississippi rivers, they received
a compassionate welcome from the Negro churches. Later,
when the numbers became too great for Wyandotte to ab-
sorb, the mayor of Lawrence offered, and then too late
reneged on the offer, to take one hundred families. These
people were regarded as political refugees by the general
populace of Lawrence, where there was already a settled
community of several hundred blacks.[19] Other towns were
not so generous. When Topeka became overcrowded, a
band of irate citizens tore down the "barracks" that had
been built to house the Exodusters and threw the lumber
into the river.[20] Leavenworth and Atchison nearly went to
war over the refugees. It is said that Leavenworth officials
bribed steamboat captains to carry the poor people upriver
to Atchison. In Atchison, in contrast to the Mississippians
who had patrolled the riverbanks to keep people from leaving, white citizens patrolled the rivers to keep them from
landing. The Leavenworth *Times* accused Atchison of being

the only town in the state to whine over taking in the migrants.[21]

One of the last things William Lloyd Garrison ever wrote was a message to a mass meeting held at Cooper Union in New York City to raise aid for the refugees. The meeting was chaired by Henry Highland Garnet. Garrison condemned the vigilantes of the South whose violence lay behind the exodus. He wrote that contrary to the slander of Southern whites who said that blacks were shiftless, irresponsible, and incompetent, they had "been the only industrious, unoffending law-abiding and loyal portion of the population in that section." None of the misery would have occurred if the United States government were "worthy of its name."[22]

Garrison was very ill at the time and destined to suffer a painful, drawn-out death. At night his family gathered at his bedroom door and sang his favorite hymns while he feebly beat time on the bed covers with his fingertips. He died on May 24, 1879.

It became clear that relief efforts for the homeless emigrants had to be coordinated. Kansas governor John P. St. John held a meeting in the Topeka Opera House to form the Central Freedman's Relief Committee, and he urged cities throughout the state and the rest of the nation to establish similar organizations. Prudence gave him her highest compliment for his actions: she called him "noble." Owing to St. John's prestige, aid flowed in the state in the form of tents, rations, and money amounting to over $100,000. Some states like Colorado sent aid so that the blacks would settle contentedly in Kansas and not move into their own state.[23]

In time, some of the black people found employment on white farms.[24] Many more settled in black colonies such as

Baxter Springs, Nicodemus, Morton City, and Singleton. The Relief Committee furnished them with initial supplies, seed, and teams of livestock. Many blacks found domestic and service jobs in cities. A substantial number were assimilated by the native Americans and settled in Indian territory. Others moved on to Oklahoma and Texas. Still others limped back to the South with such dismal tales of blizzards and dust storms that they discouraged those who were still interested in leaving.

Prudence was proud of the way Kansas had received the Exodusters. In Elk Falls, they had seen "but few colored persons" as yet, she wrote to a niece, but they had heard there was one family nearby, and she and "Aunt Clarissa," who had remarried and lived a short distance away, had decided to pay them a visit.[25]

Just about everything in Kansas pleased Prudence immensely. The land was every bit as good as in Illinois, and the climate was better. Everything grew "excepting tropical fruits." Red, white, and blue morning glories, zinnias, marigolds, and hollyhocks grew in the yard, and in spring, wildflowers carpeted the ground, the sight of which did one's "very soul good."[26] The family had nine head of cattle in the summer of 1880, and several more calves were born the following year. They sold ten of these to their rentee Henry Fraley and kept one for their own use. This one provided milk and butter, which they sold.

Reuben's daughter Josephine sent Prudence a bonnet and "a splendid brown apron" for mornings. Prudence liked it so much she cut out another just like it to wear in the afternoon. "I generally get my work done by the time the eight o'clock train comes in," she reassured Josephine, "so you see I have a pretty easy time, with no one to wait upon but Grandpa and myself."[27]

She and Hezekiah had a gay old time. One day they went to see a milk factory, which, Prudence assured Josephine, was "no small sight." Another time they visited a school in Howard, the county seat eight miles away, and had "a grand time among the profesors [*sic*]." "I saw a beautiful colored girl at the school," she told Josephine. "Her name was Calla Swindle. She said she rode into town on horseback everyday and took her dinner at the Hotel."[28]

Only one thing disappointed her. The peach trees, damaged by frost, were not bearing fruit. Then came the winter of 1881, with blizzard upon blizzard. The Providence, Rhode Island, *Evening Bulletin* and other Eastern papers printed appeals for more supplies for the black refugees. A letter from North Topeka on January 3 predicted, "Many will perish if not speedily sheltered, clothed, warmed, and fed." A further dispatch announced, "Four have died during this snowstorm; send clothing, bedding, food for the sick, speedily."

The winter of 1881 took Hezekiah too. One morning he went out to feed the animals. When he came in to breakfast, he ate little and decided he would lie down. With great fear Prudence wrote her great-nephew Obediah a few days later, "Grandpa is quite sick with numonia fever." "I have watched him all winter as you would a babe," she fretted, "begged him not to be out in the night but . . . he must do the chores to get them done before the chill of night came on." Hezekiah did as he wished. "All I could say to him made little or no difference to him—if I said a word against his working plans it made him very unhappy." She believed he had taken cold after plunging his hands into cold water while tanning hides.[29]

At the end some Baptist friends came to see him, and "he wanted the hymn sung that was sung to Mr. Garrison by his children when he was dying," which began, "Ye tribes of Adam join." His going was peaceful, "like one going to sleep."

The schools and stores of Elk Falls closed the day Hezekiah was buried. A new hymn, "The Sweet Bye and Bye," was sung at the funeral. Little Rena was less disturbed to see her great-uncle lying so still in his coffin than she was to see her great-aunt crying.

Chapter Twenty

*S*o many were gone. Two brothers and a sister, a niece, a nephew, a husband, and two stepchildren. So many old friends. Sarah Harris Fayerweather, Samuel Joseph May, Helen and William Lloyd Garrison, Arthur Tappan, Charles Burleigh. "I am the last leaf upon the tree," Prudence said.[1]

As if to find a way to stay alive in this world as well as the next, Prudence embraced yet another philosophy. Christian Science, which was founded by an Easterner, Mary Baker Eddy, in the early 1860s, emphasized the healing elements of religion and positive thinking.[2] Prudence found it in many ways compatible with spiritualism. Human beings were the spirit reflections of God and therefore eternal. Matter, including the human body, was illusion. Therefore, illness and pain were false consciousness. They represented lapses in faith, self-imposed but correctable. Death was not the end of existence but simply the gateway from one realm into another. Certainly, when she was "the last leaf," it must have been a comfort for Prudence to believe, despite appearances to the contrary, that the tree of life was evergreen.

In 1881 James H. Canfield, a professor at the University of Kansas in Lawrence, was preparing a series of lectures on the rise and growth of slave power in the United States. He read about Canterbury and was surprised to learn that Prudence was still alive and in Kansas. He sent several of his students to interview her, and from their accounts he wrote two articles for Kansas newspapers.[3]

The students traveled out to her tiny house "made of rough boards on the outside and of planed ones on the inside." There they found the seventy-eight-year-old woman keen-eyed and "full of energy." She told the students she planned to build a college on her farm for the "poor and needy" regardless of their "sex or color." "I want professorships of the highest order," she said. "I want every foot of my farm made into a garden to bless the poor of every proscribed race." Although she was very lonely, she was determined not to give in to sorrow. "I have no time to waste," she told the students. "No time to spend in grief. . . . I want to love everyone in the sense of the gospel, for true love never dies. It is as lasting as heaven."[4]

During the following year, a young man named Abraham C. Williams, identified at various times as a weather data collector, a farmer, a doctor, and a spiritualist medium, came to work on the farm. He seems to have been rather eccentric and something of a visionary, but personally he was kind and charming. He became known in the neighborhood as "Sweet William." A journalist who met Williams described him as "a man of thirty-five, with brown hair and mustache, large blue eyes, and a most sympathetic, almost affectionate manner."[5] In a short time Prudence was introducing him as her adopted son, and he was living with her.

Williams took over the heavy work on the farm, while

Prudence resumed lecturing on peace, temperance, and women's rights. She was a member of the National Arbitration League and the National Liberty League, which sought to settle disputes by negotiation rather than warfare. Peace among nations and the welfare of old soldiers, widows, and orphans were favorite poetic themes. In her reforming endeavors she was not without allies in Elk Falls. Her closest woman compatriot was Maggie Nichols, wife of Ephron Nichols, who had founded Elk Falls in 1871 with his brother Reuben. Maggie was the county superintendent of schools in 1878–80. Together, the two women battled demon rum.

Prudence specialized in organizing temperance festivals for the children of Elk Falls, where they downed crackers, apples, and cold water or sometimes bread and honeyed water. These annual festivals were first held in Prudence's house, but the fourth affair in 1885 took place in a schoolhouse to accommodate all the people.[6]

Her greatest passion, however, was women's rights. The battle for women's suffrage already had a long history in Kansas. In 1861, the year Kansas was admitted to the Union as a free state, women gained the right to vote in school elections. The further extension of suffrage, however, was checked in 1867 after a bitter and complex campaign for the enfranchisement of both women and black men in which both factions lost. Many Eastern suffragists had campaigned in the state that year, including Elizabeth Cady Stanton, the Reverend Olympia Brown, and Lucy Stone, who was known in the papers as "the petticoat chief." (She was aided by her husband, Henry B. Blackwell, referred to by the lieutenant governor of Kansas as "that seed-wart she carries around with her.")[7] In 1870 black men received the vote by national fiat, but Kansas women had to wait until 1912.[8]

On July 4, 1884, Prudence spoke on suffrage and women's rights in the grove near the Wild Cat River at a picnic organized by the ladies of Elk Falls. Thirteen young girls pranced about with printed mottoes representing the thirteen original colonies and sang a song written for the occasion. Prudence pledged before the crowd that she would vote for the best candidate, independent of party, if the day ever arrived when women could vote. The next year she spoke in Winfield, Kansas, on the same subject and was treated like a celebrity.

Suffragettes from the East occasionally visited Prudence; Helen Gougar did so in 1887.[9] Elizabeth Cady Stanton devoted several glowing paragraphs to Prudence in her monumental history of women's suffrage, published in 1886. She dubbed Prudence "a grand historic character."[10]

Meanwhile, the fate of the Exodusters continued to interest Prudence. The Reverend Alfred Fairfax had settled fifty-six families in the Little Caney Colony in the neighboring county of Chautauqua. Fairfax, a Republican politician, had fled the South after a shoot-out at his home. To save his life, he was disguised as a woman and smuggled part of the way to Kansas on a Mississippi River boat.[11] Prudence's physical frailty was the only thing that kept her from venturing out to meet him.

Her grandniece Rena remembered, nevertheless, that many black people came to the farm to visit her. Her close friend in Elk Falls the Reverend C. L. McKesson, a congregational minister who had no church, recalled that once he had come to the farm while two young girls were visiting. Prudence put her arms around their waists and called them her "dear daughters" and "walked between them as lovingly as ever did their own mother."[12] These girls, probably the daughters of Mrs. Smith, a widow, became Prudence's students, and they were, Prudence wrote one of Sarah Harris Fayerweather's daughters, "first-rate scholars to learn."

"When they come to see me," Prudence explained, "we sing and they read their compositions to me, speak pieces, and show me their hand work."[13]

She was busy, but although she adhered to the Protestant ethic of reform—work unceasingly until you succeed—she could not accomplish all that she wanted. Her restless mind was imprisoned in a slow and brittle body, and no miracle wrought of faith and correct thinking changed that. Most of the townspeople, especially the orthodox churchgoers, thought her odd and interesting, but formidable. She was a piece of history, and they tended to appreciate her, like a museum piece, from a distance. "I begin to think they are afraid of me," she said.[14]

Old age had distorted some of her qualities. Her short haircut and the men's clothes she often wore had once seemed daring and original, but now they were peculiar. Once she had been "articulate"; now she was garrulous. Once she had been "principled"; now she was opinionated.

Ties to the old days were her comfort. She valued beyond measure the correspondence with former students: "Years fled on, those gifted ones / Were as dear as life to me," she wrote in one poem.[15] Mary Harris Williams, Sarah Harris Fayerweather's younger sister, wrote to her from Greensboro, Louisiana, where she and her husband were teachers. Their oldest son was teaching in New Orleans with several teachers under him. Mary asked if Prudence was in touch with any of the children of Helen and William Lloyd Garrison, whom she compared to Christ.[16]

Prudence passed this compliment on to Wendell Phillips Garrison, the Garrisons' third son, who was the literary editor of *The Nation*. He and his younger brother Francis Jackson Garrison, a publisher, were preparing a massive biography of their father, and they had written to Prudence concerning the Canterbury section. Prudence told Wendell

Phillips that for her, his father lived on. She had received a message from him in the spiritualist paper *The Banner of Light*. "The communication I receive with my full heart, and I thank God for it."[17]

The Garrison children did not neglect her. They periodically sent newspaper clippings, and in 1887 they invited her to a family reunion back East, which she reluctantly declined. Wendell Phillips sent photographs of the likeness of an engraving that had been made from her portrait.[18] In September 1885 he sent an article he had written, "Connecticut in the Middle Ages," which appeared in the popular *Century Illustrated Monthly Magazine*, in which he recounted his father's flight from Brooklyn, Connecticut, to New York with the Canterbury pursuers right behind him.

The Canterbury affair had also been documented elsewhere. Samuel Joseph May's *Some Recollections of Our Anti-Slavery Conflict*, published in 1869, and *Memoirs of Samuel Joseph May*, published after his death, contained an account. In 1880 historian Ellen Larned published her history of Windham County, which included a long section on Prudence's school. The two women became friendly correspondents after Prudence established that Mrs. Larned held similar views on "womanly independence."

Later that same year, Abraham Payne, who had been a boy during the conflict, presented his interpretation in a paper he delivered to the Rhode Island Historical Society. The talk was printed in several Connecticut and Rhode Island newspapers. Payne said that Samuel Joseph May, if he had lived at the time, would have been "one of Cromwell's saints." Of the heroine, he said, "Miss Crandall had a little tendency to martyrdom in her constitution and did not object to trying it in a mild form." He felt that the abolitionists had acted deliberately "to provoke the persecution they endured" and that in the end Samuel Joseph May was simply "too much for Mr. Judson."

Sometime in 1885 John S. Smith from Central Village near Canterbury visited Prudence in Kansas and told her there were friends in Canterbury ready to start a campaign on her behalf to restore her good name and reimburse her for the loss of her livelihood long ago. Old and new friends soon joined the endeavor. George Burleigh, a brother of William, Charles, and Mary, wrote a petition that was eventually signed by 112 Canterbury residents. It read in part:

> We, the undersigned citizens of this State and of the town of Canterbury, mindful of the dark blot that rests upon our fair fame and name for the cruel outrages inflicted upon a former citizen of our Commonwealth, a noble Christian woman (Miss Prudence Crandall, now Mrs. Philleo) at present in straightened circumstances and far advanced in years, respectfully pray your Honorable Body to make such late reparation for the wrong done her as your united wisdom, your love of justice and an honorable pride in the good name of our noble state, shall dictate.

Even so, the Connecticut legislature was slow to respond on the grounds that Prudence had been technically guilty of a violation of the law. It took a concerted effort on the part of the press and her followers to make them act.[19]

One of Prudence's former students from Plainfield, Samuel Coit, the son of Sheriff Roger Coit, reproduced four hundred copies of the Canterbury section from Samuel Joseph May's book *Some Recollections of Our Anti-Slavery Conflict* and distributed them to every state congressman. Deacon Thomas J. Clarke, a relative of Andrew T. Judson who now lived in the Paine mansion, addressed the state legislature on her behalf.[20] In Hartford, the Reverend John Kimball delivered a sermon, later made into a pamphlet, that was effective despite its errors and exaggerations. He described Prudence as "very likely a little 'set' and obstinate in her purpose, for when God lays an axe at the root of a tree of wrong which He means to have cut down, He is very apt to make its edge not of lead or putty but of hardened steel."[21]

Prudence, who still had a bit of steel in her, made it very clear to her supporters that she would not accept charity. "I shall never plead poverty," she declared. "My plea will be for justice. When a state has falsely imprisoned an innocent citizen and passed unconstitutional laws by which they are harassed and property destroyed it [is] right they should compensate the abused . . . I think that it is a duty I owe myself and also to the state to ask for redress for such slander and abuse as I have received at their hand."[22]

Nevertheless, the humble style of her life, the contrast between the Paine mansion and her "little pioneer box house," was precisely what was illuminated in the drive to secure her pension. Senator John W. Marvin of Saybrook, Connecticut, gave a stirring speech on the senate floor in which he generously gave Prudence credit for ending slavery. Then he melodramatically pleaded, "Our heroine still lives . . . see her in her little box house of three rooms on the hillside in the West, eking out a scanty subsistence from a second-bottom farm, still in debt for the material for enclosing it."[23]

Journalists began making pilgrimages to see her. Young George Thayer of Connecticut struggled through miles of prairie mud on his bicycle to interview her for the Hartford *Evening Post*. Another reporter from the *Kansas City Journal* traveled all night on the train for his story. At dawn

Mr. Johnson, the proprietor of the Railway Hotel in Elk Falls, drove him out to Prudence's farm, assuring him he would find the eighty-three-year-old lady "bright as a pin." The house was on a little rise with a few trees planted around it, and the yard was "neatly kept." The reporter thought the inside of the house a "curiosity":

> Its dimensions were about 8 × 12. In one corner was a rude couch; at the foot of the couch was a roughly made desk covered with strong brown paper. In another corner stood a set of shelves piled full of books. . . . The stove and a table littered with papers, which she received from the East nearly filled the remaining space. Despite the corner full of books, the place bore a poverty-stricken appearance. Mrs. Philleo's dress, though neat, was worn and faded, and the furniture had seen its best days.[24]

Prudence did not apologize for her situation. Indeed she hardly seemed aware of it, although she admitted that as a result of her "own incompetency to manage designing persons" she had lost most of the property left to her by her parents.[25] But when asked what "luxuries" she would indulge in if she had some money, she replied should would like a horse and buggy and the opportunity to occasionally ride on the train—she called it the "cars"—to visit "old friends and the colored people."[26] She might consider a trip to Connecticut, but aside from those things there was nothing more she needed or wanted.

A second campaign was afoot in Connecticut to buy back the Paine mansion for her to live in, but she sent word to discourage the effort: "Home is like Heaven, it is where you find content. I think I would rather not."[27]

Prudence did not want material things; she wanted jus-

tice. As weeks went by, she grew impatient with the waiting. She worried if Mr. Clarke was "fully posted on the
particulars of the case" and competent to speak before the
legislature. "I do not know your smart lawyers," she wrote
Mr. Smith. "I suppose the case must be spoken to by somebody—I could do it myself if I was there."[28]

In the end there was little opposition. Led by the Hartford
Courant, many papers in the Northeast chanted for retri-
bution. The Springfield, Massachusetts, *Republican* affirmed that she "was right in teaching negro children." No
amount of money could repair what had been done to her,
but money could "apologize," and "the state ought not to
hesitate an instant."

The Boston *Journal* said the question was not whether
Connecticut could afford to make the grant, but, fearing
"fresh dishonor," could they afford not to. The *Advertiser*
of the same city declared that if John Brown was the most
conspicuous man associated with Kansas, then Prudence
Crandall was the most conspicuous woman.

Even the Democrats were willing to be magnanimous.
The leading Democratic paper in Connecticut, the Hartford
Times, pragmatically commented, "For over fifty years this
disgrace has remained on our state. . . . If justice is to be
done, even at this late day, it should not be long delayed,
for Prudence Crandall in the natural order of things, has
not long to live."[29]

Finally, on April 2, 1886, Prudence learned by telegram
that the bill to establish a pension for her had passed. The
next day Connecticut governor Henry B. Harrison authorized the first quarterly payment of $100 to be sent to her
out of the $400 she was to receive annually until her death.

She began collecting photographs of all the "noble" ones
who had helped with the campaign. Only then did she learn
that the famous author Mark Twain was behind the offer

to reinstate her in the mansion of "the long ago." When she wrote to thank him, she rather shyly asked if she could have a copy of *Innocents Abroad*, "that I may be able to finish the book and loan it to others who are not able to purchase it that they too may learn from you to describe the most trivial thing in such beautiful language as they can there find."[30] She also desired his photo to put under glass, "but I must not ask too much." Twain replied he would be only too glad to load her down with a number of his books.[31] As for the photo, he promptly sent her a very good one.

Chapter Twenty-One

*P*rudence did not buy a horse and buggy, nor did she take a trip back East. Her one extravagance was to buy a two-story wooden house on Osage Avenue in Elk Falls, but even with her pension arriving every three months, she had to take out a $200 mortgage.[1]

Soon she was a common sight in Elk Falls, her "bent form, clad in a coarse cotton dress made after a pattern as plain as the goods, leaning upon the top of her staff as she appeared on her way to the store."[2] Face to face with a minor legend, some of the townspeople, out of timidity or distrust, shunned her, and it was the frost of their reception that chilled her old age. "The ministers are afraid I shall upset their religious beliefs," she confided to journalist George Thayer in 1886, "and advise their congregations not to call on me, but I don't care."[3] The local churches closed their doors to her and would not let her lecture in them. In a more tolerant era she might have been called a "wise woman"; in a less tolerant one, a witch.

Her ideas had remained remarkably consistent, even undeveloped, over the years. American society had changed very much but she had changed very little. Her faith in progress, her belief that enough effort in any cause ultimately assured its success, drove her to lecture on peace in schoolhouses in the vicinity of Elk Falls up to within six months of her death at the age of eighty-seven. She carried a white flag, symbolic of peace, made of cheesecloth fastened to what had once been a map roller. But her moral position that all wars were bad because they were violent was as oversimplified as her nonresistance had been decades before. It was almost as if she regarded the revolutions and colonial wars of the age of imperialism as squabbles between hot-headed leaders who needed only to sit down together and remember their manners in order to solve their conflicts.

The problems of the 1880s were far more complex than that. The "frontier" west of the Mississippi River was no longer a land of unlimited opportunity waiting for any enterprising person to exploit. The wealth of the entire country was becoming concentrated in distant greedy hands. Debt, unstable prices, and high railroad rates plagued Kansas farmers. They had endured a decade of drought and other natural disasters, and their poverty, in most cases, had little to do with weak character. Increasingly, individuals were forming alliances, unions, political parties, and other collective entities to solve their common dilemmas.

The old-time abolitionists—and Prudence was still one of them in her heart—had rarely linked their cause for black emancipation to the struggles of the poor and working people. William Lloyd Garrison had even denounced early labor leaders for fomenting violence between the working class and the wealthy.[4] Prudence was not unconcerned with the plight of the poor, but she continued to believe that the improvement of society would result from the improvement of individual character and not, though she was not able so to articulate it, from a redistribution of wealth or a change in the balance of power. Her temperance festivals impressed upon children that liquor and loose living resulted in poverty, while other leaders were showing that it was poverty itself, resulting from debt, foreclosures, and unemployment, that turned people into alcoholics and "tramps."

Prudence, in the old Quaker way, was more comfortable aiding the victims of injustice than attacking the perpetuators. She wrote a poem for the farmers of Kansas in which she honored their humble work and urged them to be optimistic. It read in part:

> Look ahead ye noble farmer
> Fill your mission with delight
> On you depends the fate of nations
> While they jangle, strive, and fight[5]

She had never allowed factionalism to fragment her overview of what needed to be accomplished. It was therefore a contradiction of no import that she supported the Women's Christian Temperance Union, a "coercive" political organization whose position on prohibition would make abstinence a law rather than a choice. Foremost in her mind was the knowledge that women, who had so few options and rights, suffered the most when men squandered money on drink.

Similarly, although there was no specific political party she favored, she believed women would use their moral influence to transform society once they had the right to vote. In 1887, when Kansas passed the Women's Municipal Suffrage Law, which extended the vote to married women living in towns—there were about thirty of them in Elk Falls—Prudence protested its partial nature. While "it is the duty of women to be thankful for a little good," she rather sarcastically told a local paper, she would fight on until "all tax-paying women, widows, and hard-working farmers' wives, can with them celebrate their own emancipation."[6]

While her outspokenness on these political issues probably alienated conservatives in Elk Falls, spiritualism isolated her even more because, for her, spiritualism was the antithesis of orthodoxy.[7] By the late 1880s spiritualism was no longer in the mainstream. Despite intentions of moral uplift and reform, the achievements of the movement had been negligible. Part of the failure resulted from a lack of central organization and from a reliance upon the whimsical funding of benefactors. Fraud, scandal, and bad theater had further discredited spiritualists. The more profound questions spiritualism had raised were being taken over for investigation by an educated elite of scientists and philosophers.[8] Prudence challenged these thinkers with a long poem, part of which read:

> Say, what is science, ye that know
> Is it the voice of God below?
> Do all things preach, do all things pray?
> And why all the general display
> That seems to mark a full control,
> If everything has not a soul?[9]

It is possible that Prudence's brand of spiritualism was viewed as deviant behavior by the more orthodox Christians of Elk Falls. Journalist George Thayer noted she had been reading William Denton's book *Is Darwin Right?* when he visited her. Denton was a geologist, a writer, a lecturer, and a spiritualist of outlandish proportions. In 1879 he told a crowd of thousands gathered at the National Liberal League Camp Meeting in Lawrence, Kansas, that his intention was "to destroy Christianity." For Denton, the eternal spirit was a scientific law. He regarded all books besides mathematics books damaging to children, and the worst of all was the Bible, that "bloody book" from Christianity, that "bloody religion."[10]

Prudence very likely had read another of Denton's books entitled *Garrison in Heaven*, in which William Lloyd Garrison's soul is released from its body, and after paying a flying visit to abolitionist Wendell Phillips' funeral, to the huts of the poor in the South, to the Exodusters, and then to "Hayti," England, and Liberia, it is finally drawn up into heaven. Heaven is a vast skyscraper city with gates of pearl and streets of gold. The inhabitants eat oyster stew at long tables and are warmed by a central heating system vented from hell. Garrison asks his guide the whereabouts of George Thompson and is told he is in hell as "a pestilent heretic, a companion of infidels." Garrison's disappointment turns to suspicion as he learns that abolitionists Theodore Parker and Henry Wright are also in the depths along with George Washington, Thomas Paine, and Thomas Jefferson. The guide explains that admission to heaven "depends upon fitness, not upon goodness. He that believeth is saved, not he that doeth." Most of the men and women hung for murder, the guide says, are in heaven because of their last-minute repentances. At the end of the book William plots to start an Underground Railroad to get the saints out of hell: "We must empty Hell and reform Heaven."

For spiritualists like Denton and Prudence, the old debate over whether salvation was open to all or limited to a few was still very much alive. In a letter dated November 11, 1887, in the Howard *Courant* that began, "Dear Sir, How dare you . . . ," Prudence attacked a biblical literalist from Grenola, Kansas. The minister had allegedly terrorized his congregation with passages from the Bible, a book that contained, she pointed out, "thousands of acknowledged errors" and sanctioned "war, slavery and poligamy [sic]." She defended Universalists, Unitarians, and spiritualists— "of whom I am one"—and defied his authority to send "us all to hell" in "one fell swoop."[11]

In October 1889 Prudence suffered an attack of what her friends called "chronic asthma." She tried to ignore the betrayal of "clay," as she referred to her body, saying, "Mind has a great power on matter and I think I can drive away this disease." She employed a Christian Science healer and rallied briefly. Then one night in December when the healer was away at Langton, Kansas, her condition worsened. Friends pleaded with her to call a doctor, but she refused. "I want to do just what is right by this lady," she whispered, "and she does not want me to take any medicine and I will not do so until I have dismissed her."

As she grew weaker, Prudence's friend the Reverend Mr. McKesson sat with her and read aloud from a book that compared all religions and claimed that all nations had some light and truth. She kept murmuring, "That's right, that's so. God could never leave any nation without some revelation of himself."

A few days before her death she told McKesson, "You may come in anytime and find me gone and I want to say to you now that I want you to preach my funeral sermon." When he asked her what he should say, she replied, "Preach the truth." Tell them, she said, "I am no more afraid to die than I am to live." On Monday, January 28, 1890, a little before noon, with her niece Clarissa holding her hand, she died.

The funeral service was held Wednesday morning in the Baptist Church that had refused to admit her while she was alive. The casket rested in front of a wall of evergreens and white immortelles. Above this, fashioned in evergreen sprigs, was her name, Prudence Crandall. Nearby stood an evergreen cross with the word "Hope" on it. A large crowd attended. In the front row sat Mrs. Smith and her two daughters, the only black family in Elk Falls. The choir sang and then McKesson preached that a great woman had passed on: "Great, because she had deep convictions of right, and greater because neither death, life, angels, principalities, things present, things to come, heights, depth, nor any other creature could keep her from following her convictions."[12]

At first, the dates of her birth and her death[12] were marked incorrectly on her grave. Later, Clarissa put them right. But this probably would not have mattered to Prudence, for, according to her faith, she was not even there, not in the ground, not in Kansas, not in America, but in some other, infinitely better place.

Epilogue

*T*he portrait of Prudence Crandall by Francis Alexander hangs to this day in the Kirby Room of the Uris Library at Cornell University. Prudence's name lives on at a dormitory named for her at the University of Connecticut at Storrs. The name of Sarah Harris Fayerweather is similarly honored at the University of Rhode Island in Kingston.

The arguments of Prudence Crandall's lawyers, William Ellsworth and Henry Goddard, were resurrected 120 years later, in 1953, when Thurgood Marshall, chief counsel for the National Association for the Advancement of Colored People, drew upon them while arguing the landmark school desegregation case *Brown v. Board of Education of Topeka*.

The house on the green was purchased by the state of Connecticut in 1969. During the late 1970s and early 1980s it was renovated and restored. Now, as a museum and library of black and women's history, it is open daily to the public.

Notes

Prologue

1. George Thayer, *Pedal and Path*.

Chapter One

1. Rena Clisby, *Canterbury Pilgrims*. This unpublished manuscript by Prudence's grandniece contains some factual errors but provides wonderful vignettes of family life and includes several family letters unavailable elsewhere.

2. Black Hill was an elevated area near Canterbury, where a Quaker school was located. It was called Black Hill because the Indians of earlier times burned the undergrowth every year to make a pasture for the deer.

3. Rena Clisby, *Canterbury Pilgrims*.

4. Clarissa Cornell's mother, Huldah Kinne, was the daughter of David Kinne and Eunice Coggswell. The David Kinne house on Black Hill, circa 1780, is generally described as a distinguished example of the "Canterbury style." The Luther Paine house (Prudence's school) and the Thomas Benjamin Clark house are the other examples.

5. Robert Morton Hazelton, *Let Freedom Ring!*, p. 20.

6. Charles Dickens, *American Notes for General Circulation*, p. 6.

7. Marvis Olive Welch, *Prudence Crandall*, p. 12.

8. Calvin Wheeler Philleo, *Twice Married*, p. 186. This romance, published by Prudence Crandall's stepson in 1855, is set in Windham County around 1820 in the fictional village of Walbury, which closely resembles Canterbury.

9. Abraham Payne, "Prudence Crandall and Her School."

10. John Warner Barber, *Connecticut Historical Collections*, pp. 425–26. The "Christ-ians" had broken away from the Baptists.

11. Alexis de Tocqueville, *Democracy in America*, 2: 142.

12. Ellen D. Larned, *Historic Gleanings in Windham County, Connecticut*, p. 20.

13. Rena Clisby, *Canterbury Pilgrims*.

14. Reuben Crandall to Prudence Crandall, July 1, 1831, in Rena Clisby, *Canterbury Pilgrims*.

15. Ibid.

16. For a list and analysis of female seminaries at the time, see Nicholas Colucci, *Connecticut Academies for Females, 1800–1865, Ph.D.* diss., University of Connecticut, 1969.

17. A description of the Paine house and the story of its restoration are found in Eleanor Edelman, "Restoration and Renascence." Another description and a picture are found in Lee and Virginia McAlester, *A Field Guide to American Houses*, pp. 153–67. For other descriptions of the Paine house, the Congregational Church, and other significant Canterbury buildings, see Richard H. Dana, Jr., "An Architectural Monograph on Old Canterbury on the Quinebaug."

18. Richard H. Dana, Jr., "An Architectural Monograph on Old Canterbury on the Quinebaug."

19. According to David O. White, "Prudence Crandall," Canterbury land records show she didn't actually purchase the house until January 5, 1832, when she paid for it with $500 in cash and a $1,500 mortgage from Samuel Hough.

20. Other students mentioned by Marvis Welch in her biography are Miss Avery, Miss Seth, and Frances Ensworth. Richard M. Bayles, in *History of Windham County, Connecticut*, p. 1098, states that there was one boy among the girls, Dwight Barstow, born in Canterbury Plains on August 8, 1820. He was the son of Hezekiah Barstow. Eleanor Edelman, in her thesis, adds another boy to the list, Charles J. Aspenwall.

Chapter Two

1. *Freedom's Journal* was published weekly in New York from March 16, 1827, to March 29, 1829. The editors were John B. Russwurm, the first black American to graduate from college (Bowdoin, 1826), and Samuel E. Cornish.

2. Edward S. Abdy, *Journal*, 1:122.

3. Martin Delany, *Colored People of the United States*, pp. 24–25.

4. Leonard L. Richards, *"Gentlemen of Property and Standing,"* p. 44: "For many Northerners, the probable alternative to slavery and African colonization, was *either* race war *or* miscegenation."

5. Oliver Johnson, *William Lloyd Garrison and His Times*, p. 44.

6. Samuel May, Thomas James Mumford, and George B. Emerson, *The Memoirs of Samuel Joseph May*, p. 14.

7. Samuel Joseph May, *A Discourse on Slavery in the United States*.

8. Francis Scott Key, *Oration Delivered in the Rotunda of the Capitol of the United States on the Fourth of July, 1831*. Key was the author of the lyrics to "The Star-Spangled Banner." A personal friend of President Andrew Jackson, he was United States District Attorney for the District of Columbia from January 29, 1833, until July 3, 1841. Key was also one of the founders of the Colonization Society. He prosecuted Dr. Reuben Crandall for seditious libel in 1836. (See chapter 15.)

9. Simeon Jocelyn in *The Liberator*, September 24, 1831.

10. Biographical data on the Harris family come from Carl R. Woodward, "A Profile in Dedication." Part of the large Harris family may have remained in Norwich. Woodward says that William Harris was listed on the tax records for both towns. *Norwich Vital Statistics* states that Frederick Olney, the *Liberator* agent for Norwich, married Olive Harris of Norwich on July 16, 1844. According to the 1830 census, there were sixty-nine black people in Canterbury. Among these would have been the Harris family, a servant named Mary Barber who worked at the Jedidiah Shephard house, and Eben, Frances, and Adaline Freeman, who are listed as attending the district school in 1827 along with Almira Crandall. Another source identifies one of Prudence's subsequent black students as Polly Freeman, and she may also have been from this family.

11. Abraham Payne, "Prudence Crandall and Her School." Payne went to Brown University and had a career in law. According to 1828 Canterbury School records, he and his sisters, Mary and Sarah, attended the district elementary school along with Almira Crandall.

12. Ibid.

13. Some historians refer to Mariah as Marcia, but this is probably a misreading of Prudence's handwriting in a letter to Ellen Larned on May 15, 1869. Her name is recorded as Mariah Davis at the time of her marriage to Charles Floreval Harris on November 28, 1833. Also, *The Liberator* of December 21, 1833, in its report of the marriage, calls her Ann Maria Davis.

14. Edward S. Abdy, *Journal*, 1:197. Prudence described Sarah to a reporter from the *Kansas City Journal* in an interview on March 28, 1886: "She was regarded as a colored girl, though in reality she was part white, part Indian, and part negro. Her complexion was quite light."

15. If the schoolroom was located on the second floor, as the curator of the Prudence Crandall Museum believes it was, this explains why Hezekiah and others during the first trial testified they had never seen or been in the classroom. (See chapter 10.)

16. *Windham County Advertiser*, May 7, 1833.

17. Calvin Wheeler Philleo, *Twice Married*, p. 140.

18. *The Liberator*, November 17, 1832.

Chapter Three

1. Ellen Larned, *The History of Windham County, Connecticut*, p. 491. In Larned's account, Prudence calls this woman Mrs. Peters, but J. C. Hubbard, in "Prudence Crandall, a Philanthropic Matron of Elk Falls," refers to her as Mrs. White. George S. White, possibly this woman's husband, was a Congregational minister who was active in the temperance movement. Hubbard says he was on the board of school examiners of the First Ecclesiastical Society of Canterbury (the church on the green), which enabled him to be a pedagogue in school district matters. There was another George White in the village, but he was a tanner by trade.

2. Prudence's letter of January 13, 1833, to William Lloyd Garrison is in Francis Jackson Garrison and Wendell Phillips Garrison, *William Lloyd Garrison*, 1: 315–16.

3. Ibid.

4. William Lloyd Garrison to Henry Benson, July 30, 1831, in Walter M. Merrill and Louis Ruchames, eds., *The Letters of William Lloyd Garrison*.

5. In addition to raising money for the manual labor school, Garrison also wished to debate the Colonization Society's agent, Elliot Cresson, who was in England at the time.

6. Josiah Copley in *United Presbyterian*, June 5, 1879, printed in Francis Jackson Garrison and Wendell Phillips Garrison, *William Lloyd Garrison*, 1: 220–21.

7. George M. Frederickson, ed., *William Lloyd Garrison*, p. 116.

8. Samuel Joseph May, *Some Recollections of Our Anti-Slavery Conflict*, pp. 18–20.

9. Helene G. Baer, *The Heart Is Like Heaven*, p. 64.

10. *Creative Survival*, p. 43.

11. Henry Benson to William Lloyd Garrison, February 8, 1833, Boston Public Library.

12. Prudence Crandall to William Lloyd Garrison, February 12, 1833, in Francis Jackson Garrison and Wendell Phillips Garrison, *William Lloyd Garrison*, 1:316–17.

13. Ibid.

14. Prudence Crandall to Simeon Jocelyn, February 26, 1833, in Captain Arthur B. Springarn, "Abolition Letters."

15. Rena Clisby, *Canterbury Pilgrims*.

16. See the letter from the "Society Committee" on July 26, 1833, and Prudence's reply, dated July 29, 1833, in Edward S. Abdy, *Journal*, 1: 200–2.

17. Prudence Crandall to Simeon Jocelyn, February 26, 1833, in Captain Arthur B. Springarn, "Abolition Letters."

18. An account of the March 1 meeting is found in a letter from George Benson to William Lloyd Garrison, March 5, 1833, Boston Public Library.

Chapter Four

1. *A Statement of Facts*, a pamphlet published by the *Brooklyn Advertiser Press* in 1833.

2. George Benson to William Lloyd Garrison, March 5, 1833, Boston Public Library.

3. William H. Pease and Jane H. Pease, "Samuel J. May: Civil Libertarian."

4. Catherine Beecher, *An Essay on Slavery and Abolitionism*, p. 102.

5. Helen Benson to William Lloyd Garrison, March 13, 1834, Villard Papers, Houghton Library, Harvard University.

6. Samuel Joseph May, *Some Recollections of Our Anti-Slavery Conflict.* p. 43.

7. Edward S. Abdy, *Journal*, 1:208.

8. William Lloyd Garrison to George Benson, March 13, 1833, in Walter M. Merrill and Louis Ruchames, eds., *The Letters of William Lloyd Garrison.*

9. The composite account of the March 9 meeting is derived from a letter from George Benson to Samuel Joseph May, March 30, 1833, Boston Public Library; *The Liberator*, April 6, 1833; Samuel Joseph May, *Letters to Andrew T. Judson, Esquire, and Others in Canterbury*; undated letter from Pardon Crandall to Selectmen and Civil Authority; and Abraham Payne, "Prudence Crandall and Her School."

Chapter Five

1. Abraham Payne, "Prudence Crandall and Her School." Payne wrote that the village was in an "uproar" over anti-Masonry: "My father was a Royal Arch Mason, and had just come out of a violent quarrel with his next neighbor. . . . When I asked him what Masonry was, his reply was, 'Boy, it is the foolishest thing in this world except anti-Masonry.' "

2. Edward S. Abdy, *Journal*, 1:205.

3. Leonard Richards, *"Gentlemen of Property and Standing,"* p. 45: "For Americans who desperately dreaded being cut off from deep and permanent ties of family, clan, class, community, and position—amalgamation touched the heart of their passions: their dread of sinking below their forefathers' station and their nightmare of becoming cogs in a mass society."

4. Catherine Beecher, "On the Peculiar Responsibilities of American Women," p. 176.

5. "An Appeal to the Colonization Society," *Norwich Courier*, March 27, 1833.

6. Undated letter from Pardon Crandall to Canterbury Selectmen. The original is in the possession of Mrs. Jessica Nashold.

7. Samuel Joseph May, *Letters to Andrew T. Judson, Esquire, and Others in Canterbury.*

8. Petition of Pardon Crandall to Andrew T. Judson and Chester Lyon, printed in "Prudence Crandall," *Kansas City Journal*, March 28, 1886.

9. Catherine Beecher, *An Essay on Slavery and Abolitionism*, pp. 30–31.

10. Abraham Payne, "Prudence Crandall and Her School."

11. Andrew T. Judson to Gideon Welles, Esquire, March 29, 1830, Hartford Public Library.

12. Gentleman Committee from Canterbury to President Andrew Jackson, February 5, 1833, printed in the Hartford *Courant*, March 26, 1833.

13. Lawrence J. Friedman, *Inventors of the Promised Land*, p. 271, suggests that the coalition that blocked the New Haven School became prominent overnight, and by leading a similar campaign Judson thought he might get ahead.

14. Leonard Richards, "The Jacksonians and Slavery," p. 105: "Historians have unearthed a few who sympathized with blacks or worried much about Catholics, but generally speaking the party of Jackson was the party of the Catholic immigrant, and Democrats marched shoulder to shoulder on the race question."

15. Leonard Richards, *"Gentlemen of Property and Standing,"* pp. 80–81: "The proportion of mobs generally decreased after antislavery organizers established a beachhead. . . . The amount of violence in any given area, then, depended not only on the number of societies being organized, but also on the number of societies already organized. . . . Violent resistance decreased as an antislavery beachhead became an antislavery stronghold."

16. David O. White, "The Crandall School."

17. William Lloyd Garrison, *Thoughts on African Colonization*, pp. 12–14.

18. Prudence Crandall Philleo to Ellen Larned, May 15, 1869, Larned Collection, Hartford Public Library.

19. Samuel Joseph May, *Some Recollections of Our Anti-Slavery Conflict*, pp. 46–50.

20. Undated letter from Pardon Crandall to Canterbury Selectmen, in possession of Mrs. Jessica Nashold.

21. Helen Benson to William Lloyd Garrison, June 18, 1834, Villard Papers, Houghton Library, Harvard University.

22. Lucretia Coffin May to Samuel May, February 1, 1833, Olin Library, Cornell University.

23. William Kinne, a prominent citizen, was probably related to the father of Hezekiah Crandall's wife, David Kinne. William Kinne had briefly conducted a boy's school on the Canterbury green shortly after the turn of the century. He had also for many years been principal of a high school in Maine. He pledged to start a school for black boys in Canterbury to complement Prudence's, but the idea never got off the ground.

Chapter Six

1. Prudence Crandall to William Lloyd Garrison, March 19, 1833, Boston Public Library.

2. Henry Benson to William Lloyd Garrison, March 23, 1833, Boston Public Library.

3. Samuel Joseph May to Andrew T. Judson, Esquire, March 29, 1833, in *Letters to Andrew T. Judson, Esquire, and Others in Canterbury.*

4. Francis Jackson Garrison and Wendell Phillips Garrison, *William Lloyd Garrison*, 1:336.

5. Almira Crandall to Henry Benson, April 30, 1833, Boston Public Library.

6. Abraham Payne, "Prudence Crandall and Her School."

7. Helen Catterall, ed., *Judicial Cases Concerning American Slavery and the Negro*, 4:429.

8. William Jay, *American Colonization and American Anti-Slavery Societies*, p. 32: "Mr. Judson had indeed a certain LAW in reserve, but it was necessary that *certain influences* should be previously brought into action before a civilized and Christian people could be induced to tolerate the application of that law."

9. Samuel Joseph May, *Letters to Andrew T. Judson, Esquire, and Others in Canterbury.*

10. Ibid.

11. David Lee Child, *The Despotism of Freedom: Or the Tyranny and Cruelty of American Republican Slave-Masters, Shown to Be the Worst in the World, in a Speech Delivered at the First Anniversary of the New England Anti-Slavery Society, 1833*, in Anne C. Loveland, "Evangelicalism and Immediate Emancipation in American Antislavery Thought," p. 186.

12. William Lloyd Garrison to Joseph Gales and William M. Seaton, September 23, 1831, in Walter M. Merrill and Louis Ruchames, eds., *The Letters of William Lloyd Garrison.*

13. Prudence Crandall to Simeon Jocelyn, April 17, 1833, in Captain Arthur B. Springarn, "Abolition Letters."

14. Henry Benson to Isaac Knapp, April 16, 1833, Boston Public Library.

15. The arrival dates of the students vary with different sources. This date for Eliza Glasko (or Glasco) comes from David O. White, "Prudence Crandall." Most sources agree there were eventually twenty to thirty students at the school. The following girls are generally agreed upon: Henrietta Bolt, M. E. Carter, Jeruska Congdon, Theodosia De Grass (or De Grasse), G. C. Marshall, Ann Peterson, Catherine Ann Weldon, from New York City; Amy Fenner (Parker), Eliza Glasko and her sister, from Griswold, Connecticut; Ann Eliza Hammond and her sister Sarah Hammond, Mariah Robinson, Elizabeth N. Smith, from Providence; Polly Freeman, Sarah Harris (Fayerweather) and her sister Mary Harris (Williams), from Canterbury; Elizabeth Henley, J. K. Johnson, from Philadelphia; Harriet Rosetta Lamson, from New Haven; and Julia Williams (Garnet). Because of confusion in historical records, the spelling of the following names is disputed: Amelia Elizabeth Wilder, Emila Willson (or Wilson), Eliza Weldon, and Mary Elizabeth Wiles.

16. The Canterbury Masonic Hall hardly seems like neutral ground for a meeting. This choice of place might suggest that many or a majority of Prudence

Crandall's opponents approved of or were Masons. A fascinating article on this subject is David Brion Davis' "Some Themes of Counter-Subversion: An Analysis of Anti-Masonic, Anti-Catholic, and Anti-Mormon Literature." On several occasions Garrison notes in *The Liberator* that anti-Masonic papers had reacted favorably to the antislavery cause. The petition committee consisted of Andrew T. Judson, William Lester, Chester Lyons, Rufus Adams, Solomon Paine, Andrew Harris, Ashael Bacon, George White (an Episcopal clergyman), Isaac Backus, and Daniel Packer. Why Packer, a supposed sympathizer, is on this list is a puzzle.

17. William Jay, *American Colonization and American Anti-Slavery Societies*, p. 33.

18. Henry Benson to William Lloyd Garrison, August 30, 1833, in Francis Jackson Garrison and Wendell Phillips Garrison, *William Lloyd Garrison*, 1:321. Despite Payne's opinion, the partial boycott did cause some inconvenience and humiliation. It is documented that Dr. Andrew Harris refused to cross the street to attend a student, and Prudence had to seek Dr. Clark, who lived three miles away. Pardon did have to cart water to the school from his farm after the well was fouled. Frederick Olney did have to drive students places on occasion.

19. Abraham Payne, "Prudence Crandall and Her School."

20. Henry Benson to Isaac Knapp, April 9, 1833, Boston Public Library.

21. Helen Benson to William Lloyd Garrison, March 21, 1834, Villard Papers, Houghton Library, Harvard University.

22. Ibid.

23. William Lloyd Garrison, *Helen Eliza Benson*, p. 18.

24. Prudence Crandall to Simeon Jocelyn, April 9, 1833, in Arthur B. Springarn, "Abolition Letters."

25. William Lloyd Garrison to Isaac Knapp, April 11, 1833, in Walter M. Merrill and Louis Ruchames, eds., *The Letters of William Lloyd Garrison*.

26. The writs would not be served until November 2, 1833, after Garrison returned from England.

27. James Forten was a very prosperous sail maker in Philadelphia. A leader of Philadelphia's large black community, he greatly influenced Garrison's thinking on the Colonization Society. His son-in-law, Robert Purris, was a close personal friend of Garrison as well.

28. Wendell Phillips Garrison, "Connecticut in the Middle Ages," p. 785.

29. Ibid.

30. John Malcolm Brinnin, *The Sway of the Grand Salon*, p. 16.

Chapter Seven

1. Calvin Wheeler Philleo, *Twice Married*, p. 64.

2. David O. White, in "Prudence Crandall," says it is likely Almira did more running of errands than teaching, and it is probably an exaggeration to call her a teacher. She also handled correspondence when Prudence was away.

3. The other fifteen towns, besides Canterbury, that signed petitions were Bethany, Brooklyn, Colchester, Hampton, Hebron, Killingly, Middleton, New London, Norwich, Sterling, Plainfield, Stafford, Thompson, Waterbury, and Windham.

4. Pardon Crandall to Andrew T. Judson and Chester Lyons, "Representatives of the Town of Canterbury in the General Assembly now in session at Hartford, May 5, 1833," reprinted in the *Kansas City Journal*, March 28, 1886.

5. Undated letter by Pardon Crandall. Original in the possession of Mrs. Jessica Nashold.

6. *The Liberator*, May 18, 1833.

7. Pardon Crandall to Andrew T. Judson and Chester Lyons, "Representatives of the Town of Canterbury."

8. Ibid.

9. Alfred Thurston Child, Jr., "Prudence Crandall and the Canterbury Experiment."

10. Esther Baldwin to Amy Baldwin, May 4, 1833, Baldwin Collection, Connecticut Historical Society, Hartford.

11. Amy Baldwin to Mary Clark, undated letter, Baldwin Collection, Connecticut Historical Society, Hartford.

12. The account of Reuben and Judson's encounter is from *The Trial of Reuben Crandall, M.D.*

13. Prudence Crandall to Simeon Jocelyn, April 17, 1833, in Captain Arthur B. Springarn, "Abolition Letters."

14. Calvin Wheeler Philleo, *Twice Married*, p. 64.

Chapter Eight

1. Andrew T. Judson and Rufus Adams, *Answers to Aspersions*, printed in *The Unionist*, August 8, 1833, New-York Historical Society.

2. Pardon Crandall to the General Assembly of Connecticut in "Prudence Crandall," *Kansas City Journal*, March 28, 1866.

3. Hartford *Courant*, June 24, 1833.

4. Jay quoted from an article, "Evidences Against the Views of the Abolitionists, Consisting of Physical and Moral Proofs of the Natural Inferiority of the Negroes," in *American Colonization and American Anti-Slavery Societies*.

5. The action of the Maryland legislature was reported in the *Emancipator*, June 22, 1833.

6. Report of Phillip Pearl to the May 1833 session of the Connecticut General Assembly on changes to "An Act for the Admission and Settlement of Inhabitants in Towns," printed in Edmund Fuller, *Prudence Crandall*, pp. 35–37.

7. A copy of this petition was sent to Festus Baldwin of Canterbury and is in the Baldwin Collection at the Connecticut Historical Society.

8. It is hard to know with certainty the identities behind the pseudonyms of many letters to the editors of newspapers. However, the identity of "Canter-

bury," whether it was William Burleigh, Pardon Crandall, or some other supporter, was probably obvious to many people in the village at the time.

9. The account of the visit is found in one of Pardon's circulars reprinted in the *Kansas City Journal*, March 28, 1886.

10. An anonymous student wrote a letter dated May 24, 1833, that appeared in the June 22, 1833, issue of *The Liberator*: "There are thirteen scholars now in the school."

11. *Kansas City Journal*, March 28, 1886.

12. Edward S. Abdy, *Journal*, 1:200.

13. Calvin Wheeler Philleo, *Twice Married*, p. 14.

14. The description of the arrest and jailing of Prudence comes from Samuel Joseph May, *Some Recollections of Our Anti-Slavery Conflict*, pp. 52–57.

Chapter Nine

1. *Windham County Advertiser*, July 20, 1833.

2. William Leete Stone, editor of the New York *Commercial Advertiser*, and James Watson Webb, editor of the New York *Courier and Enquirer*, were rabid anti-abolitionists who hated William Lloyd Garrison. Stone is quoted in William Jay, *American Colonization and American Anti-Slavery Societies*, p. 38.

3. *Niles' Weekly Register*, July 27, 1833. Editor Hezekiah Niles was a great respecter of law and order. He believed in obeying the will of the majority. Thus, he was sometimes caught in the middle, for although he strenuously opposed abolitionism, he also opposed vigilantism.

4. Edward S. Abdy, *Journal*, 1:204.

5. *The Liberator*, August 10, 1833.

6. *Shadow of the Elms: Reminiscences of Moses Brown School, 1784–1984*, P. 27.

7. Edward S. Abdy, *Journal*, 1:195.

8. Ibid., 1:218.

9. *The Unionist*, reprinted in *The Liberator*, April 5, 1834.

10. *The Liberator*, July 6, 1833. From an article written by one of the Connecticut students for the *Religious Intelligencer* and forwarded to *The Liberator* by "A. T." (Arthur Tappan?)

11. Prudence Crandall Philleo to Ellen Larned, March 7, 1870, Larned Collection, Hartford Public Library.

12. *The Liberator*, July 6, 1833.

13. *The Liberator*, August 3, 1833.

14. The church incident, including Prudence's reply of July 29, 1833, to the Society Committee, is in Edward S. Abdy, *Journal*, 1:202.

15. Esther Baldwin to Hannah Baldwin, July 28, 1833, Baldwin Collection, Connecticut Historical Society, Hartford.

16. *The Unionist*, August 29, 1833, reprinted in the Hartford *Courant*.

17. The carriage incident was related as oral history to Marvis Olive Welch

years ago by an elderly member of the Packerville Baptist Church. Ms. Welch kindly permitted me to include it here.

18. Esther Baldwin to Hannah Baldwin, July 28, 1833, Baldwin Collection, Connecticut Historical Society, Hartford.

19. Almira Crandall to George Benson, July 9, 1833, Boston Public Library.

20. *A Statement of Facts.*

21. *The Liberator*, June 22, 1833.

22. Herbert Aptheker, *American Negro Slave Revolts*, p. 21.

23. Samuel Joseph May, "A Tribute to the Memory of Arthur Tappan," from the *New York Independent*, reprinted in Lewis Tappan, *The Life of Arthur Tappan*, p. 155.

24. Samuel Joseph May, *Some Recollections of Our Anti-Slavery Conflict*, p. 156. Tappan's fortunes were severely reversed in the Panic of 1837.

25. Ibid., p. 60.

26. Ibid., p. 64.

27. Edward S. Abdy, *Journal*, 1:221.

Chapter Ten

1. Lydia Maria Child was married to abolitionist David Lee Child. Her novels *The Rebels of Boston Before the Revolution* and *Hobomok: A Tale of Early Times*, among others, were very popular. However, with the publication of *An Appeal*, she lost the patronage of Boston's elite. Subscriptions to the children's magazine she edited dwindled, and the gentlemen of the Boston Atheneum, who had given her the special privilege of access, withdrew it.

2. Samuel May et al., *Memoirs of Samuel Joseph May*, p. 152.

3. *Dictionary of American Biography*, 6:115.

4. Information about the lawyers is scanty. Chauncey Fitch Cleveland was governor of Connecticut from 1842 to 1844. He studied law with Daniel Frost, Jr., of Canterbury. Ichabod Bulkley came from Ashford, Connecticut, and later became a state senator and judge. Defense lawyer Calvin Goddard lived in Plainfield and later became a state supreme court judge.

5. *A Statement of Facts.* Other sources list additional girls as witnesses, but only partial records of the trial exist, and it is not certain how many students testified.

6. Samuel Joseph May, *Some Recollections of Our Anti-Slavery Conflict*, p. 59.

7. Calvin Wheeler Philleo, *Twice Married*, p. 2.

8. H. T. Sheldon to Prudence Crandall Philleo, December 6, 1880, Sheldon Collection, Kent Memorial Library, Suffield, Connecticut.

9. Edward S. Abdy, *Journal* 1:205.

10. Hartford *Courant*, August 26, 1833.

11. The account of the trial comes from the Hartford *Courant*, August 26 and September 1, 1833; Samuel Joseph May, *Some Recollections of Our Anti-*

Slavery Conflict, pp. 66–69; Edward S. Abdy, *Journal*, 1:205; and *A Statement of Facts*.

12. Abraham Payne, "Prudence Crandall and Her School."

13. Ralph Foster Weld, *Slavery in Connecticut*, pp. 24–25.

14. Edward S. Abdy, *Journal*, 1:203.

15. Abraham Payne, "Prudence Crandall and Her School."

16. Edwin and Miriam Small, "Prudence Crandall, Champion of Negro Education."

17. Esther Baldwin to Hannah Baldwin, July 28, 1833, Baldwin Collection, Connecticut Historical Society, Hartford.

18. Edwin and Miriam Small, "Prudence Crandall, Champion of Negro Education."

19. Nathaniel Paul to Andrew T. Judson, Esq., August 29, 1833, in Carter Woodson, *The Mind of the Negro*, p. 167.

Chapter Eleven

1. William Lloyd Garrison to "The Patrons of the Liberator and the Friends of Abolition," October 11, 1833, in Walter M. Merrill and Louis Ruchames, eds., *The Letters of William Lloyd Garrison*.

2. New York *Commercial Advertiser* in *Niles' Weekly Register*, October 12, 1833.

3. Gurley is quoted in Leonard Richards, *"Gentlemen of Property and Standing,"* p. 26.

4. Ibid.

5. Ibid.

6. An account of the chaotic founding of the New York Anti-Slavery Society can be found in *Niles' Weekly Register*, October 12, 1833.

7. Lewis Tappan, like his brother Arthur, was a businessman and philanthropist. In 1840 the two brothers broke with Garrison over the issues of women's rights, political action, anticlericalism, and nonresistance. The Tappans formed the American and Foreign Anti-Slavery Society. Arthur Tappan and Garrison were reconciled in 1863 when Garrison invited Tappan to participate in a commemorative meeting of those who had founded the American Anti-Slavery Society.

8. Henry Benson to Samuel Joseph May, September 30, 1833, Boston Public Library.

9. Samuel Joseph May, *Some Recollections of Our Anti-Slavery Conflict*, p. 69.

10. Edwin and Miriam Small, "Prudence Crandall, Champion of Negro Education."

11. William G. McLoughlin, *New England Dissent*, p. 1045.

12. Bernard C. Steiner, "History of Slavery in Connecticut," p. 4.

13. Samuel Bradlee Daggett, *A History of the Dagget-Daggett Family*, p. 155.

14. Helen Catterall, ed., *Judicial Cases Concerning American Slavery and the Negro*, 4:415–16.

15. *Windham County Advertiser*, December 19, 1833.

16. *The Liberator*, November 2, 1833, reprinted from the *Emancipator*.

17. *The Liberator*, November 2, 1833. Garrison's libel case was postponed several times and never came to trial.

18. William Lloyd Garrison to George Benson, November 25, 1833, in Walter M. Merrill and Louis Ruchames, eds., *The Letters of William Lloyd Garrison*.

19. David O. White, "The Crandall School."

20. Calvin Wheeler Philleo, *Twice Married*, p. 170.

21. Lucretia May to Samuel Joseph May, December 5, 1833, Olin Library, Cornell University. May and Garrison were attending the Philadelphia Convention to form a national organization, the American Anti-Slavery Society. Garrison wrote the Declaration of Sentiments for the new society, but worked little with the organization thereafter. He continued to confine his activities mainly to the Northeast, although he was elected secretary of foreign correspondence. Arthur Tappan was elected president. The New England Anti-Slavery Society, Garrison's own group, became the Massachusetts auxiliary of the larger society. The *Emancipator* was made the publication of the American Anti-Slavery Society. *The Liberator* became the organ of the state organization but was later printed under Garrison's name again.

Chapter Twelve

1. *The Liberator*, February 15, 1834; also in William Jay, *American Colonization and American Anti-Slavery Societies*.

2. In 1844 Frederick Olney married Olive Harris, a sister of Charles, Mary, and Sarah Harris. The events of Olney's visit and the subsequent fire are gleaned from the transcript of his arson trial, printed in *The Unionist* of March 13, 1834, a copy of which is in the New-York Historical Society. Unfortunately, only the prosecution half of the trial is recorded. The jury seems to have been convinced that the arsonist introduced the fire from outside the house in a space where the mortar was removed from the sill above the parlor window on the first floor. There was apparently enough wet rot so that the fire smoldered several hours before catching.

3. Henry Benson to [Samuel Joseph May], February 14, 1834, Boston Public Library: "If Olney is bound over to county court, brother wishes to be summoned as a witness."

4. Henry Benson to Isaac Knapp, February 14, 1834, Boston Public Library.

5. Helen Benson to William Lloyd Garrison, February 18, 1834, Villard Papers, Houghton Library, Harvard University.

6. William Lloyd Garrison to Helen Benson, February 18, 1834, in Walter M. Merrill and Louis Ruchames, eds., *The Letters of William Lloyd Garrison*.

7. William Lloyd Garrison to Helen Benson, March 25, 1834, ibid.
8. William Lloyd Garrison to George Benson, Sr., May 31, 1834, ibid.
9. Ibid.

Chapter Thirteen

1. *The Liberator*, April 19, 1834.
2. D. H. Van Hoosear, *The Fillow, Philo, and Philleo Genealogy.*
3. Calvin Philleo, *A Sermon from Pawtucket*, p. 3.
4. Emeline Whipple to H. S. Sheldon, June 5, 1881, Sheldon Collection, Kent Memorial Library, Suffield, Connecticut.
5. Rena Clisby, *Canterbury Pilgrims.*
6. H. C. Sheldon, "Calvin Philleo," unpublished monograph, Sheldon Collection, Kent Memorial Library, Suffield, Connecticut.
7. Calvin Philleo, *A Sermon from Pawtucket*, p. 10.
8. Brendan Francis Gilbane, *A Social History of Samuel Slater's Pawtucket*, p. 446. The Universalist Society of Pawtucket was in debt over the construction of their meeting house. In January 1830 the General Assembly authorized the society to hold a lottery to raise $4,000 to pay their debts, but the lottery was never held and the meeting house passed into other hands. The society dissolved in the early 1830s and was not revived until 1840.
9. Helen Benson to William Lloyd Garrison, March 1, 1834, Villard Papers, Houghton Library, Harvard University.
10. Jacob Frieze, *Two Discourses Delivered in the Universalist Church*, p. 33.
11. Ibid.
12. Jacob Frieze, *"Letter to Rev. Mr. Philleo."* Calvin had his church in Pawtucket from January 1830 to May 1833.
13. Ibid.
14. Helen Benson to William Lloyd Garrison, June 16, 1834, Villard Papers, Houghton Library, Harvard University.
15. Ibid., March 13, 1834.
16. Ibid., June 9, 1834.
17. Ibid., March 1, 1834.
18. Ibid., April 3, 1834.
19. William Lloyd Garrison to Helen Benson, April 5, 1834, in Walter M. Merrill and Louis Ruchames, eds., *The Letters of William Lloyd Garrison.*
20. Ibid., April 7, 1834.
21. Helen Benson to William Lloyd Garrison, May 22, 1834, Villard Papers, Houghton Library, Harvard University.
22. Ibid., April 9, 1834.
23. Calvin Wheeler Philleo, *Twice Married*, p. 64.
24. Henry Benson to George Benson, April 23, 1834, Boston Public Library.

25. William Lloyd Garrison to Helen Benson, June 2, 1834, in Walter M. Merrill and Louis Ruchames, eds., *The Letters of William Lloyd Garrison.*

26. Helen Benson to William Lloyd Garrison, June 9, 1834, Villard Papers, Houghton Library, Harvard University.

27. Ibid., June 2, 1834.

28. Ibid., June 18, 1834.

29. Ibid., June 9, 1834.

30. William Lloyd Garrison to George Benson, June 16, 1834, in Walter M. Merrill and Louis Ruchames, eds., *The Letters of William Lloyd Garrison.*

31. Ibid. Apparently Philleo's plan was new. Helen had written on June 9 that she thought it was Prudence's intention to marry as soon as possible and leave the school.

32. William Lloyd Garrison to Helen Benson, June 21, 1834, in Walter M. Merrill and Louis Ruchames, eds., *The Letters of William Lloyd Garrison.*

33. Lucretia May to Samuel Joseph May, June 3, 1834, Olin Library, Cornell University.

34. Helen Benson to William Lloyd Garrison, April 14, 1834, Villard Papers, Houghton Library, Harvard University.

Chapter Fourteen

1. *Niles' Weekly Register*, November 16, 1833. Niles was not the only editor to feel this way.

2. Ibid., May 3, 1834.

3. Ibid., June 7, 1834.

4. Job Roberts Tyson, *A Discourse Before the Young Men's Colonization Society, 1834,* in Leonard Richards, *"Gentlemen of Property and Standing,"* p. 67. I am using Richards' interpretation of the "British plot."

5. *Niles' Weekly Register*, May 3, 1834.

6. Leonard Richards, *"Gentlemen of Property and Standing,"* p. 116.

7. *Niles' Weekly Register*, July 12, 1834.

8. H. B. Robbins to Hannah Pearl, March 28, 1834, Baldwin Collection, Connecticut Historical Society, Hartford.

9. *The Liberator*, June 21, 1834.

10. *Niles' Weekly Register*, August 2, 1834.

11. The account of the third trial is found in *Report of the Arguments of Counsel in the Case of Prudence Crandall.*

12. Abraham Payne, "Prudence Crandall and Her School."

13. William Lloyd Garrison to Helen Benson, August 18, 1834, in Walter M. Merrill and Louis Ruchames, eds., *The Letters of William Lloyd Garrison.*

14. Edward S. Abdy, *Journal*, 3:213; also, Prudence Crandall Philleo to Ellen Larned, July 2, 1869, Larned Collection, Hartford Public Library.

15. William Lloyd Garrison to Helen Benson, August 18, 1834, in Walter M. Merrill and Louis Ruchames, eds., *The Letters of William Lloyd Garrison.*

16. Lucretia Mott to James McKim, in Otelia Cromwell, *Lucretia Mott* (Cambridge: Harvard University Press), p. 53.

17. *Niles' Weekly Register*, August 23, 1834.

18. It is not known if Charles Stuart brought the lithograph of Daniel O'Connell, but it is likely because Edward Abdy saw it shortly thereafter on the mantel.

19. There were four windows in each of the two front parlors. Each window had twenty-four small panes of glass.

20. "Prudence Crandall," *Kansas City Journal*, March 28, 1886.

21. *Kansas City Journal*, March 28, 1886; also, Samuel May et al., *Memoirs of Samuel Joseph May*, p. 151. There may have been an attempt to set the house on fire again. Prudence mentions this in the Kansas article.

22. Samuel Joseph May, *Some Recollections of Our Anti-Slavery Conflict*, p. 71.

23. *The Liberator*, September 20, 1834.

Chapter Fifteen

1. Lewis Tappan, *The Life of Arthur Tappan*, p. 222.

2. Ibid., p. 248.

3. Leonard Richards, *"Gentlemen of Property and Standing,"* pp. 71–73. The "revolution" included the development of the steam press, the paper-cutting machine, new techniques for recycling colored rags into usable paper, and advances in transportation.

4. Southern opinion on slavery was by no means unanimous, but after the Nat Turner insurrection in 1831, abolition societies had all but disappeared in the South. Many sympathetic whites kept silent or, like many Quakers, moved away from such "unholy places." See Herbert Aptheker, "The Quakers and Negro Slavery," p. 34.

5. William Lloyd Garrison to George Benson, September 4, 1835, in Walter M. Merrill and Louis Ruchames, eds., *The Letters of William Lloyd Garrison*.

6. President Andrew Jackson to Postmaster General Amos Kendall, August 9, 1835, in John Spencer Bassett, *The Correspondence of Andrew Jackson*, 5:360–61.

7. Edward S. Abdy, *Journal*, 2:90.

8. The account of Reuben's journey, arrest, and trial comes from two transcripts of the trial. The first, forty-eight pages long, is *The Trial of Reuben Crandall, M.D. Charged with Publishing and Circulating Seditious and Incendiary Papers, etc. in the District of Columbia, with the Intent of Exciting Servile Insurrection.* The second, sixty-two pages long, is *The Trial of Reuben Crandall, M.D., Charged with Publishing Seditious Libels by Circulating the Publications of the American Anti-Slavery Society.* Dr. Crandall had the latter published at his own expense.

9. In February 1836 the case of John Arthur Bowen came before Judge Cranch. District Attorney Francis Scott Key prosecuted. The prisoner was con-

victed and sentenced to hang, but the sentence was reprieved several times, and he was finally pardoned at the insistence of his mistress, Mrs. Thornton. See Helen Catterall, cd., *Judicial Cases Concerning American Slavery and the Negro*, 4:167.

10. Reuben Crandall to "My dear Father," January 29, 1836, in Rena Clisby, *Canterbury Pilgrims*.

11. Ibid.

12. Almira [Crandall] Rand to "Dear Sister," August 26, 1835, in Rena Clisby, *Canterbury Pilgrims*.

13. D. H. Van Hoosear, *The Fillow, Philo, and Philleo Genealogy*, p. 68.

14. Pardon Crandall to "My Dear Son Reuben," January 25, 1836, in Rena Clisby, *Canterbury Pilgrims*.

15. Reuben Crandall to "My dear Father," January 29, 1836, ibid.

16. The prosecution's precedent was the Sedition Act of July 14, 1798, against "any person guilty of uttering a seditious libel against the Government of the United States, with intent to defame the same and bring it into contempt and disrepute." Attorney General Key maintained that this law was repealed only because "the offences which it punished were sufficiently provided for already by the common law as it stood." The defense, however, held that the Sedition Act was repealed not because it was redundant, but because it was "tyrannical, oppressive, [and] unconstitutional of the liberty of speech and press."

17. Although none were read at the trial, abolitionists had printed many disclaimers asserting that the postal campaign was not aimed at a black audience. An example is from the *Fourth Annual Report of the Board of Managers of the New England Anti-Slavery Society* in 1836:

> We declare unequivocally, that we have never known or heard of an Abolitionist, who has sent a tract, a page, or a word, to any of the slaves. . . . We have refrained from sending our publications to them, not because they contain any sentiments which the slaves ought not to know we cherish. . . . We have refrained from sending our publications to the slaves for four reasons. First—They are not addressed nor adapted to the slaves, but to their masters. Secondly—if sent, they probably would never reach the slaves, so vigilant is the espionage of their oppressors. Thirdly—If they should get safely into their hands, they could not read them. Fourthly— We fear, if any of our publications should be found in their hands, they would be as fuel to the fire of their afflications. For similar reasons, we have never sent from the office in Boston, and the Secretary of the Society at New York assures us, he has never knowingly sent anything to the free colored people south of Washington City. In that city, there were two or three colored men who were subscribers to our publications. (pp. 17–18)

18. Andrew T. Judson was a member of the U.S. House of Representatives from March 1835 until July 1836, when he was appointed United States Judge

for the District of Connecticut by President Andrew Jackson. He served in that position until his death in 1853.

19. Reuben Crandall to Hezekiah Crandall, April 26, 1836, in Rena Clisby, *Canterbury Pilgrims*.

20. William Lloyd Garrison to Helen Benson Garrison, July 2, 1836, in Walter M. Merrill and Louis Ruchames, eds., *The Letters of William Lloyd Garrison*.

Chapter Sixteen

1. Reuben Crandall to "Dear Sister," July 17, 1837, Rena Clisby, *Canterbury Pilgrims*.

2. John Rand to Pardon and Esther Crandall, November 1, 1837, ibid.

3. Reuben Crandall to parents, November 10, 1837, ibid.

4. David S. Ingrasham to Pardon and Esther Crandall, January 20, 1838, ibid.

5. Marvis Olive Welch, *Prudence Crandall*, pp. 125–26.

6. Troy Grove was originally named from a founder from Troy, New York. The description of Pardon's journey comes from a letter to Prudence from her mother dated February 23, 1838, and printed in Marvis Olive Welch, *Prudence Crandall*, p. 126. Rena Clisby in *Canterbury Pilgrims* speculated, "He might have gone by coach part of the way, likely went across New York by the Erie Canal. If there was no regular coach travel from there on, he might have bought a horse and rode horseback the rest of the way."

7. Michael Cyprian O'Bryne, *History of LaSalle County*, p. 105.

8. Ibid.

9. George Benson to Samuel Joseph May, June 13, 1839, Boston Public Library.

10. Pearl's quote is found in a letter by Theodore Weld to Lewis Tappan, June 8, 1837, in Gilbert H. Barnes and Dwight L. Dumond, eds., *The Letters of Theodore Weld, Angelina Grimke Weld, and Sarah Grimke, 1822–1844*, p. 397–400.

11. Abraham Payne, "Prudence Crandall and Her School."

12. Samuel May et al., *Memoirs of Samuel Joseph May*, pp. 174 and 178. May only stayed at the Lexington Normal School for two years.

13. Lewis Tappan, *The Life of Arthur Tappan*, p. 301.

14. Jessica Nashold to Mrs. Sellers, March 9, 1949, Shain Library, Connecticut College, New London. Jessica Nashold is a descendant of Prudence Crandall. Helen Sellers was researching a book on Prudence, which was never printed.

15. Prudence Crandall Philleo to "Dear Friends," September 9, 1841, Shain Library, Connecticut College, New London.

16. Hezekiah Crandall to Prudence Crandall Philleo, November 29, 1842. Part of this letter is printed in *Magnificent Whistle Stop*.

17. Calvin Philleo to Calvin Wheeler Philleo, October 10, 1844, quoted in Welch, *Prudence Crandall*, p. 136.

18. Calvin Philleo to Calvin Wheeler Philleo, October 22, 1844, quoted in Welch, *Prudence Crandall*, p. 137.

19. There are differences of opinion among historians as to the year Esther took Clarissa to Illinois. Some put it several years later, but Rena Clisby, Clarissa's daughter, says it was 1844. In addition, one of Emeline's letters to Calvin Wheeler states that when Prudence left Boston in 1847, she intended to "present" herself to her mother (in Illinois) and hoped for a cordial reception. Otherwise she would "take to the prairies." I doubt Prudence would have left Obediah alone in Illinois. Clisby also says another of Hezekiah's daughters, Huldah, went out to Illinois in 1846. In all likelihood, she would not have gone unless Esther was there to receive her.

20. Rena Clisby, *Canterbury Pilgrims*.

21. Prudence Crandall Philleo to Calvin Wheeler Philleo, November 16, 1844, Shain Library, Connecticut College, New London.

22. *The Liberator*, May 1, 1846.

23. Emeline Goodwin to Calvin Wheeler Philleo, February 2, 1847, Connecticut Historical Society, Hartford.

24. The Garrison children were George Thompson, b. 1836; William Lloyd, b. 1838; Wendell Phillips, b. 1840; Charles Follen, b. 1842; and Helen Francis, b. 1844. Two more babies followed: Elizabeth Pease, b. 1846, and Francis Jackson, b. 1848. Charles and Elizabeth died as children.

25. Emeline Goodwin to Calvin Wheeler Philleo, July 18, 1847, Connecticut Historical Society, Hartford.

Chapter Seventeen

1. Lillian Schlissel, *Women's Diaries of the Westward Journey*, p. 6.

2. Dawn Lander Gherman, "From Parlor to Teepee," p. 14. Of particular interest are Gherman's views on "feminine wildness" and female wanderlust.

3. Ibid. Prudence went to Illinois thirty years before the Indian wars of extermination. For the most part, before the Civil War, women found native Americans nonthreatening and often helpful and kind.

4. Ibid., p. 15.

5. Rena Clisby, *Canterbury Pilgrims*. Brooks Farm was founded by transcendentalist George Ripley in 1841 in West Roxbury, Massachusetts. It was a community of artists of every variety and collapsed after several years. Margaret Fuller (1810–50) was a transcendentalist and a noted author, critic, and feminist.

6. After the failure of the Northampton experiment, George Benson turned the site into a hydropathic spa that catered to ailing abolitionists. Later he went to Kansas.

7. The term "Philleo Academy" comes from C. C. Tisler, "Prudence Crandall, Abolitionist," p. 205.

8. Mrs. Charles McDougal to Rena Keith Clisby, May 23, 1948, Shain Library, Connecticut College, New London. These two women are descendants of Prudence.

9. Ibid., May 2, 1948.

10. Rena Clisby, *Canterbury Pilgrims*.

11. Mary Bull, "Women's Rights and Other Reforms in Seneca Falls," *Good Company* (1870), in Andrew Sinclair, *The Emancipation of the American Woman*, p. 106.

12. All six of Hezekiah's children with his first wife, Clarissa Cornell, went west and married there. They all settled in La Salle County, Illinois, within a few miles of one another. Esther married Joseph Worsley, an Englishman, in 1847. Reuben married Amanda Smith in 1852. Huldah married George Webster, a member of the family Pardon first boarded with, in 1853. Mary married Henry Bass, who came from Windham County, in 1854. Obediah married Myra Bowers in 1856. Clarissa married Henry Keith in 1858.

13. Calvin Philleo to Calvin Wheeler Philleo, November 1847, Connecticut Historical Society, Hartford.

14. Calvin Wheeler Philleo to Calvin Philleo, January 19, 1850, Shain Library, Connecticut College, New London.

15. Calvin Wheeler Philleo to Hon. Richard Hernidien, November 1, 1852, ibid.

16. Calvin Wheeler Philleo to Calvin Philleo, January 19, 1850, ibid.

17. Jessica Nashold to Mrs. Helen Sellers, September 29, 1948, ibid.

18. Ibid., March 9, 1949.

19. Ibid., September 29, 1948.

20. Samuel W. Taylor, *Nightfall at Nauvoo*, p. 127.

21. John Hauberg, "Black Hawk's Mississippi," p. 101.

22. Cecil Eby, *"That Disgraceful Affair,"* p. 277.

23. Ibid., p. 152.

24. Ibid., p. 234. Eby documents other atrocities committed by Dr. Philleo.

25. Prudence Crandall Philleo to Calvin Wheeler Philleo, October 18, 1857, Connecticut Historical Society, Hartford.

26. Ibid.

27. Calvin Philleo to Emeline Goodwin Whipple, December 10, 1857, Connecticut Historical Society, Hartford.

28. Prudence Crandall Philleo to Elizabeth Norton Philleo, December 3, 1859, Shain Library, Connecticut College, New London.

29. Emeline Goodwin Whipple to Calvin Wheeler Philleo, April 26, 1855, Connecticut Historical Society, Hartford.

30. Prudence Crandall Philleo to Calvin Wheeler Philleo, October 18, 1857, ibid.

31. The Kansas-Nebraska Act of 1854 created two territories west of the Mississippi River and ostensibly gave to each "popular sovereignty" over the slavery question. It was assumed the northern part (Nebraska) would be against

slavery and the southern part (Kansas) would be for it. By this "compromise," politicians hoped to placate Southerners into supporting the building of a transcontinental railroad across the entire region. Nebraska did as expected, but trouble began in Kansas when New Englanders tried to outnumber the proslavery forces from Missouri and Arkansas who had brought large numbers of slaves with them. Five thousand armed Missourians swarmed into the territory before the election of 1855 and made even antislavery talk a crime. When an assassin killed a proslavery sheriff in the antislavery town of Lawrence, eight hundred Southerners sacked the place. In holy revenge, John Brown raided Pottawatomie Creek and murdered five Southerners. A three-month war ensued. By the late 1850s the free-state forces dominated, and in 1861 Kansas was admitted to the Union as a free state.

32. Senator Douglas is quoted in Leon Litwack, *North of Slavery*, p. 67.

33. Vera Cooley, "Illinois and the Underground Railroad to Canada," and N. D. Wight Harris, *Negro Servitude in Illinois*, p. 137.

34. An article from *The Monthly Miscellany of Religion and Letters*, reprinted in *The Liberator*, December 20, 1839, quoted in John Demos, "The Antislavery Movement and the Problem of Violent Means," p. 51.

35. Samuel May et al., *Memoirs of Samuel Joseph May*, pp. 219–20.

36. Prudence Crandall Philleo to Elizabeth Norton Philleo, December 3, 1859, Shain Library, Connecticut College, New London.

Chapter Eighteen

1. Third stanza of a poem Prudence composed in Troy Grove, Illinois, in 1861. Rena Clisby, *Canterbury Pilgrims*.

2. Prudence Crandall Philleo to Elizabeth Norton Philleo, December 3, 1859, Shain Library, Connecticut College, New London.

3. Laurence Moore, *In Search of White Crows*, p. 55.

4. Ibid., p. 38.

5. Ibid., p. 17.

6. William Lloyd Garrison to J. S. Adams, January 31, 1871, in Walter M. Merrill and Louis Ruchames, eds., *The Letters of William Lloyd Garrison*. Helen Benson Garrison did not believe in spiritualism.

7. Laurence Moore, *In Search of White Crows*, p. 51.

8. Prudence Crandall Philleo to the Reverend Mr. Gibson, November 11, 1887, in the Howard (Kansas) *Courant*, November 18, 1887. The phrase "original act" means miracle.

9. *The Christian Register*, July 6 and August 8, 1867. Emma Hardinge originally came from England. After failing as an actress, she billed herself as a healing medium and went into trances for mixed male and female audiences. She believed spiritualism was a religion and its purpose was the improvement of individual character.

10. Laurence Moore, *In Search of White Crows*, p. 83.

11. James Malin, *A Concern About Humanity*, p. 61.

12. Calvin Philleo to Elizabeth Philleo, August 28, 1864, Shain Library, Connecticut College, New London.

13. *Magnificent Whistle Stop*, p. 139.

14. Senator Stephen Douglas is quoted in Leon Litwack, *North of Slavery*, p. 268.

15. Ibid., p. 278.

16. *Magnificent Whistle Stop*, p. 332.

17. *The Liberator*, May 23, 1862.

18. Calvin Philleo to Elizabeth Philleo, March 8, 1865, Shain Library, Connecticut College, New London.

19. Calvin Philleo to Elizabeth Philleo, August 28, 1864, ibid.

20. *The Christian Register*, July 6 and August 8, 1867.

21. Emeline Whipple to Elizabeth Philleo, quoted in Marvis Olive Welch, *Prudence Crandall*, p. 163.

22. Calvin Philleo to Elizabeth Philleo, August 28, 1864, Shain Library, Connecticut College, New London.

23. Prudence Crandall Philleo to Sarah Harris Fayerweather, December 2, 1869, quoted in Carl R. Woodward, "A Profile in Dedication."

24. Mrs. Charles McDougall to Rena Keith Clisby, May 23, 1948, Shain Library, Connecticut College, New London.

25. Ibid.

26. Hallie Q. Brown, *Homespun Heroines and Other Women of Distinction*, p. 27.

27. Emeline Whipple to Elizabeth Philleo, June 1, 1862, quoted in Carl R. Woodward, "A Profile in Dedication."

28. Samuel May et al., *Memoirs of Samuel Joseph May*, p. 291. Samuel Joseph May died on July 1, 1871.

29. Prudence Crandall Philleo to Sarah Harris Fayerweather, July 26, 1871, Kingston, Rhode Island, Free Library.

30. Prudence Crandall Philleo to Obediah Crandall, September 9, 1872, quoted in Marvis Olive Welch, *Prudence Crandall*, p. 177.

31. Ibid.

32. Rena Clisby, *Canterbury Pilgrims*.

33. Last lines of "Hope's Soliloquy," quoted in Marvis Olive Welch, *Prudence Crandall*, p. 186.

Chapter Nineteen

1. Rena Clisby, *Canterbury Pilgrims*.

2. Ibid.

3. Prudence Crandall Philleo to Huldah Webster, November 1, 1877, Shain Library, Connecticut College, New London.

4. Hallie Q. Brown, *Homespun Heroines and Other Women of Distinction*, p. 28. Sarah Harris Fayerweather died on November 16, 1878.

5. Prudence Crandall Philleo to William Lloyd Garrison, March 20, 1879, Boston Public Library.

6. John L. Thomas, *The Liberator: William Lloyd Garrison*, p. 451.

7. Prudence Crandall Philleo to William Lloyd Garrison, April 20, 1879, Boston Public Library.

8. Julia Ward Howe was the wife of Samuel Gridley Howe of the Perkins Institute for the Blind, where Emeline had worked. Both of the Howes were active in the antislavery and women's rights movements. Julia Ward Howe wrote the lyrics for "The Battle Hymn of the Republic."

9. Prudence Crandall Philleo to William Lloyd Garrison, April 20, 1879, Boston Public Library.

10. The lithograph appears in the Vicksburg (Mississippi) *Daily Advertiser*, May 6, 1879, and is reprinted in John G. Van Deusen, "The Exodus of 1879," p. 119.

11. Carter Woodson, *A Century of Negro Migration*, pp. 133–36.

12. Nudie Williams, "Black Newspapers and the Exodusters of 1879."

13. John G. Van Deusen, "The Exodus of 1879," p. 118.

14. Quoted in William Loren Katz, *The Black West*, p. 170.

15. Nell Painter, *Exodusters*, p. 245.

16. John G. Van Deusen, "The Exodus of 1879," p. 121, and Carter Woodson, *A Century of Negro Migration*, pp. 138–39.

17. Nudie Williams, "Black Newspapers and the Exodusters of 1879."

18. D. A. Beckwith, "The Wandering Refugees," p. 355.

19. Glen Schwendemann, "The 'Exodusters' on the Missouri," pp. 29–30.

20. John G. Van Deusen, "The Exodus of 1879," p. 125.

21. Glen Schwendemann, "The 'Exodusters' on the Missouri," p. 38.

22. *New York Daily Herald*, April 24, 1879.

23. Sherman Savage, *Blacks in the West*, p. 98.

24. There was sometimes difficulty in placing blacks on white farms because white employers often wanted only the adults and not the children. See Herbert Gutman, *The Black Family in Slavery and Freedom*, p. 436.

25. Prudence Crandall Philleo to Josephine Crandall, July 25, 1880, Shain Library, Connecticut College, New London.

26. Prudence Crandall Philleo to "A. Natick," May 15, 1881, in the Providence (Rhode Island) *Morning Star*, June 6, 1881.

27. Prudence Crandall Philleo to Josephine Crandall, July 25, 1880, Shain Library, Connecticut College, New London.

28. Ibid.

29. The description of Hezekiah's illness and death is from Prudence Crandall Philleo to Obediah Crandall, March 15, 1881, Shain Library, Connecticut College, New London; Prudence Crandall Philleo to "Esther and Huldah," April 12, 1881, ibid.; Rena Clisby, *Canterbury Pilgrims*.

Chapter Twenty

1. Prudence Crandall Philleo to "A. of Natick," May 25, 1881, Providence (Rhode Island) *Morning Star*, June 6, 1881.

2. It appears that Prudence became interested in Christian Science around the time Esther was dying and they were living at Obediah's. Relatives reported finding "pounds" of Christian Science literature and receipts and correspondence with Christian Science healers years later in the attic of the house.

3. James H. Canfield, "A Whole-Souled Woman" and "Prudence Crandall."

4. James H. Canfield, "A Whole-Souled Woman."

5. George Thayer, *Pedal and Path*. For an interesting account of Abraham Williams, especially after Prudence's death, see Rodney O. Davis, "Prudence Crandall, Spiritualism, and Populist-Era Reform in Kansas."

6. Rodney O. Davis, "Prudence Crandall, Spiritualism, and Populist-Era Reform in Kansas"; Marvis Olive Welch, *Prudence Crandall*, p. 198.

7. Charles V. Eskridge, lieutenant governor of Kansas, on June 7, 1867, in the *Emporia News*.

8. After black men got the vote, women, children, and lunatics were still excluded. Kansas was the eighth state in the Union to grant women's suffrage.

9. Helen Gougar (1843–1907) was a suffrage and temperance leader from Indiana who undertook an extensive lecture tour in 1884. In Kansas she presided at the convention that organized a state suffrage association.

10. Elizabeth Cady Stanton et al., *The History of Woman Suffrage*, 3:703.

11. Nell Painter, *Exodusters*, pp. 163–70; *Historic Preservation in Kansas*, p. 21.

12. Moline *Republican*, February 7, 1890.

13. Prudence Crandall Philleo to Mrs. George Mitchell, March 14, 1888, Kingston, Rhode Island, Free Library.

14. George Thayer, *Pedal and Path*.

15. From "Early Love of Friends," in Marvis Olive Welch, *Prudence Crandall*, p. 185.

16. Prudence Crandall Philleo to Wendell Phillips Garrison, May 5, 1881, Alma Lutz Collection, Schlesinger Library, Radcliffe College.

17. Prudence Crandall Philleo to Wendell Phillips Garrison, February 6, 1887, Boston Public Library.

18. The plate of the engraving made of her painting by W. C. Ormsby was in the family of Francis Jackson Garrison.

19. *Kansas City Journal*, March 28, 1886.

20. The identity of Mr. Clark (or Clarke) is somewhat foggy. Bayles' history of Canterbury says Deacon Thomas Clarke was the Judson relation who was active in the pension campaign. Marvis Olive Welch in her biography identifies Thomas Clark as Andrew Judson's nephew (p. 50). Edwin and Miriam Small in their article refer to a nephew, Andrew Judson Clarke, as the promoter. Eleanor

Edelman says Thomas B. Clarke bought the house in 1870 for $3,400. She says he was Judson's son-in-law, but Abraham Payne states that Andrew Judson had no daughter and therefore could not have a son-in-law. In existing correspondence Prudence simply refers to "Mr. Clark."

21. Reverend John Kimball, *Connecticut's Canterbury Tale*.

22. Prudence Crandall Philleo to John S. Smith, November 3, 1885, Shain Library, Connecticut College, New London.

23. "Prudence Crandall," *Connecticut Magazine*, pp. 386–88.

24. "Prudence Crandall," *Kansas City Journal*.

25. Prudence Crandall Philleo to John S. Smith, January 30, 1886, Shain Library, Connecticut College, New London.

26. Ibid., November 3, 1885.

27. Prudence Crandall Philleo to "Dear Sir," Hartford *Courant*, March 5, 1886.

28. Prudence Crandall Philleo to John S. Smith, November 3, 1885, and January 9, 1886, Shain Library, Connecticut College, New London.

29. J. C. Hubbard, "Prudence Crandall, a Philanthropic Matron of Elk Falls."

30. Prudence Crandall Philleo to Mark Twain, April 14, 1886, Mark Twain Papers, Berkeley Library, University of California at Berkeley.

31. George Thayer, *Pedal and Path*.

Chapter Twenty-one

1. David O. White, "Prudence Crandall."

2. Reverend C. L. McKesson's funeral sermon is found in the Moline *Republican*, February 7, 1890.

3. George Thayer, *Pedal and Path*.

4. Conversely, many white workers and their leaders were slow to help the black cause. They thought that their own struggle had primacy and that the slavery issue detracted workers from confronting their own situation. See Philip S. Foner, *History of the Labor Movement in the United States*, p. 273.

5. Poem dated June 16, 1886, to George T. Thompson, Kansas State Agricultural College, in David O. White, "Letters from Kansas."

6. Howard *Courant*, March 11, 1887.

7. Rodney O. Davis, "Prudence Crandall, Spiritualism, and Populist-Era Reform in Kansas." Davis says she felt isolated as a spiritualist in Elk Falls (p. 243). While it was largely a separate concern from her other causes, by 1890 spiritualism was becoming "a positively deviant belief system" (p. 244). It should be noted, however, that Prudence was not the only spiritualist in Elk Falls or in the area. Indeed, as Davis notes, spiritualism had a brief revival in Elk County after Prudence's death.

8. Laurence R. Moore, *In Search of White Crows*, pp. 67–69.

9. Marvis Olive Welch, *Prudence Crandall*, p. 183.

10. James C. Malin, *A Concern About Humanity*, pp. 69–70.

11. Howard *Courant*, November 18, 1887.

12. Reverend C. L. McKesson's funeral sermon, in Moline *Republican*, February 7, 1890.

Bibliography

Abdy, Edward S. *A Journal of a Residence and Tour in the United States of North America.* London: J. Murray, 1835.

Aptheker, Herbert. *American Negro Slave Revolts.* New York: International, 1943.

———. "The Quakers and Negro Slavery." *The Journal of the American Negro* 25, no. 3 (1940).

Baer, Helene. *The Heart Is Like Heaven: The Life of Lydia Maria Child.* Philadelphia: University of Pennsylvania Press, 1964.

Baldwin, Elmer. *The History of La Salle County, Illinois.* Chicago: Rand McNally, 1877.

Barber, John Warner. *Connecticut Historical Collections, Containing a General Collection of Interesting Facts, Traditions, Biographical Sketches, Anecdotes, Etc., Relating to the History and Antiquities of Every Town in Connecticut, with Geographical Descriptions.* New Haven: Durries and Peck, 1838.

Barnes, Gilbert Hobbs. *The Anti-Slavery Impulse, 1830–1844.* New York and London: D. Appleton-Century, 1933.

Barnes, Gilbert H., and Dumond, Dwight L., eds. *The Letters of Theodore Weld, Angelina Grimke Weld, and Sarah Grimke, 1822–1844.* New York: Da Capo Press, 1970.

Bassett, John Spencer. *The Correspondence of Andrew Jackson. Vol. 5:*

1833–1838. Washington, D.C.: Carnegie Institution of Washington, 1931.

Bayles, R. M. *The History of Windham County, Connecticut*. New York: W.W. Preston, 1889.

Beckwith, D. A. "The Wandering Refugees." *The Western Homestead* (May 1879).

Beecher, Catherine. *An Essay of Slavery and Abolitionism with Reference to the Duty of American Females*. Philadelphia: H. Perkins, 1837.

———. "On the Peculiar Responsibilities of American Women." *A Treatise on Domestic Economy for the Use of Young Ladies at Home and at School (3d ed.)*. New York: Harper's, 1856.

Birdsall, Richard. "The Second Great Awakening and the New England Social Order." *Church History* 39, no. 3 (September 1970).

Brinnin, John Malcolm. *The Sway of the Grand Salon: A Social History of the North Atlantic*. New York: Macmillan, 1972.

Brown, Hallie Q. *Homespun Heroines and Other Women of Distinction*. 1926.

Burleigh, Charles, ed. *The Unionist* (Brooklyn, Conn.), August 3, September 5, 1833.

Canfield, James H. "A Whole-Souled Woman." Topeka *Daily Capital*, November 19, 1881.

———. "Prudence Crandall: The Continuation of the Story of an Interesting Life." Topeka *Daily Capital*, October 18, 1885.

Canterbury Land Records. Book 21 and 22. Connecticut State Library.

Catterall, Helen, ed. *Judicial Cases Concerning American Slavery and the Negro*. Vol. 4: *Cases from the Courts of New England, the Middle States, and the District of Columbia*. Washington, D.C.: Carnegie Institution of Washington, 1936.

Child, Alfred Thurston, Jr. "Prudence Crandall and the Canterbury Experiment." *Friends Historical Bulletin* 22 (1933).

Child, Lydia Maria. *An Appeal in Favor of That Class of Americans Called Africans*. Boston: Allen and Ticknor, 1833.

———, ed. *The Oasis*. Boston: B. C. Bacon, 1834.

Clisby, Rena. *Canterbury Pilgrims*. Unpublished manuscript, 1947.

———. *Memoirs of Rena Keith Clisby Written for Her Son Keith*. Unpublished manuscript.

Cooley, Vera. "Illinois and the Underground Railroad to Canada." *Transactions of the Illinois Historical Society for the Year 1917*. No. 23.

Cott, Nancy. *The Bonds of Womanhood: "Women's Sphere in New England," 1780–1835*. New Haven: Yale University Press, 1977.

Cottrol, Robert J. *The Afro-Yankees: Providence's Black Community in the Antebellum Era.* Westport, Conn.: Greenwood Press, 1982.

Crandall, John Cortland. *Elder John Crandall of Rhode Island and His Descendants.* New Woodstock, N.Y., 1949.

Creative Survival: The Providence Black Community in the 19th Century. Rhode Island Black Heritage Society. Rhode Island Historical Society.

Crummell, Alexander. *The Eulogy of Henry Highland Garnet, D.D., Presbyterian Minister; Late Minister Resident of the United States to the Republic of Liberia.* Washington D.C.: Union Bethel Literary and Historical Association, 1882.

Custer, Milo. "Asiatic Cholera in Central Illinois, 1834–1873." *Journal of the Illinois Historical Society* (April 1930).

Daggett, Samuel Bradlee. *A History of the Dagget-Daggett Family.* Boston: Rockwell and Churchill, 1894.

Dana, Richard H. "An Architectural Monograph on Old Canterbury on the Quinebaug." *White Pine Series of Architectural Monographs* 9, no. 6 (1923).

Davis, David Brion. "Some Themes of Counter-Subversion: An Analysis of Anti-Masonic, Anti-Catholic, and Anti-Mormon Literature." *Mississippi Valley Historical Review* (September 1960).

Davis, Rodney O. "Prudence Crandall, Spiritualism, and Populist-Era Reform in Kansas." *Kansas History: A Journal of the Central Plains* 3, no. 4 (Winter 1980).

Delany, Martin. *The Condition, Elevation, Emigration, and Destiny of the Colored People of the United States.* New York: Arno Press, 1968 (reprint of 1852 edition).

Demos, John. "The Antislavery Movement and the Problem of Violent Means." *New England Quarterly* 37, no. 4 (December 1964).

Denton, William. *Garrison in Heaven: A Dream.* Wellesley, Mass.: Mrs. E. M. F. Denton, 1882.

Dickens, Charles. *American Notes for General Circulation.* London: Chapman and Hall, 1842.

Dictionary of American Biography. Vol. 6. New York: Scribner's, 1931.

Duberman, Martin. "Abolitionists and Psychology." *Journal of Negro History* 47, no. 3 (July 1962).

———, ed. *The Anti-Slavery Vanguard: New Essays on the Abolitionists.* Princeton: Princeton University Press, 1965.

Dumond, Dwight L. *Anti-Slavery: The Crusade for Freedom in America.* Ann Arbor: University of Michigan Press, 1961.

Dwight, Timothy. *Travels in New England and New York.* Published by Timothy Dwight, 1821.

Eby, Cecil. *"That Disgraceful Affair": The Black Hawk War.* New York: Norton, 1973.

Edelman, Eleanor. "Restoration and Renascence: The House and Spirit of Prudence Crandall." Master's thesis, Graduate School of Architecture and Planning, Columbia University, 1983.

Edwards, Frances. "Connecticut's Black Law." *New England Galaxy* 5, no. 2 (Fall 1963).

Flexner, Eleanor. *Century of Struggle: The Woman's Rights Movement in the United States.* Cambridge: Belknap Press of Harvard University Press, 1959.

Foner, Eric, ed. *Nat Turner.* Englewoods Cliffs, N.J.: Prentice Hall, 1972.

Foner, Phillip S. *History of the Labor Movement in the United States from Colonial Times to the Founding of the American Federation of Labor.* Vol. 1. New York: International, 1947.

Foner, Phillip S., and Pachico, Josephine F. *Three Who Dared: Prudence Crandall, Margaret Douglas, Myrtilla Miner—Champions of Antebellum Black Education.* Westport, Conn.: Greenwood Press, 1984.

Fowler, William C. *The Historical Status of the Negro in Connecticut: A Paper Read Before the New Haven Colony Historical Society.* New Haven: Tuttle, Morehouse, and Taylor, 1875.

Fox, Early Lee. "The American Colonization Society." *Johns Hopkins Studies* 37. Baltimore: 1919.

Frederickson, George M., ed. *William Lloyd Garrison.* Englewoods Cliffs, N.J.: Prentice Hall, 1968.

Friedman, Lawrence J. *Inventors of the Promised Land.* New York: Knopf, 1975.

———. "Racism and Sexism in Ante-Bellum America: The Prudence Crandall Episode Reconsidered." *Societas* 4, no. 3 (Summer 1974).

Frieze, Jacob. *Two Discourses Delivered in the Universalist Church in Pawtucket on Sunday, August 30, 1829, on the Subject of Religious Excitements. Includes "Letter to Rev. Mr. Philleo: Dedicated to the People of Pawtucket."* Pawtucket: Chronicle Press, 1829.

Fuller, Edmund. "Prudence of Canterbury." *American Scholar* 18, no. 3 (Summer 1949).

———. *Prudence Crandall: An Incident of Racism in Nineteenth Century Connecticut.* Middletown, Conn.: Wesleyan University Press, 1971.

Fuller, Frank E., ed. *Shadow of the Elms: Reminiscences of Moses Brown School, 1784–1984.* Providence: Moses Brown School, 1983.

Garrison, Francis Jackson, and Garrison, Wendell Phillips. *William Lloyd Garrison, 1805–1879: The Story of His Life, Told by His Children.* Boston: Century Press, 1885.

Garrison, Wendell Phillips. "Connecticut in the Middle Ages." *Century Illustrated Monthly Magazine* 25 (September 1885).

Garrison, William Lloyd. *An Address Delivered Before the Free People of Color in Philadelphia, New York, and Other Cities, During the Month of June, 1831.* Boston: S. Foster, 1831.

————. *An Address Delivered in Boston, New York, and Philadelphia, Before the Free People of Color in April, 1833.* New York: Printed for the Free People of Color, 1833.

————. *Helen Eliza Garrison: A Memorial.* Boston: Riverside Press, 1876.

————. *Thoughts on African Colonization.* Boston, 1832.

————, ed. *The Liberator.* 1831–1865.

Gherman, Dawn Lander. "From Parlor to Teepee: The White Squaw on the American Frontier." Ph.D. diss., University of Massachusetts, 1975.

Gilbane, Brendan Francis. *A Social History of Samuel Slater's Pawtucket, 1790–1830.* Typewritten manuscript, 1969. Rhode Island Historical Society.

Goodell, William. *Slavery and Anti-Slavery: A History of the Great Struggle in Both Hemispheres, with a View of the Slavery Question in the United States.* New York: Negro Universities Press, 1968 (reprint of 1852 edition).

Grieve, Robert. *An Illustrated History of Pawtucket, Central Falls, and Vicinity: A Narrative of the Growth and Evolution of the Community.* Pawtucket: Pawtucket Gazette and Chronicle, 1897.

Gutman, Herbert G. *The Black Family in Slavery and Freedom, 1750–1925.* New York: Vintage Books, 1976.

Handbook of Elk and Chautauqua Counties. C. S. Burch, 1886.

Harris, N. D. Wight. *Negro Servitude in Illinois, 1719–1864.* Chicago: A. C. McClurg, 1904.

Harwood, Pliny LeRoy. *History of Eastern Connecticut Embracing the Counties of Tolland, Windham, Middlesex, and New London.* Chicago and New Haven: Pioneer Historical Publishing, 1932.

Hauberg, John. "Black Hawk's Mississippi." *Journal of the Illinois State Historical Society* (April 1929).

Hazelton, Robert Morton. *Let Freedom Ring! A Biography of Moses Brown*. New York: New Voices, 1957.

Hetrick, Rev. Andrew J. "A Historical Discourse Preached October 27, 1895, in the Meeting House on Canterbury Green in Recognition of Its Renovation." Prudence Crandall Museum, Canterbury, Connecticut.

Historic Preservation in Kansas. Black Historical Sites: A Beginning Point. Topeka: Historic Sites Survey, Kansas State Historical Society, September 1977.

Hubbard, J. C. "Prudence Crandall, a Philanthropic Matron of Elk Falls." Topeka *Daily Capital*, April 14, 1886.

James, Edward T., ed. *Notable American Women*. Cambridge: Harvard University Press, 1971.

Jay, William. *An Inquiry into the Character and Tendency of the American Colonization and American Anti-Slavery Societies*. New York: Leavitt, Lord, 1835.

Johnson, Oliver. *William Lloyd Garrison and His Times*. Miami: Menemosyne, 1969 (reprint of 1881 edition).

"Judgement Binding Prudence Crandall over to Superior Court, September, 1833." Hartford, Connecticut, State Library.

Judson, Andrew T., and Adams, Rufus. *Answers to Aspersions*. Broadside Press, June 19, 1833.

Katz, William Loren. *The Black West*. New York: Doubleday, 1977.

Key, Francis Scott. *Oration Delivered in the Rotunda of the Capitol of the United States, July 4, 1831*. New-York Historical Society.

Kimball, Rev. John C. *Connecticut's Canterbury Tale: Its Heroine Prudence Crandall and Its Moral for Today*. Hartford: Plimpton Press, 1886.

Larned, Ellen. *The History of Windham County*. 2 vols. Worcester, Mass.: C. Hamilton, 1874–1900.

———. *Historic Gleanings in Windham County, Connecticut*. 1899.

Litwack, Leon. *North of Slavery: The Negro in the Free States, 1790–1860*. Chicago: University of Chicago Press, 1961.

———. "The Abolitionist Dilemma: The Antislavery Movement and the Northern Negro." *New England Quarterly* 34, no. 1 (March 1961).

Loveland, Anne C. "Evangelicalism and Immediate Emancipation in American Antislavery Thought." *Journal of Southern History* 32, no. 2 (May 1966).

Magnificent Whistle Stop: The 100 Year Story of Mendota. Mendota Centennial Committee, 1953.

Malin, James C. *A Concern About Humanity: Notes on Reform, 1872–1912, at the National and Kansas Levels of Thought.* Lawrence, Kansas, 1964.

May, Samuel; Emerson, George B.; and Mumford, Thomas James. *Memoirs of Samuel Joseph May.* Boston: Roberts, 1873.

May, Samuel Joseph. *A Discourse on Slavery in the United States, Delivered in Brooklyn, July 3, 1831.* Boston: Garrison and Knapp, 1832.

———. *The Right of Colored People to Education Vindicated: Letters to Andrew T. Judson, Esquire, and Others in Canterbury Remonstrating with Them on Their Unjust and Unjustifiable Procedure Relative to Miss Crandall and Her School for Colored Females.* Brooklyn, Conn.: Advertiser Press, 1833.

———. *Some Recollections of Our Anti-Slavery Conflict.* New York: Arno Press, 1968 (reprint of 1869 edition).

McAlester, Lee, and McAlester, Virginia. *A Field Guide to American Houses.* New York: Knopf, 1984.

McCarron, Anna T. "The Trial of Prudence Crandall for the Crime of Educating Negroes in Connecticut." *Connecticut Magazine* 12, no. 2 (Second Quarter 1908).

McLoughlin, William G. *New England Dissent, 1630–1883: The Baptists and the Separation of Church and State.* Vols. 1 and 2. Cambridge: Harvard University Press, 1971.

McMurtrie, Douglas C. "The First Printers of Illinois." *Journal of the Illinois Historical Society* 26, no. 31 (October 1933).

McPherson, James M. "The Fight Against the Gag Rule: Joshua Leavitt and Antislavery Insurgency in the Whig Party, 1839–1842." *Journal of Negro History* 48, no. 3 (July 1963).

Merrill, Walter M. "A Passionate Attachment: William Lloyd Garrison's Courtship of Helen Eliza Benson." *New England Quarterly* 29 (June 1956): 190.

———. *Against Wind and Tide: A Biography of William Lloyd Garrison.* Cambridge: Harvard University Press, 1963.

Merrill, Walter M., and Ruchames, Louis, eds. *The Letters of William Lloyd Garrison.* Cambridge: Belknap Press of Harvard University Press, 1971–1981.

Moore, Laurence R. *In Search of White Crows: Spiritualism, Parapsy-*

2

64 *Bibliography*

chology, and American Culture. New York: Oxford University Press,
  1977.
Nashold, Jessica. "The Final Years of Prudence Crandall's Life." *Mendota
  Reporter*. April 29, 1981.
Niles, Hezekiah. *Niles' Weekly Register*. Baltimore, Washington, D.C.,
  September 7, 1811–September 28, 1849. (First published as *Weekly
  Register*, then *Niles' Weekly Register*, finally *Niles' National Register*.)
Norval, Neil Luxon. *Niles' Weekly Register: 19th Century News Magazine*.
  Baton Rouge: Louisiana State University Press, 1947.
O'Bryne, Michael Cyprian. *The History of La Salle County, Illinois*.
  Chicago and New York: Lewis Publishing, 1924.
Painter, Nell. *Exodusters: Black Migration to Kansas After Reconstruction*.
  New York: Knopf, 1977.
Payne, Abraham. "Prudence Crandall and Her School." Paper read be-
  fore the Rhode Island Historical Society. December 28, 1880.
Pease, Jane, and Pease, William. "Anti-Slavery Ambivalence, Immedia-
  tism, Expediency, and Race." *American Quarterly* 27, no. 4 (Winter
  1965).
———. "Samuel J. May: Civil Libertarian." *Cornell Library Journal*
  (Autumn 1967).
*Petition of the Citizens of the Town of Canterbury and Others to the Con-
  necticut General Assembly for Aid for Miss Prudence Crandall*. House
  Petition no. 48. January session, 1886.
Philleo, Calvin. *Light on Masonry and Anti-Masonry and a Renunciation
  of Both, with Undissembled Esteem for Masons and Anti-Masons*.
  Providence: H.H. Brown, 1831.
———. *A Sermon from Pawtucket*. Pawtucket, R.I.: H.H. Brown, n.d.
Philleo, Calvin Wheeler. *Twice Married: A Story of Connecticut Life*. New
  York: Dix and Edwards, 1855.
Providence City Directories 1824, 1826, 1828, 1830.
"Prudence Crandall." *Connecticut Magazine* 5, no. 7 (July 1899).
"Prudence Crandall." *Kansas City Journal*, March 28, 1886.
Quarles, Benjamin. *Black Abolitionists*. New York: Oxford University
  Press, 1969.
Ratner, Lorman. *Powder Keg: Northern Opposition to the Anti-Slavery
  Movement, 1831–1840*. New York: Basic Books, 1969.
Records of the Packerville Baptist Church. 3 vols. Hartford, Connecticut,
  State Library.
Remarks of Andrew T. Judson to the Jury in the Case of the State vs.

Prudence Crandall Before Superior Court, October Term, 1833. Hartford, 1833.

Report of the Arguments of Counsel in the Case of Prudence Crandall, Plaintiff in Error vs. the State of Connecticut, Before the Supreme Court of Errors at Their Session at Brooklyn, July Term, 1834. By a Member of the Bar. Boston: Garrison and Knapp, 1834.

Richards, Leonard. *"Gentlemen of Property and Standing": Anti-Abolition Mobs in Jacksonian America.* New York: Oxford University Press, 1970.

———. "The Jacksonians and Slavery." In Lewis Perry and Michael Fellman, eds. *Anti-Slavery Reconsidered: New Perspectives on the Abolitionists.* Baton Rouge: Louisiana State University Press, 1979.

Rosenberg, Carroll Smith. "Beauty, the Beast, and the Militant Woman: A Case Study in Sex Roles and Social Stress in Jacksonian America." *American Quarterly* 23, no. 4 (October 1971).

———. "The Female World of Love and Ritual: Relations Between Women in Nineteenth Century America." *Signs, Journal of Women and Culture and Society* 1, no. 1 (Autumn 1975).

Ruchames, Louis, ed. *The Abolitionists: A Collection of Their Writings.* New York: Putnam, 1963.

Savage, Sherman. *Blacks in the West.* Westport, Conn.: Greenwood Press, 1976.

Schlissel, Lillian. *Women's Diaries of the Westward Journey.* New York: Schocken, 1982.

Schwendemann, Glen. "The 'Exodusters' on the Missouri." *Kansas Historical Quarterly* 29 (1963).

Sheldon, H. S. "History of the Second Baptist Church of Suffield, Connecticut." Kent Memorial Library, Suffield, Connecticut.

———. "A Biographical Sketch of Prudence Crandall, Who Married Calvin Philleo." Kent Memorial Library, Suffield, Connecticut.

Sinclair, Andrew. *The Emancipation of the American Woman.* New York: Harper and Row, 1965.

Small, Edwin, and Small, Miriam. "Prudence Crandall, Champion of Negro Education." *New England Quarterly* 17, no. 4 (December 1944).

Snow, Edwin N. *Alphabetical Index of Births, Marriages, and Deaths Recorded in Providence from 1636 to 1850 Inclusive.* Providence, 1879.

Springarn, Captain Arthur B. "Abolition Letters Collected by Captain

Arthur B. Springarn." *Journal of Negro History* 18, no. 1 (January 1933).

Stanton, Elizabeth Cady; Anthony, Susan B.; and Gage, Matilda Joslyn, eds. *The History of Woman Suffrage.* Vol. 3. New York: Fowler and Welles, 1881.

A Statement of Facts, Respecting the School for Colored Females in Canterbury, Connecticut, Together with a Report of the Late Trial of Miss Prudence Crandall. Brooklyn, Conn.: Advertiser Press, 1833.

Staudenraus, Phillip J. *The American Colonization Movement, 1816–1865.* New York: Columbia University Press, 1961.

Steiner, Bernard C. "History of Slavery in Connecticut." *Johns Hopkins University Studies in Historical and Political Science.* Vol. 11. Baltimore: Johns Hopkins Press, 1893.

Stillman, Elisha. "Prudence Crandall and Her Work." Paper read before the Westerly, Rhode Island, Historical Society, December 13, 1913.

Strother, Horatio T. *The Underground Railroad in Connecticut.* Middletown, Conn.: Wesleyan University Press, 1962.

Tappan, Lewis. *The Life of Arthur Tappan.* Cambridge: Riverside Press, 1870.

Taylor, Samuel W. *Nightfall at Nauvoo.* New York: Macmillan, 1971.

Thayer, George B. *Pedal and Path: Across the Continent Awheel and Afoot.* Hartford: Hartford Evening Post Association, 1887.

Thomas, John L. *The Liberator: William Lloyd Garrison, a Biography.* Boston: Little, Brown, 1963.

Tisler, C. C. "Prudence Crandall, Abolitionist." *Journal of the Illinois State Historical Society* 33, no. 2 (June 1940).

Tocqueville, Alexis de. *Democracy in America.* 4th ed. New York: J. and H. G. Langley, 1841.

Trachtenberg, Leo. "The Canterbury Tale." *Negro History Bulletin* (March 1949).

Tremain, Mary. *Slavery in the District of Columbia: The Policy of Congress and the Struggle for Abolition.* New York: Negro Universities Press, 1969 (reprint of 1892 edition).

The Trial of Reuben Crandall, M.D., Charged with Publishing and Circulating Seditious and Incendiary Papers, etc., in the District of Columbia, with the Intent of Exciting Servile Insurrection. Carefully Reported and Compiled from the Written Statements of the Court and the Counsel by a Member of the Bar. Washington, 1836.

The Trial of Reuben Crandall, M.D., Charged with Publishing Seditious Libels by Circulating the Publications of the American Anti-Slavery

Society. Before the Circuit Court for the District of Columbia, Held at Washington, in April 1836, Occupying the Court the Period of Ten Days, 1836. New York: H. R. Piercy, 1836.

Van Deusen, John G. "The Exodus of 1879." *Journal of Negro History* 21, no. 2 (April 1936).

Van Hoosear, D. H. *The Fillow, Philo, and Philleo Genealogy: A Record of the Descendants of John Fillow, a Huguenot Refugee from France.* Albany: John Munsell, 1888.

Wade, Richard C. *Slavery in the Cities: The South, 1820–1860.* New York: Oxford University Press, 1964.

Walsh, Jeannine B. "Prudence Crandall: A Clarification of the Canterbury Tale and Its Heroine." Master's thesis, Southern Connecticut State College, 1976.

Welch, Marvis Olive. *Prudence Crandall: A Biography.* Hartford, Conn.: Jason, 1983.

Weld, Ralph Foster. *Slavery in Connecticut.* New Haven: Tricentenary Commission of the State of Connecticut, Committee on Historical Publications, 1935.

White, David O. "The Crandall School and the Degree of Influence by Garrison and the Abolitionists Upon It." *Connecticut Historical Society Bulletin* 43, no. 4 (October 1978).

———. "A Guide to Resources Relating to the Court Trials of Prudence Crandall." Connecticut Historical Commission, 1971.

———. "Prudence Crandall." Mimeographed manuscript. Connecticut Historical Society.

———. "Prudence Crandall Philleo: Letters from Kansas." Connecticut Historical Commission, January 1972.

Writ of Arrest of Prudence Crandall, June 27, 1833. Hartford, Connecticut, State Library.

Williams, Nudie. "Black Newspapers and the Exodusters of 1879." *Kansas History: A Journal of the Central Plains* 8, no. 4 (Winter 1985–86).

Woodson, Carter. *A Century of Negro Migration.* New York: Russell and Russell, 1918.

———. *The Education of the Negro Prior to 1861: A History of the Education of the Colored People of the United States from the Beginning of Slavery to the Civil War.* New York: Putnam's, 1915.

———. *Free Negro Heads of Families in the United States in 1830, Together with a Brief Treatment of the Free Negro.* Washington, D.C.: Association for the Study of Negro Life and History, 1929.

————. *The Mind of the Negro as Reflected in Letters Written During the Crisis 1800–1860*. Washington, D.C.: Association for the Study of Negro Life and History, 1929.

————. *The Negro in Our History*. Washington, D.C.: Associated Publishers, 1945.

Woodward, Carl R. "A Profile in Dedication: Sarah Harris and the Fayerweather Family." *New England Galaxy* 25, no. 1 (Summer 1973).

Wormley, G. Smith. "Prudence Crandall." *Journal of Negro History* 8, no. 1 (January 1923).

Zorn, Roman J. "The New England Anti-Slavery Society: Pioneer Abolition Organization." *Journal of Negro History* 43, no. 3 (July 1957).

Index